D0898108

★ ★ ★ ★ ★ ★ ★ ★ ★ ★ ★

THE
MILITARY
FAMILY
IN
PEACE AND WAR

★ ★ ★ ★ ★ ★ ★ ★ ★ ★ ★

Florence W. Kaslow, PhD, ABPP, is Director of the Florida Couples and Family Institute, and President of Kaslow Associates, P.A., in West Palm Beach, Florida. She is a Visiting Professor of Medical Psychology in the Department of Psychiatry at Duke University Medical School and a Visiting Professor in the Graduate School of Psychology at Florida Institute of Technology and the California Graduate School of Family Psychology. Dr. Kaslow received her PhD from Bryn Mawr College and is the author of over 150 publications, including 13 books, has guest lectured in more than 30 countries, and has had her work translated into many languages. She received the Family Psychologist of the Year Award in 1986 and in 1987 became the first President of the International Family Therapy Association, a position she held until 1990. In 1989 Dr. Kaslow was the recipient of the American Psychological Association's Distinguished Contribution to Applied Psychology Award and in 1991 received the AAMFT's Outstanding Contribution to the Field of Family Therapy Award.

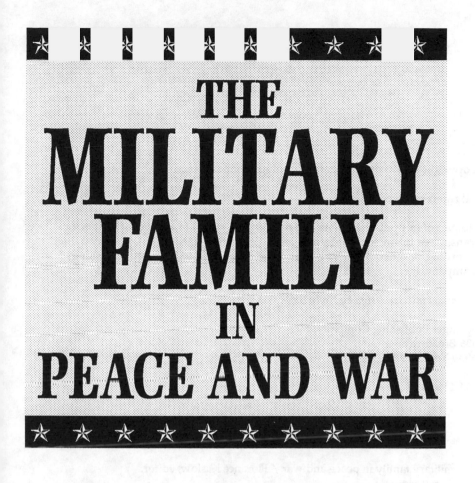

THE
MILITARY
FAMILY
IN
PEACE AND WAR

Florence W. Kaslow, PhD, ABPP
Editor

SPRINGER PUBLISHING COMPANY
NEW YORK

Cover and interior design by Holly Block

Springer Publishing Company, Inc.
536 Broadway
New York, NY 10012-3955

93 94 95 96 97 / 5 4 3 2 1

Library of Congress Cataloging-in-Publication Data

The military family in peace and war / Florence Kaslow, editor.
    p.   cm.
    Includes bibliographical references and index.
    ISBN 0-8261-8270-4
    1. Soldiers—United States—Family relationships. 2. Sociology, Military—United States.   I. Kaslow, Florence Whiteman.
    U21.5.M47 1993
    306.2'7'0973—dc20

                              93-14560
                                 CIP

Printed in the United States of America

Contents

Contributors

Richard W. Bloom III, PhD, Diplomate in Clinical Psychology, ABPP, is the Chairperson, Psychology and National Security Affairs Committee, Military Psychology Division of the American Psychological Association. He is a past president of this APA division and a Fellow of the Society of Air Force Clinical Psychologists.

Richard J. Brown III, PhD, is the Chief of the Family Matters Division in the Center for Professional Development at Air University, Maxwell Air Force Base, Montgomery, Alabama, and has over 15 years experience in the military family arena. He holds a B.A. in psychology, a B.D. in theology, an M.A. in clinical psychology, and a Ph.D. in child development and family relations.

Charles R. Figley, PhD, is a Professor and Director of the Interdivisional PhD program in Marriage and Family, Florida State University Marriage and Family Therapy Center, and Psychosocial Stress Research Program, Florida State University, Tallahassee.

Rex A. Frank, PhD, is the former Chief, Outpatient Mental Health Services, Wilford Hall USAF Medical Center, Lackland Air Force Base, Texas, and President of the Applied Psychology Institute in San Antonio, Texas.

Edna J. Hunter-King, PhD, is currently Deputy Chairman of the Congressionally mandated Advisory Committee on Former Prisoners of War, Department of Veterans Affairs. From 1971 until her retirement in 1989, Dr. Hunter-King was Acting Director and Administrative Director, San Diego Center for Prisoners of War; Professor and Head, Marriage and Family Therapy Graduate Programs, United States International University; Visiting Distinguished Professor, United States Military Academy, West Point; and Fulbright Scholar, Ministry of Defense (New Zealand and Australia). She has over 200 professional publications to her credit, including 10 books.

Diana L. Kupchella, MEd, MS (Nursing), is a Congressional Fellow in Washington, DC, assigned to the Senate Subcommittee on Defense Appropriations (1992–93), working in the office of Senator D. Inouye, Chairman of the Subcommittee. She is a Lieutenant Colonel in the U.S. Air Force Nurse Corp.

Colonel Jose Florante J. Leyson, MD, MS, is Commander, SCI Service and Director, Sex Clinic/NeuroUrology, VA Medical Center, East Orange, NJ, and Chief of Urology, Hospital Center of Essex County, Cedar Grove, NJ.

Commander Thomas C. Mountz, PhD, is a psychologist who is currently stationed at the United States Marine Corps, Quantico, Virginia. He serves in the Special Forces.

D. Stephen Nice, PhD, is Head of the Health Sciences and Epidemiology Department, Naval Health Research Center, San Diego, CA, and an Adjunct faculty member, Graduate School of Public Health, San Diego State University.

Captain Lindsay B. Paden, MD, MC, USN, is Head of the Child Psychiatry Division and Assistant Director of the Psychiatry Residency Training Program at the Naval Hospital, San Diego, CA, and is Assistant Clinical Professor of Psychiatry, University of California, San Diego.

LCDR Laurence J. Pezor, MD, MC, USN, is Head of the Child, Adolescent, and Family Psychiatry Division, and Assistant Director of Residency Training at the National Naval Medical Center, Bethesda, MD, and is Assistant Professor of Psychiatry, Uniformed Services University of the Health Sciences, Bethesda.

Patricia J. Thomas, MS, is the Director of the Office of Women and Multicultural Research at the Navy Personnel Research and Development Center, San Diego, California. She holds an MS degree in psychology from San Diego State University.

Marie D. Thomas, PhD, is a Personnel Research Psychologist at the Navy Personnel Research and Development Center, San Diego, California. She works in the Office of Women and Multicultural Research. Dr. Thomas holds an MA degree in psychology and a PhD in psychometrics from Fordham University.

Foreword

The cold war is over! The military is undergoing a major reduction in personnel and budget. And some wonder why there is a need for a significant armed force at all. Aren't the military issues receding? Have the issues affecting families changed?

The answer is that in recent years dramatic changes have taken place within the services and society, and although the threats have changed, the military is as important to the country as it has ever been and its role is expanding greatly. The national interest has involved us in major armed conflict, best exemplified by the Gulf War. Trouble spots throughout the world, as in the former Yugoslavia, and in Russia and North Korea, to mention just a few, require readiness. United Nations peacekeeping (currently in 13 different trouble spots throughout the world) and our involvement in support of major humanitarian efforts, as in Somalia, appear to be increasing. The military services are being utilized for drug interdiction, border control, and even civil disturbances. Societal changes have always had direct impact on the military: thus the changing roles of women and single parents and the problem of discrimination against homosexuals are among the issues affecting the fabric of service life and the military family.

Politicians, policymakers, government officials, service members, and medical and mental health providers who work with military families need the information provided here and can make good use of it.

The ability to understand and work effectively with or for military families requires, most importantly, a knowledge of the military culture. One would not expect a policymaker or a therapist to go into another country and work effectively without first having a significant comprehension of the traditions, values, mores, and requirements of that country. So too, those involved with military families must under-

stand things like "duty," "going in harm's way," "good order and discipline," "unit cohesiveness," the necessity of "separations," and the paramount importance of "the mission." Uninformed policymakers who tread
here can do irreparable harm, and therapists with excellent intentions
and even outstanding clinical skills can increase turmoil and produce
bad outcomes unless they understand the military's unique culture.

This book makes a significant contribution towards a fuller understanding of this culture and the issues involved. The unique nature of
the military is perhaps best exemplified in Mountz' chapter on the
"special warrior." In fact, after reading this chapter, one is left somewhat suspended because of what would appear to be the author's perception of a need for less than full revelation of the "secret" nature of
the duties involved.

The military services are often the first to be called on to confront—
on a large scale—some of the critical social issues in our society. Successful racial integration of the services is an early example. Effective
programs for identification and treatment of alcohol abuse and family
violence were first accomplished in a major military success story in
the early eighties. And most recently the awareness and confrontation
of sexual harassment and gender issues have been undertaken by the
services.

Paden and Pezor, two Navy child psychiatrists, do a marvelous job
in describing the children of military families and the special and
unique stresses that they face. They have done a thorough review of
the literature and speak cogently of the effects on these children of such
issues as parental absence, frequent geographic moves, and war. Although essentially no research has been done, they raise interesting
questions about the relatively new phenomenon seen during the Gulf
War namely—the effect on children of the mother going to war, or more
dramatically, what happens when both parents go to war. They suggest further study of the impact of television coverage of armed conflict on all children and especially preschoolers and those whose
parent(s) are deployed in the war zone. The chapter also describes the
debate over whether or not military children and military families have
a greater incidence of psychopathology than their civilian counterparts.
They conclude that the evidence points strongly towards the conclusion that there is not a greater incidence of serious psychopathology
and, in fact, that military families provide children many opportunities for healthy development and maturation.

The centerpiece of this book is Kaslow's chapter, "Attitudes, Knowledge Base, and Skills Essential to Treat Military Families." Although
appropriate for many audiences, the central purpose of this book is to

educate and inform those who provide mental health services to the
military family and its members. This chapter is a tour de force. Its
discussion of training and supervisory techniques is really valuable for
any setting where family therapy is being taught, but the added gems
pertinent for those working with military families make it a classic.

Although the chapters in this book are uniformly good, some stand out
as exceptional and unique contributions. One such chapter is "Mothers
in Uniform," written by Patricia and Marie Thomas, research psychologists at the Navy Personnel Research and Development Center in San
Diego. It is to date the defining piece about the controversial issue of
women and mothers in the military and in combat. The chapter is well-
researched and thoroughly documented, and is a comprehensive treatment of the issue and beautifully written. The history it traces is fascinating and leads to the inexorable conclusion that mothers in uniform
will one day in the not-too-distant future be an accepted component of
military life. The authors estimate that 12,000 mothers served in Desert
Storm. They proceed to debunk each objection that was created to discourage allowing mothers to serve.

The military services are currently undergoing the largest downsizing since the end of the Vietnam era. Thousands of soldiers, sailors,
airman, and marines will be leaving active service—some by regular
retirement, but many involuntarily through early retirement, and
many before they are eligible for retirement. The transition from service life to civilian life can be one of the most stressful passages these
individuals will experience. Rex Frank, a retired Air Force psychologist, writes knowingly of the many issues involved in this life change.
This chapter should be required reading for the policymakers managing this dragon, the mental health professions who will be called to
work with those struggling to make this change, and, most especially,
the retiree who will benefit by understanding the dynamics of this
phenomenon.

Many families, and especially military families, use the health care
system as a significant part of their support system. A very significant
contribution in this volume is Steven Nice's chapter on the military
family and the maintenance of health. He suggests that the organizational perspective on the active duty service person be broadened so
as to consider the individual in his or her fundamental family and family priorities in health care planning and other strategic processes. And
finally, he recommends "enjoining these family resources in the development of a fundamental paradigm shift toward wellness."

The next iteration of this book needs to be in the works immediately.
As Kaslow points out in the preface, issues such as the homosexual in

the military, the handling of persons who are HIV positive, and the special dilemmas of military spouses are not fully dealt with. There will need to be evaluations of how well the policy makers and the military leaders do in bringing about the many changes that are currently underway and no doubt will arise as national policy and social challenges change in the coming years. There will need to be reports on how well leadership supports the military family both in policy and dollars for needed programs. We can all hope that Kaslow will rise to meet this challenge again and produce another volume to take its place alongside the two volumes she has already created on the subject of military families.

I feel honored to have been asked to write this foreword. Most of my professional life has been devoted to dealing with these issues, and my family has lived through many of the phenomena described herein. I feel responsible in large part for Florence Kaslow's involvement with the military family, since I was responsible for the final decision to bring her aboard as supervisor and consultant in the Department of Psychiatry at the Philadelphia Naval Hospital in 1973. It turned out to be one of the best decisions I have made, for she has so positively influenced many generations of Navy residents and mental health staff members as well as similar groups in the other services. Her many publications, and especially the two books she has now edited on the military family have been invaluable contributions in this subject area and serve as the source documents. Military families, in all their variations and over all times, have played a vital role in our nation's defense. They deserve the best we can give to understand them and to promote their healthy functioning. This book is a major contribution towards that end.

H. JAMES T. SEARS, MD, FAPA
Rear Admiral, Medical Corps
U.S. Navy, Retired

Preface

Every country in the world that maintains armed forces has military families in its midst. Whether the services are peopled predominantly by young single men or comprised also of married men and women, the military has an ethical and existential responsibility to be mindful of the impact the service member's activities and whereabouts have on his/her parents, siblings, spouse, children, and grandparents. Similarly, the mental and physical well-being (or lack of it) of civilian significant others profoundly influences the emotional state and on-the-job performance of the soldier, sailor, or marine.

Since 1973, when I first began treating military families and training psychiatric residents and senior staff at the Philadelphia Naval Hospital to do the same, I have found the military family to be a fascinating and compelling topic. My experiences and observations, combined with those of then Lieutenant Commander Richard Ridenour, MD, led to the co-editing of (and authoring chapters for) *The Military Family: Dynamics and Treatment* (1984). Now, almost 10 years later, and with continuing involvement with military families as a clinician, consultant, and trainer of other professionals to understand military families here and abroad, it seemed time for another book.

The volume is divided into two interrelated sections. Part I deals with the personal and interpersonal issues that affect military families and structures and encompasses family dynamics and treatment issues, as well as a bevy of clinical and philosophic concerns. However, since military families are vitally influenced by legislation and other social policy decisions, Part II was incorporated to deal with these subjects and the larger context that impacts on the lives of all military personnel and their loved ones.

Several chapters deal with substantive issues like retirement, where new major legislation has been promulgated in the past decade. There are chapters that deal with prisoners of war and training civilian and military therapists to treat military families; these incorporate new ideas and findings.

This book encompasses features of the military family in wartime and its aftermath, as well as in peacetime. There is also an international perspective—that is, on issues that affect military families in many countries. The impetus came from the recent conflicts in Afghanistan, China, Iraq/Kuwait, Panama, South Africa, and what were formerly the Soviet Union and Yugoslavia, to mention but a few battles of the past decade. Many, but not all, of the concerns are similar, in civil as in intercountry wars. One major difference is that in civil wars families may be divided and fighting on opposite sides, causing profound worry and dissension as brother may kill brother. This is less likely, though certainly still possible, in intercountry struggles. A book that deals solely with our own troopers and their families would be myopic, given today's global community. Therefore, chapters dealing with governmental, university-sponsored, and private programs instituted to help families cope with the strife and stresses of the Persian Gulf War (1991) and its aftermath have been included. It appears that the kinds of programs established were quite viable and could be quickly duplicated if and when another war breaks out and escalates to the point where we become involved, and they are adaptable by other countries.

Some of the special features of this book are highlighted here. The volume opens with attention to children in the military family. They have always been a much-talked-about group, often designated (not so kindly) as "military brats." The special life circumstances that engulf the child raised in the military family are addressed.

Mothers on active duty in the front lines, a new phenomenon for our country, is another important new topic. The role of women vis-à-vis their husbands, children, and "comrades in arms" was and remains a highly controversial subject.

The sequelae of wars in the form of psychosexual scars is another topic that has received scant attention, yet it is one aspect of posttraumatic stress disorder and a lingering symptom that affects marital functioning; thus, the inclusion of a chapter on this complex subject.

There is a certain mystique that surrounds the special warrior. Because of the very nature of the assignments he undertakes, the chapter is shrouded in secrecy; to reveal all is not permissible—a fact of daily life for the special warrior and one that is often exceedingly difficult for his wife and children to accept unquestioningly.

The final chapter attempts to integrate the many threads and themes encompassed in the book into a coherent whole. Although every effort was made to be reasonably inclusive, the book is far from exhaustive. This is partially attributable to space restrictions and partly to how quickly these subjects are changing. We recognize and regret the lack of inclusion of chapters on such topics as homosexuality in the military, the handling of personnel who are HIV positive, and special dilemmas of military wives. We are pleased that Rear Admiral H. James T. Sears (U.S.N., Ret.) kindly consented to write the foreword.

Acknowledgments

My sincere appreciation is expressed to all of the authors for their significant contributions to this volume and their willingness to rewrite chapters many times; to my secretary, Gladys Adams, for her diligent cooperation and continuous encouragement; to my patient husband, Sol, who tolerates my editing and writing late into the night and on many weekends; and to Mary Grace Luke and others on the staff at Springer for enabling us to bring this volume to fruition.

PART I

Personal and Interpersonal Issues That Affect Military Families

CHAPTER ONE

Uniforms and Youth: The Military Child and His or Her Family

Lindsay B. Paden, MD, and
Laurence J. Pezor, MD

CONTROVERSY SURROUNDS THE LABEL OF "DIFFERENT" WHEN APPLIED TO THE military child and his or her family. Although many negative attitudes toward military life have abated (Rodriguez, 1984), the idea that military children are psychologically "sicker" than their civilian peers has persisted. As this chapter explores the unique social system of the military and its effect on the children and families, we suggest an alternative orientation in assessing a military child: he or she may not be all that different from civilian age counterparts (Chess & Thomas, 1984). A firm understanding of the unique structure and function of the military system is essential for accurate assessment of and meaningful interventions with a military family. In this chapter, we will outline the current knowledge base, ongoing investigations, available resources, and future directions aimed at understanding and responding to the special needs of the military child.

Family patterns within the military, as within the general population, have experienced a great deal of change since the 1970s. The shift

The views expressed in this chapter are those of the authors and do not reflect the official policy or position of the Department of the Navy, Department of Defense, nor the United States government.

from "traditional" family structures to those involving working couples, active-duty mothers, and single parents have necessitated a readjustment in the expectations of and services required by active-duty military members. The past two decades have witnessed increasing attention to the needs and rights of our youth. In 1977 the first National Conference on Military Family Research was organized in San Diego, California, and was attended by representatives of all of the military services; 1984 was declared "The Year of the Military Child" by the Department of the Army and was followed in 1985 by "The Year of the Military Family." This focus on the emotional needs of children continued into 1990, as the American Psychiatric Association chose the theme "Our Children: Our Future" for their annual meeting.

In addition to the increased professional and military awareness of the uniqueness and special needs of children, especially in the military, the lay community responded with several recent books and articles in the popular press on the subject of "military brats" (Long, 1986; Truscott, 1989; Wertsch, 1991) and with the formation of support groups such as Adult Children of Military Personnel (*Navy Times*, 12 August 91).

Increased attention to the needs and rights of all children, especially those within the military, must continue throughout the 1990s. Health care providers and child advocates will need to persist in the pursuit of improved support and educational services for military families and better access to mental health care for their children.

DEVELOPMENTAL ISSUES

When one considers the effect of either peacetime or wartime stressors on military children, a developmental perspective should be utilized. Various stages of development present new tasks for the child to master and new defenses to employ. Thus, responses to specific stressors may be quite different, depending on a child's developmental stage. The following brief examples of this process will provide a general framework for evaluating the effect of some specific stressors of military family life.

The first few years of life are crucial for the formation of attachment and the development of basic trust in the world as a safe and predictable place (Erickson, 1963). Most attachment theorists agree that separation from a parent, particularly the major attachment figure, during the first 2 years of life can be highly detrimental (Bowlby, 1988). Even more crucial may be the almost daily presence of both parents during the entire time of the process of separation and individuation, as described by Mahler and colleagues (Mahler, Pine, & Bergman,

1975). Clinically, a child whose parent is absent during this stage of development may manifest a variety of symptoms, including disruption of biological rhythms, loss of previously gained developmental abilities, eating and sleeping difficulties, general irritability, and poor social skills.

Preschool children do not have a fully developed sense of time and may react to even brief absences of a parent as if they were forever. Children of this age possess a magical sense of omnipotence, feeling that "whatever happens is under my control" (Fraiberg, 1959). Thus, children may attribute the absence of mother or father to their occasional wish to be rid of them when angry or to their own ongoing misbehavior. Oedipal-aged children (3–6 years) may have difficulty resolving the "family romance" if one of the parents is absent. In fact, it may be at the time of the father's return that boys of this age have the most difficulty. Aggression, toileting difficulties, sleep disturbances (including nightmares), and defiance are typical behaviors of an overstressed toddler.

Healthy school-age children are actively expanding their relationships outside the family, often looking for a "buddy" or "chum." It is expected that a family move, particularly one involving a major geographic relocation, would be most challenging for this age group. Clinically, their struggle for acceptance within a peer group may be disrupted by symptoms of withdrawal, regression, and perhaps overt depressive symptomatology.

Likewise, while struggling with identity issues and separation from their parents, adolescents will be placed at a great disadvantage if there is an interruption of important peer relationships because of a move (Shaw, 1979a). Adolescents searching for a sense of identity (Erickson, 1963) frequently rebel or challenge authority within the rigid structure of the military. How better to embarrass one's parents or make them angry than to misbehave or cause trouble on a military installation? Clinically troubled adolescents present with symptoms of aggression, anger, social withdrawal, and depression. Other externalizing behaviors—including substance abuse, promiscuity, and illegal activities—are often the product of externally induced stress at this developmental stage.

PEACETIME STRESSES AND STRENGTHS

Children from military families are subjected to a variety of unique peacetime stresses, including frequent, often sudden moves; forced adaptation to new communities and schools (many in foreign countries); regular separation from at least one parent due to deployments or remote assignments; potentially dangerous occupations for parents; and the probability of middle-age retirement for at least one parent. Additionally, they may be aware of the haunting possibility of war, with the attendant risks of a parent being injured, killed, captured, or reported missing in action. Particularly when they live on a military base, children inhabit a highly structured and often rigid environment, a patriarchal society with a well-defined hierarchy based on rank and a formalized social caste system (Shaw, 1979b). In this setting, a curious, independent, and occasionally stubborn child may experience significant conflict and frustration, which may result in behavioral disturbance. Children in civilian families may experience one or more of these same stressors but rarely all at once or for a similarly extended period.

The effect of these stressors may be mitigated, however, by additional resources provided by the military to which civilian children may not have access: a relatively stable family income, adequate housing, a supportive extended community, low-cost or free medical care, military-sponsored activities and recreational facilities, and Department of Defense (DOD) schools (Rodriguez, 1984; Shaw, 1987). The consistency of expectations and regulations that typify many of these patriarchal families may also prove beneficial to the children; that is, the rules do not shift in a confusing manner.

PARENT ABSENCE

Virtually all research to date addressing the response of military children to the absence of a parent has looked at the absence of the father. Initially, most studies suggested that father absence was universally detrimental to children. The effects are usually described as more significant for boys than for girls, contingent on the age and developmental stage of the child, and related to the quality of the preexisting relationship between the child and the father. There have been reports of decreased school performance, increased visits to base clinics by both spouses and children, and of depression and behavioral problems (Jensen, Grogan, Xenakis, & Bain, 1989).

In one of the earliest studies, Lynn and Sawrey (1959) found that 8–9-year-old Norwegian boys whose sailor-fathers were absent were more immature and showed poorer peer adjustment and impaired masculine identification. Crumley and Blumenthal (1973) considered the cycle of separation and reunion to be one of gross developmental interference, which would leave psychological scars on the developing psyche. Among a group of psychiatric referrals, they found a higher incidence of emotional problems for persons who experienced paternal absence during childhood than for those who did not. Hillenbrand (1976) summarized the findings of several studies related to father absence. Males tended to react to father absence with increased dependency, lower scores on intelligence and achievement tests, a "feminine" cognitive pattern, and feminine sex-role preferences. She found that absence of the father beginning before age 5 was associated with future aggressiveness and increased dependency in boys who had older brothers. First-born boys showed increased quantitative ability the longer the father was gone. There were no apparent effects on girls.

Yeatman (1981) reported transient symptoms in at least one child of 61% of families in which the service member went away on an unaccompanied tour. These included disciplinary problems, phobias (particularly fear of the dark), somatic complaints, and a decline in school grades. Chandler (1981) also documented temporary declines in school performance for boys whose fathers had been absent for 1 year or more. These declines gradually subsided on the father's return.

Father absence due to death, divorce, combat duty, or prisoner-of-war status has been thought to be more detrimental to the emotional adjustment of children than absence under less traumatic conditions. (Studies related to prisoner-of-war status are discussed in a later chapter of this book.) Anecdotal evidence also suggests increased difficulties for children from cross-cultural families (Cottrell, 1978).

Shaw (1987) described six factors that are important in the reaction of a child to the absence of the father: the length of the father's absence, the developmental stage of the child, the child's gender, the ability of the mother to expand her parental role, the availability of male (father) surrogate models, and the quality of the relationship of the child with the father prior to the separation. Clearly, it is not merely the absence of a parent that is significant. In fact, some studies report that children raised in single-parent families show little difference in emotional/behavioral problems from children raised in traditional two-parent families (Compas & Williams, 1990).

Several authors have found evidence of improved or higher functioning in certain children while their fathers were gone (Dahl & McCubbin, 1975; Nice, 1978; Pedersen, 1966). They theorize that the absence of the father encourages the child to become more independent, more active in the operation of the family, and more self-confident. Of significance is the impact of mother's psychopathology and her coping skills during the absence of father. For example, children of dominant mothers who provide a high level of supervision show fewer symptoms, while boys of mothers who "lack empathy and positive regard" are more likely to have low self-esteem (Jensen et al., 1989).

Pedersen (1966) suggested that a psychologically healthy mother can significantly counteract the effect of the father's absence. He concluded that "the extent of father-absence in the child's history bears no relationship to the adequacy of the child's emotional adjustment" (p. 326). Similarly, Jensen et al. (1989) concluded that "the effects of father absence under routine conditions in relatively healthy samples may exert no significant effects independent of intervening family stressors or maternal psychopathology" (p. 171). They found that the longer the father was away, the greater were the symptoms in the child but that "relatively brief absences under routine, non-extreme conditions exert minimal effects on children's behavior and emotional development" (p. 174). Children's symptoms may be mediated by their mother's psychiatric symptoms and other family stresses occurring during the absence. But we doubt that prolonged father absence can be totally discounted, as Pedersen suggested, as a contributory factor.

What happens when it is mother who is on active duty and is sent away? Subsequent to the Iraqi invasion of Kuwait in August 1990 and during Operation Desert Shield/Storm, 13% of the troops deployed were women (Embry, 1991), many of whom were mothers. Was it more difficult for children to be separated from their mothers? Does it matter if the children are boys or girls? Are there critical ages where the mother's absence is most disruptive? What about the uncommon situation of having both mother and father deployed? How does this affect the development of their children? These and other questions can certainly be topics of speculation, but answers will come only through research and further evaluation, and there has been little of either to date. One would expect that these events would be very stressful to children, particularly those at sensitive developmental stages. Amen et al. (Amen, Jellen, Merves, & Lee, 1988) have described ways to minimize the negative effects of parent absence.

Sometimes the reunion is more difficult than the separation (Gonzalez, 1970), and frequent partings and reunions may have a cumulative effect. Baker et al. (1968) found that the stress of the father's return after a prolonged absence is as great as that experienced at the time of his departure. In fact, some children remain symptom-free during the separation, only to experience nightmares and clingy behavior when the parent returns. Yeatman (1981) described readjustment problems in 38% of children whose fathers had been on an unaccompanied tour of duty. They displayed fear and resentment, shyness, and separation anxiety. In this survey, children less than 2 years of age were at greatest risk.

Case Examples

Sean, an 11-year-old son of an active-duty marine couple, was referred for evaluation of attentional and behavioral problems manifested at home and school. Review of his past history revealed that his father frequently accepted assignments away from home. In fact, at the time of his presentation, Sean's father was stationed several hundred miles from home. This separation was necessitated in part by the family's need to remain near a major medical center for Sean's chronic medical problems. Over the course of the evaluation, it became clear that Sean's emotional and physical distance from his father played a major role in the aggravation of his decreased attention, poor concentration, and dysphoria. Although medication alleviated much of his difficulty with attention and concentration at school, therapy centered on exploring feelings of abandonment and loss as they applied to the relationship with his father. As both parents began to better understand the importance of their physical presence, they were able to make significant changes in their career plans and to better balance the attention paid to family needs.

Steven, an intelligent 10-year-old, was referred when he became significantly more defiant and difficult to handle at school. After his father's deployment to the Persian Gulf, Steven became the "man of the house." Quickly overwhelmed by this role, Steven became very anxious and feared for his father's safety. At times of his greatest fear and anxiety, Steven would "see" an "old man in a tree," who would comfort him. Over time, dynamically oriented psychotherapy reduced his anxiety and alleviated the visual hallucinations. No medications were necessary, and therapy expanded to include the father upon his return.

GEOGRAPHIC MOBILITY

With the average military assignment lasting only 3 to 4 years and many requiring more frequent changes, children of the military are subjected to regular geographic relocations, with the attendant stresses of making new friends, severing ties with old ones, adapting to new schools and curricula (and often entire cultures), and the disruption of what is familiar. Also, during a stressful move, parents and siblings are likely to be more irritable and less supportive. This may be partially countered by the excitement and anticipation of change.

Kurlander et al. (Kurlander, Leukel, Palevsky, & Kohn, 1961) found that military children who were referred to a child guidance clinic had already experienced a median of 6 geographic moves, compared to only 1.5 for civilian children. Darnauer (1976) found that by the age of 16 to 18 years, a sample of military adolescents had experienced an average of 5.8 moves. In a comparison survey of civilian and military adolescents, one-half of the military youth had moved in the past year, compared to one-fifth of the civilians (Long, 1986).

Case Example

Melissa, the 16-year-old daughter of an army lieutenant colonel, presented with an 8-month history of severe depressive symptoms. Her social withdrawal, poor school performance, low energy level, and suicidal ideation arose in the context of her father's change of duty orders. Having experienced relatively few moves with her military family, this adolescent perceived the trauma as devastating. The severity of her depression necessitated aggressive management with outpatient psychotherapy, medication, and firm, consistent structure and support from the family. As therapy progressed and depressive symptoms lessened, issues of separation–individuation, resentment of authority, and the family's identity within the military system were addressed.

Pedersen and Sullivan (1964) found that it was not the incidence of geographic relocation that predicted emotional disturbances in military officers' children but, more important, the parents' attitudes toward the move and toward the military in general. Most effects were described as time-limited. Jensen et al. (Jensen, Lewis, & Xenakis, 1986) summarized the studies by saying that "relocations do not cause psychopathology; rather, the difficulties of families with preexisting psychosocial dysfunction may be exacerbated by a stressful move" (p. 229). In fact, O'Connell (1981) suggested that mobility may be a positive experience for children, exposing them to new stimuli and challenging their resourcefulness.

EFFECTS OF RETIREMENT

With the possibility that the serviceperson has to retire after as few as 20 years of service, many military families face the prospect of an out-of-work provider or one who undergoes a major career change in his or her late 30s or early to mid-40s—much earlier than their civilian counterparts. Giffen and McNeil (1967) described lower pay (with attendant lower social status) and the loss of security as major stressors for the young retiree and his or her family. These factors, combined with midlife issues for men, menopause and/or returning to the work force for women, and separation issues for adolescents, can create a crisis for the family. Symptoms often include an increase in psychosomatic complaints, anxiety, depression, and, in children, behavioral disturbances. As adolescents attempt to define their identity, the primary wage earner also faces uncertainty about his or her status, occupation, and finances (Strange, 1984). Any therapeutic interventions with a military family at this developmental juncture must address the issues of loss, money concerns, insecurity, role confusion, and fears about the future.

ADVANTAGES

While there are many stresses unique to being raised in a military family, there are also many advantages. The opportunity to travel, to see different parts of the world and a variety of cultures, to share an identity with a large and often stimulating "family," to feel a sense of patriotism—that you are directly contributing to the protection of your country while having your basic needs (food, shelter, medical care) provided—is unusual. Maybe that is why many military children go on to join the military themselves. It is estimated that over 50% of our current troops were raised in military families (Embry, 1991).

Hillenbrand (1976) concluded that adverse life experiences can result in maladjustment in children, or they may actually provide an opportunity for maturation. Similarly, Shaw (1987) said:

> Frequent family moves, transcultural experiences, transient father absence, and early sponsor retirement represent crisis situations that are temporarily upsetting, not always in an unpleasant sense, which require reorganization and mobilization of the individual's adaptive capacities. In this context these experiences imply neither good nor ill. Some individuals arrive at higher levels of adaptation with effective coping and problem solving patterns of behavior. Others achieve a less adaptive equilibrium. In those instances where the parents have identified with the military way of life and assimilated the shared network of values and loyalties, many of these stresses can be significantly mitigated if not offset by the other psychosocial advantages of this community. (p. 544)

EFFECTS OF WAR ON CHILDREN

The specific stresses of war present an extraordinary challenge for the military child. Some of the earliest studies related to military children involved the exploration of the effects of war. Anna Freud participated in the evaluation and care of children who were separated from their parents during the German bombing of Great Britain (Freud & Burlingham, 1943). In most homes, separation from the mother was more traumatic than separation from the father, probably due to stronger prior attachment. According to Igel (1945) separation from parents is a traumatic experience which creates more serious problems for the child than that created by an external disaster, including bombing. After World War II there were several books and articles describing how children coped with wartime stresses and the potential harmful effects (Escolona, 1975; MacDonald, 1943; Rosenblatt, 1983).

During the 1970s two new sources of information became available. The war in Vietnam resulted in many American prisoners of war being separated for prolonged periods from their families. Those studying these men also studied their wives and children (McCubbin, Hunter, & Metres, 1974). (See chapter 3 for additional information on prisoners of war.) Also, the Middle East wars involving the Israelis in 1967 and 1973, the continued unrest in the Middle East, and conflicts in Central America and Northern Ireland have provided additional information about the ways children cope with the unpleasantness of war (Arroyo & Eth, 1985; Rosenblatt, 1983; Ziv, Kruglanski, & Shulman, 1974).

Naturally, one assumes that war is stressful for all human beings. MacDonald (1943) suggested that war would intensify preexisting emotional disturbances in children, thus contributing to increased delinquency. Escalona (1975) commented on the confusion that a child must face when his or her culture expects an internalization of kindness and tolerance and the control and channeling of aggressive and hostile feelings, while at the same time demonstrating cruelty and aggression toward another nation.

Milgram and Milgram (1975) described a two-fold increase in anxiety in fourth- and fifth-grade students during the Yom Kippur War in Israel. Arroyo and Eth (1985) proposed that "war and extreme civil strife can adversely affect the local children and adolescents psychologically and disrupt their normal development" and that "the more intimately (or personally) and catastrophically the youth are victimized, the greater is the risk of developing seriously disabling psychiatric symptoms" (p. 107).

Baker (1990) described the mental health of 796 Palestinian children living in the occupied territories. There was an increase in depression and anxiety as well as in conduct problems, including disobedience to parents, fighting with and disturbing others, and irresponsibility. There was a predictable increase in the fear of Israeli soldiers and a reluctance to leave home. A different observation was that children who were involved in the fighting themselves had an increase in self-esteem.

Dreman (1989) described a 10-year follow-up of children whose parents had been killed by terrorist activities in Israel. His findings suggest that children exposed to violence, war, or other traumatic events may experience posttraumatic stress disorder (PTSD) symptoms, which may become chronic if there are no interventions. These findings are similar to those from the excellent long-term studies of children exposed to civilian traumas by Terr (1990).

Arroyo and Eth (1985) studied 30 children referred to an outpatient psychiatry clinic who had emigrated from Central America to southern California. All of these children had been exposed to warfare and violence. Ten had symptoms of PTSD, and nine were diagnosed as having adjustment disorders. They described different manifestations at various developmental levels, with regression and somatic complaints more prevalent in younger children and serious acting out and suicide attempts more common in adolescents.

Embry (1991), a consultant for the Department of Defense, found that having a parent go to the Persian Gulf initially created symptoms of separation anxiety in military children. These symptoms resembled chronic grief and persisted even after reunion occurred. Children who had suffered prior traumas experienced a reactivation of symptoms. The Gulf War was unique in that far greater numbers of women were involved, and many of these women were single parents and/or had left behind infants or toddlers. Sixty percent of the deployed were married, and an additional 20% were in committed relationships. This is in sharp contrast to those who served in wars as recent as Vietnam, in which 85% of the troops were unmarried.

If a parent is killed in a military activity, the child will likely experience bereavement similar to what they would experience in the loss of a parent from other causes (Kreuger, 1983). However, the military, the government, or an opposing country or its leader could serve as targets for the displacement of anger generated by the loss.

TELEVISION COVERAGE OF WAR

Beginning with Vietnam and continuing with the war in the Persian Gulf, children were subjected to immediate, live portrayal of the power, excitement, and horror of war. Television literally brought the Gulf War into everyone's living room, shrinking any geographic distance. Children, particularly preschoolers, given their cognitive developmental level, had difficulty discerning that the actual fighting was thousands of miles away. These distortions resulted in unrealistic fears of danger and potential fighting in their own neighborhood. Clinically, this was manifested by fear of leaving home, nightmares, and insomnia. The trauma of the graphic depiction of violence, injury, death, and destruction may have potentiated worry that their parent was directly involved, thus activating fears of abandonment. Adolescents questioned their own and society's values as they saw the death and destruction portrayed, at a time when they were being directed and encouraged to exercise control and to respect property and human life.

During the 1973 Middle East war, Israeli children viewed more TV with their parents but spent a significantly decreased amount of time in play (Cohen & Dotan, 1976). Many became frightened by the constant threat portrayed and were reluctant to go outside their homes.

The direct effects of televised armed conflict, intertwined with the fact that one or both parents have been sent to a combat zone, require further study. How children of military families react in comparison to children in civilian families is still unknown. Clinical experience suggests that children of nonmilitary families also were deeply affected by television accounts of the Gulf War. Virtually no child with a TV was immune. This phenomenon presents a potential for widespread traumatic reactions reaching far beyond just military families.

PSYCHOPATHOLOGY AND MILITARY CHILDREN

Given these peacetime and wartime stressors, how do military children compare with other children? Is there any such thing as a military brat?

The literature pertaining to the occurrence of psychopathology in military children contains two opposing theoretical stances. The first is that children of the military are subjected to unique, unusual, and life-altering stresses, and as a result they experience a significantly increased incidence of psychopathology (Cantwell, 1974; LaGrone, 1978; Yeatman, 1981). The opposing view is that the children of the military are similar to children in the general population, and in spite of hardships or adversity, they function just as well and experience no greater incidence of psychopathology (Crain & Stamm, 1965; Jensen, Xenakis, Wolf, & Bain, 1991; Kenny, 1967; Morrison, 1981).

The incidence of psychopathology in children from military families has been estimated to be from 1% to 35% of the total population (Jensen et al., 1986). There have been reports of increased behavioral problems in military children, and LaGrone (1978) described a "military family syndrome" characterized by out-of-control children, depressed mothers, and authoritarian fathers. Other studies have been more optimistic. Kenny (1967) and White (1976) found lower or similar rates of conduct disorders and behavioral problems in their studies of military children, compared to age-matched civilian control groups. Kenny also found military children to have lower delinquency rates, higher achievement scores, and a higher median IQ than their civilian counterparts. Morrison (1981) found a similar incidence of conduct disorders but a *lower* incidence of psychosis and drug or alcohol abuse in military children, compared with their civilian counterparts.

Jensen et al. (Jensen, Bloedau, & Davis, 1990; Jensen, Bloedau, Degroot, Ussery, & Davis, 1990) looked at various risk factors for the development of psychopathology in military children. They found that the levels of parental psychopathology and the extent of the life stresses in the family were most predictive. A history of divorce and smaller family size also helped to distinguish children in the clinical group from controls.

In a more recent study, Jensen et al. (Jensen, Richters, Ussery, Bloedau, & Davis, 1991) used multiple informants (child, teacher, and both parents) to survey symptoms of psychopathology in military children. This study did not find evidence of greater psychopathology in these children. It did find a correlation between the parent's level of stress and their assessment of their children. Parents who described themselves as being under significant stress reported higher levels of symptomatology in their children, although the children, in self-reports, did not differ from controls. The conclusion was that there was no evidence of a military family syndrome.

CURRENT SERVICES AND FUTURE NEEDS

The magnitude of needed services for military children and families should be no surprise. Conservative estimates from the Defense Medical Information System (DMIS) indicate that during fiscal year (FY) 1990 there were over 2.1 million military dependent children 17 years of age or younger. Of these, approximately 1.6 million were children of active-duty members, and nearly 600,000 were children of reserve, retired, or deceased members (see Table 1.1).

The Institute of Medicine (1989) estimated that approximately one-quarter of the general population of the United States is under the age of 18 years and at least 12% has a diagnosable mental illness at any given time. Extrapolating this to the DMIS estimates, almost 250,000 military children would be in need of mental health services. Ninety percent of these children are under 13 years of age, with an overall median age of 5.3 years (Ursano, Holloway, Jones, Rodriguez, & Belenky, 1989).

Table 1.1   Worldwide Military Dependent Children

AGES	ARMY	NAVY	AIR FORCE	OTHER[a]	TOTAL
0–4	223,977	201,758	169,246	12,278	607,259
5–14	448,013	359,830	352,691	25,958	1,186,492
15–17	120,688	96,662	108,444	6,831	332,625
Totals	792,678	658,250	630,381	45,067	2,126,376

[a]Includes Coast Guard, Public Health Service, and National Oceanic and Atmospheric Administration.
Source: Defense Medical Information System, FY90 Population Report, Computer Data Base.

In his analysis of the mental health resources needed by the military to provide for its children, Srabstein (1983) recommended a ratio of one military child and adolescent psychiatrist for every 5,200 children. He projected that the army needs 49 active-duty child psychiatrists; the navy, 16; the air force, 17; and joint military commands, 6; for a total of 88 in all branches. In light of these figures, how well does the military provide for its children? As shown in Table 1.2, at the end of 1991 there were few military mental health providers, particularly for children. Child psychiatrists were in short supply (1/33,800 children). These shortfalls were echoed across the disciplines of general psychiatry, psychology, social work, and pediatrics.

Partially offsetting this deficiency was a fairly liberal insurance program, the Civilian Health and Medical Program of the Uniformed Services (CHAMPUS). In FY 90 the total expenditure for psychiatric/psychotherapeutic services under this program was $517,841,002, of which nearly $350 million was spent for children and adolescents (OCHAMPUS, 1991). Given that military psychiatric care is less costly

Table 1.2   Tri-service Comparison of Medical Resources for Military Children, December 1991

	ARMY	NAVY	AIR FORCE
Active duty population	842,126	808,305	556,191
Children ages 17 and under	792,678	658,250	630,381
Pediatricians	436	285	263
Billets, general	275*	109	215
Billets, specialty		52	50
Child psychiatrists,	38	13	12
full-time billets[a]	23	8	13

[a]Includes both general and specialty billets.
Source: Compiled from DMIS; army, air force, and navy detailers (December 1991).

than civilian care (Grant, 1978), there has been renewed interest both in providing services for children and in "recapturing" some of these dollars. We will discuss some initiatives to do this in the section on resource sharing.

Despite the lack of military mental health manpower, special services exist specifically for military families addressing their unique needs within the military system. These include Family Service Centers, Family Advocacy Programs, and the Exceptional Family Member Program; they are widely available and invaluable to the health care provider, military or civilian, as well as to the families and children he or she serves.

FAMILY SERVICE CENTERS

Within the military system, comprehensive family support for dependent children and spouses remains a major goal. As early as 1965, and more consistently since the early 1980s, each branch of service has established one or more entities to offer education, support, and counseling for military families. These augment the services available through other civilian and military agencies (O'Keefe, Eyre, & Smith, 1984). Under administrative control of major commands, these centers rely on a variety of full- and part-time professional staff and volunteers.

Never since their inception have these organizations faced a tougher challenge than during the military involvement in the liberation of Kuwait and Operation Desert Shield/Desert Storm. Rising to the occasion, several centers served as clearinghouses for information and referral for services for families of deployed forces, both reserve and active duty. The rapid, well-organized, and effective response during this trying time further proved to commanders and dependents alike the utility and necessity of these services. (See chapter 8, "Military Family Service Centers," for additional information.)

EXCEPTIONAL FAMILY MEMBER PROGRAM

The DOD-wide Exceptional Family Member Program (EFMP), implemented in the late 1980s, provides special detailing consideration to eligible families. Any military member who has a dependent with special medical, psychiatric, or educational needs (including speech and occupational or physical therapy) is required to enroll. This will ensure that the service member is assigned only to duty stations where these needs can be met.

Furthermore, there are several worldwide central screening committees (CSCs) through which all applications are reviewed. In addition to registering deserving families, these CSCs provide specialized evaluations in speech and language pathology and occupational and physical therapy, as well as social work, psychology, and psychiatry. These multidisciplinary teams also provide evaluative and consultative services to isolated commands. The EFMP not only ensures that military families are able to access all needed services but also safeguards the medical treatment facilities from having to provide services for which they do not have the capability.

With over 160,000 school-age children within the DoD's Dependents' School (DoDDS) system overseas (Shaw, 1987), identification of the special educational needs of the child as well as knowledge of each overseas school's capabilities is paramount to providing legally mandated services. Avoiding the placement of a known special-needs child (learning-disabled, severely emotionally disturbed, physically handicapped) in a DoDDS school without acceptable services saves a family from further stress and disruption and also saves the military unnecessary relocation costs.

Through this program, military personnel commands demonstrate their commitment to the needs of the family, thereby increasing retention and diminishing undue hardship. Since enrollment is required by regulation, medical personnel, individual service members, their commands, and civilian health care providers are responsible for utilizing this important resource.

FAMILY ADVOCACY PROGRAMS

Another specialized service, the Family Advocacy Program, expands the civilian model of child and adult protective services. Since 1981 the military has mandated reporting of family violence. Allegations of physical or sexual abuse are evaluated through the Family Advocacy Division of social work departments utilizing a multidisciplinary team of social workers, physicians, and legal personnel. Within the navy, centralized family advocacy committees track allegations of abuse and recommend treatment options via case review subcommittees. More complete and comprehensive than their civilian counterparts, these committees allow for world-wide sharing of information and anticipated needs of involved families.

In 1989, the DoD established a central, multidisciplinary, tri-service team designed to respond to and coordinate interventions for multi-victim, out-of-home, sexual abuse cases. This Family Advocacy Command Assistance Team (FACAT) consists of highly trained experts standing ready to assist any military community worldwide.

Although rates of family violence within the military are not necessarily higher than those of the civilian populations (Jensen et al., 1986), the identification of family violence within the military receives significant command support and attention, thus increasing reported cases as well as improving interventions and treatment. Although occasionally criticized for taking early administrative action in cases of family violence, overall the military goes to great lengths to provide support and treatment for both victims and offenders.

Interventions include on-site counseling or community referral for victims and offenders, often at government expense. These treatment plans are closely tracked, and *families are not transferred in the middle of treatment*. Although it is necessary to criminally punish the perpetrator in some cases, the military family advocacy system strives for early recognition and treatment intervention. For example, within the closed military system, it is not unusual for a health care provider, co-worker, or neighbor in government housing to refer a family. The sensitivity and concern of the military system for family advocacy issues acts as a primary preventive factor.

RESOURCE SHARING AND COORDINATED CARE

Changing family patterns and the advent of managed health care have heightened awareness of the need for cooperative services between the military treatment facilities (MTFs) of all branches, private civilian providers, and those under contract to the MTFs. The various CHAMPUS demonstration projects in California, Hawaii, Texas, Virginia, and North Carolina are examples of concerted efforts to provide quality care within budgetary constraints.

Some of these projects operate like health maintenance organizations (HMOs) or preferred provider organizations (PPOs), with care being provided to the children and families by contracted civilian mental health professionals. Under resource sharing, child psychiatrists, pediatricians, and social workers are brought into the MTFs to provide services that would not be available through military providers. With coordinated care, the commander of the MTF has overall control of the health care dollars for his area (both military and CHAMPUS) and is responsible for providing all of the required care. These variations are intended to provide the highest quality of care at a reasonable cost. Additionally, there has been a move to reexamine and utilize available resources from a regional tri-service perspective.

One comprehensive program, the Fort Bragg Evaluation Project, provides an example of how these initiatives can have direct impact on the mental health needs of military children. The project was established by the Department of the Army and funded by a grant from the National Institute of Mental Health to provide *all* mental health services for the 22,000 military dependent children in the Fort Bragg, North Carolina, area. Established in 1989, it provides comprehensive diagnostic evaluations and complete therapeutic services, including inpatient care; outpatient individual, family, and group psychotherapy; day treatment; residential care; and foster care. Unique in the military, it employs 150 persons, including 3 child psychiatrists, and has an annual budget of $12 to 14 million. This project is being evaluated by an independent contractor to establish its cost-effectiveness and therapeutic efficacy. A comparison is being made with Fort Campbell, Kentucky, which is providing services under the traditional CHAMPUS model (Leonard Bickman, Ph.D., personal communication, April, 1991).

FUTURE NEEDS

We have outlined some of the research efforts that have surveyed the military child and summarized the currently available mental health resources. Several aspects of mental health care remain unaddressed.

First, the DoD and individual military services must establish a complete and more accurate picture of the military child, including total population, geographic location, and distribution within service branches and, most important, must make an assessment of collective and individual mental health needs. This should be accomplished in conjunction with an assessment of general and specialty pediatric needs. With the probability of military downsizing, a projection of trends and anticipated changes is required.

Once the needs are identified, the next question is how to provide for them: Can the needs best be met by prevention, education, or more traditional therapeutic interventions? Should additional child psychiatrists and psychologists, social workers, and family therapists be brought into active duty, or should the care be contracted—worldwide, nationally, or locally? Can resource sharing between the military and civilian health insurers work? What about the consolidation of care under a tri-service model? Do projects like the CHAMPUS Reform Initiative and the Fort Bragg Evaluation Project provide better care at a lower cost? These and other questions remain unanswered at present.

Should the military continue to expand the role of women, especially in combat? Does this have too negative an effect on their children's developmental process? If the commitment to women and single parents is made, can the military also provide adequate educational resources, mental health services, and affordable day care?

What is certain is that *child advocates within the military and civilian community must continue to lobby for and encourage expansion of services and attention to the needs of military children.* A strong, deployable military force can be maintained only on a solid foundation of family support. Providing for military youth promotes more stable functioning and encourages the retention of those in uniform.

REFERENCES

Amen, D. G., Jellen, L., Merves, E., & Lee, R. E. (1988). Minimizing the impact of deployment separation on military children: Stages, current preventive efforts, and system recommendations. *Military Medicine, 153,* 441–446.

Arroyo, W., & Eth, S. (1985). Children traumatized by Central American warfare. In S. Eth & R. S. Pynoos (Eds.), *Post-traumatic stress disorder in children* (pp. 103–120). Washington, DC: American Psychiatric Press.

Baker, A. M. (1990). The psychological impact of the Intifada on Palestinian children in the occupied West Bank and Gaza: An exploratory study. *American Journal of Orthopsychiatry, 60,* 496–505.

Baker, S. L., Fischer, E. G., Cove, L. A., Master, F. D., Fagen, S. A., & Janda, E. J. (1968). Impact of father absence: Problems of family reintegration following prolonged father absence. *American Journal of Orthopsychiatry, 8,* 347. (Abstract)

Bowlby, J. (1988). *A secure base: Parent-child attachment and healthy human development.* New York: Basic Books.

Cantwell, D. P. (1974). Prevalence of psychiatric disorder in a pediatric clinic for military dependent children. *Journal of Pediatrics, 85,* 711–714.

Chandler, J. L. (1981, May). *Down to the sea in ships: A study of father absence.* Symposium presented at the Annual Meeting of the American Psychiatric Association, New Orleans.

Chess S., & Thomas, A. (1984). *Origins and evolution of behavior disorders: From infancy to early adult life.* NY: Bruner/Mazel.

Cohen, A. A., & Dotan, J. (1976). Communication in the family as a function of stress during war and peace. *Journal of Marriage and the Family, 38,* 141–148.

Compas, B. E., & Williams, R. A. (1990). Stress, coping, and adjustment in mothers and young adolescents in single- and two-parent families. *American Journal of Community Psychology, 18,* 525–545.

Cottrell, A. B. (1978). Mixed children: Some observations and speculations. In E. J. Hunter & S. D. Nice (Eds.), *Children of military families* (pp. 61–81). Washington, DC: U.S. Government Printing Office.

Crain, A. J., & Stamm, C. S. (1965). Intermittent absence of fathers and children's perceptions of parents. *Journal of Marriage and the Family, 27,* 344–347.

Crumley, F. E., & Blumenthal, R. S. (1973). Children's reactions to temporary loss of the father. *American Journal of Psychiatry, 130,* 778–782.

Dahl, R. B., & McCubbin, H. I. (1975). *Children of returned prisoners of war: The effects of long-term father absence.* (Tech. Rep. No. 75–30). San Diego: Naval Health Research Center, Center for POW Studies.

Darnauer, P. F. (1976). The adolescent experience in career army families. In H. I. McCubbin, B. B. Dahl, & E. J. Hunter (Eds.), *Families in the military system* (pp. 42–66). Beverly Hills, CA: Sage Publications.

Dreman, S. (1989). Children of victims of terrorism in Israel: Coping and adjustment in the face of trauma. *Israel Journal of Psychiatry and Related Sciences, 26,* 212–222.

Embry, D. D. (1991, July). *Readjustment problems experienced by Desert Storm military personnel and their families.* Testimony before the Senate Committee on Veterans' Affairs, Washington, DC.

Erickson, E. H. (1963). *Children and society* (2nd ed.). New York: W. W. Norton.

Escalona, S. (1975). Children in a warring world. *American Journal of Orthopsychiatry, 45,* 765–772.

Fraiberg, S. (1959). *The Magic Years.* New York: Charles Scribner's Sons.

Freud, A., & Burlingham, D. T. (1943). *War and children.* New York: Ernest Willard.

Giffen, M. B., & McNeil, J. S. (1967). Effect of military retirement on dependents. *Archives of General Psychiatry, 17,* 717–722.

Gonzalez, V. R. (1970). *Psychiatry and the army brat.* Springfield, IL: Charles C. Thomas.

Grant, D. H. (1978). Monetary parameters in military child psychiatry. *Military Medicine, 143,* 123–124.

Hillenbrand, E. D. (1976). Father absence in military families. *The Family Coordinator, 25,* 451–458.

Igel, A. (1945). The effect of war separation on father-child relations. *The Family, 26,* 3–9.

Institute of Medicine. (1989). *Research on children and adolescents with mental, behavioral and developmental disorders.* Washington, DC: National Academy Press.

Jensen, P. S., Bloedau, L., & Davis, H. (1990). Children at risk: 2. Risk factors and clinic utilization. *Journal of the American Academy of Child and Adolescent Psychiatry, 29,* 804–812.

Jensen, P. S., Bloedau, L., Degroot, J., Ussery, T., & Davis, H. (1990). Children at risk: Risk factors and child symptomatology. *Journal of the American Academy of Child and Adolescent Psychiatry, 29,* 51–59.

Jensen, P. S., Grogan, D., Xenakis, S. N., & Bain, M. W. (1989). Father absence: Effects on child and maternal psychopathology. *Journal of the American Academy of Child and Adolescent Psychiatry, 28,* 171–175.

Jensen, P. S., Lewis, R. L., & Xenakis, S. N. (1986). The military family in review: Context, risk, and prevention. *Journal of the American Academy of Child Psychiatry, 25,* 225–234.

Jensen, P. S., Richters, J., Ussery, T., Bloedau, L., Davis, H. (1991). Child psychopathology and environmental influences: Discrete life events versus ongoing adversity. *Journal of the American Academy of Child and Adolescent Psychiatry, 30,* 303–309.

Jensen, P. S., Xenakis, S. N., Wolf, P., & Bain, M. W. (1991). The Military Family Syndrome Revisited: By the numbers. *Journal of Nervous and Mental Disorders, 179,* 102–107.

Kenny, J. A. (1967). The child in the military community. *Journal of the American Academy of Child Psychiatry, 6,* 51–63.

Kreuger, D. W. (1983). Childhood parent loss: Developmental impact and adult psychopathology. *American Journal of Psychotherapy, 37,* 582–592.

Kurlander, L. D., Leukel, D., Palevsky, L., & Kohn, F. (1961, March). *Migrations: Some psychological effects on children.* Paper presented at the annual meeting of the American Orthopsychiatric Association, New York.

Lagrone, D. M. (1978). The military family syndrome. *American Journal of Psychiatry, 135,* 1040–1043.

Long, P. (1986, December). Growing up military. *Psychology Today,* pp. 31–37.

Lynn, D. B., & Sawrey, W. (1959). The effects of father absence on Norwegian boys and girls. *Journal of Abnormal and Social Psychology, 59,* 258–262.

MacDonald, M. W. (1943). Impact of war on children and youths: Intensification of emotional problems. *American Journal of Public Health, 33,* 336–338.

Mahler, M. S., Pine, F., & Bergman, A. (1975). *The psychological birth of the human infant.* New York: Basic Books.

McCubbin, H. I., Dahl, B. B., & Hunter, E. J. (Eds.). (1976). *Families in the military system.* Beverly Hills, CA: Sage.

Milgram, R., & Milgram, N. (1975, January). *The effects of the Yom Kippur war on anxiety level in Israeli children.* Paper presented at the International Conference on Psychological Stress and Adjustment in Time of War and Peace, Tel Aviv, Israel.

Morrison, J. (1981). Rethinking the military family syndrome. *American Journal of Psychiatry, 138,* 354–357.

Nice, D. S. (1978). The androgynous wife and the military child. In E. J. Hunter & D. S. Nice (Eds.), *Children of military families* (pp. 25–37). Washington, DC: U.S. Government Printing Office.

O'Connell, P. V. (1981). *The effect of mobility on selected personality characteristics of ninth and twelfth grade military dependents.* Unpublished doctoral dissertation, University of Wisconsin, Milwaukee.

O'Keefe, R. A., Eyre, M. C., & Smith, D. L. (1984). Military family service centers. In F. W. Kaslow & R. I. Ridenour (Eds.), *The Military Family* (pp. 254–268). New York: Guilford Press.

Pedersen, F. A (1966). Relationships between father-absence and emotional disturbance in male military dependents. *Merrill-Palmer Quarterly, 12,* 321–331.

Pedersen, F. A., & Sullivan, E. J. (1964). Relationships among geographical mobility, parental attitudes and emotional disturbance in children. *American Journal of Orthopsychiatry, 34,* 575–580.

Rodriguez, A. R. (1984). Special treatment needs of children of military families.

In F. W. Kaslow & R. I. Ridenour (Eds.), *The military family* (pp. 46–72). New York: Guilford Press.

Rosenblatt, R. (1983). *Children of war.* New York: Doubleday.

Shaw, J. A. (1979a). Adolescents in the mobile military community. In D. X. Freedman et al. (Eds.), *Adolescent psychiatry* (Vol. 7, pp. 191–198). Chicago: University of Chicago Press.

Shaw, J. A. (1979b). The child in the military community. In J. D. Noshpitz (Ed.), *Basic handbook of child psychiatry* (pp. 310–316). New York: Basic Books.

Shaw, J. A. (1987). Children in the military. *Psychiatric Annals, 17,* 539–544.

Shaw, J. A., Duffy, J. C., & Privitera, C. R. (1978). The military child: A developmental perspective. In E. J. Hunter & D. S. Nice (Eds.), *Children of military families* (pp. 1–14). Washington, DC: U.S. Government Printing Office.

Srabstein, J. (1983). Geographic distribution of military dependent children: Mental health resources needed. *Military Medicine, 148,* 127–132.

Strange, R. E. (1984). Retirement from the service: The individual and his family. In F. W. Kaslow & R. I. Ridenour (Eds.), *The military family* (pp. 217–225). New York: Guilford Press.

Terr, L. (1990). *Too scared to cry.* New York: Harper & Row.

Trunnell, T. L. (1968). The absent father's children's emotional disturbances. *Archives of General Psychiatry, 19,* 180–188.

Truscott, M. (1989). *Brats.* New York: E. P. Dutton.

Ursano, R. J., Holloway, H. C., Jones, D. R., Rodriguez, A. R., & Belenky, G. L. (1989). Psychiatric care in the military community: Family and military stressors. *Hospital and Community Psychiatry, 40,* 1284–1289.

Wertsch, M. E. (1991). *Military brats: Legacies of childhood inside the fortress.* New York: Harmony Books.

White, J. H. (1976). An analysis of first year referrals to a new military child psychiatry clinic. *U.S. Navy Medicine, 67,* 18–21.

Yeatman, G. W. (1981). Paternal separation and the military dependent child. *Military Medicine, 146,* 320–322.

Ziv, A., Kruglanski, A. W., & Shulman, S. (1974). Children's psychological reactions to wartime stress. *Journal of Personality and Social Psychology, 30,* 24–30.

CHAPTER Two

Mothers in Uniform

Patricia J. Thomas, MS, and
Marie D. Thomas, PhD

*Striking a reasonable balance between the new
realities of our force composition and the primary
responsibilities of our service personnel to defend our
country is not an easy task. . . . But, gone are the days
when service members had to get permission from
their commanding officer before they got married.
Gone are the days when we relied
solely on young males to defend our country.*
*—Representative Jill Long before the
House Veterans Affairs Committee, February 1991*

BACKGROUND

Mothers in uniform are an anomaly in the military—symbols of self-
less love and lifegiving femininity immersed in a masculine institution that is devoted to conflict and destruction. Military managers who
must achieve a balance between concern for mothers and their young
children and for the mission of the armed forces face unique problems.
Twenty years ago there were no mothers in the uniform, and military
families that included children consisted of a male service member, his
civilian spouse, and their offspring. What sociopolitical forces brought
about the change? How have the military and the mothers adapted to
the inevitable role conflict? Can the relationship withstand the unique
pressures that war imposes? Are attitudes about military mothers related to beliefs about women in general?

The opinions expressed in this chapter are those of the authors, are not official, and do not
necessarily represent the views of the Navy Department.

Growth in Representation of Women in the Armed Forces

A phenomenal change in the gender mix of the military occurred during the 1970s, brought about by the initiation of the all-volunteer force, the declining pool of men eligible for military service, and the civil rights movement. As shown in Table 2.1, while women represented only 2.5% of all military personnel in 1973, their numbers had grown to almost 11% by 1989. Moreover, military women of today are more like their civilian age cohorts than was true 20 years ago and, in some respects, also more like military men. Marital and parental status are stark examples of this transition. While in 1973 only 18% of the enlisted women were married, compared to 52% of the men, by 1991 the marriage rate for women had risen to 47% (56% for men) (Office of the Assistant Secretary of Defense, 1992).

Parenthood among military women follows a similar trend to that of marriage, but the start of the growth curve came later. The erosion of restrictions on women with dependents was more gradual and lagged behind the removal of restrictions on women being married, as will be discussed in the next section.

Law and Policy Regarding Motherhood Since World War II

The basic legislation authorizing and regulating cadres of women in the United States armed forces is the Women's Armed Services Integration Act of 1948 (Public Law 625). This act established a policy of differential treatment of military women and men, with regard to age at enlistment or commissioning, highest rank, maximum number, and

Table 2.1   Change in Representation of Military Women in Department of Defense

SERVICE	1973		1989 TO 1991	
	NO. OF WOMEN	% OF FORCE	NO. OF WOMEN	% OF FORCE
Air Force	19,750	2.9	71,863	13.9
Army	20,736	2.6	79,164	11.5
Marine Corps	2,288	1.2	8,872	4.6
Navy	12,628	2.3	56,060	10.0
Department of Defense	55,402	2.5	215,959	11.0

other restrictions. It also stated that children of military women were not to be considered dependents unless their father was dead or their mother was their chief support. Executive Order 10240 (27 April 1951) provided the basis for, but did not mandate, the discharge of military women for pregnancy or if they had custody of a child for 30 or more days per year. Regulations that were subsequently implemented by the services interpreted this order in its most restrictive sense and prevented mothers from enlisting or being commissioned and required the discharge of a woman who became pregnant or who acquired a child through marriage or adoption. The rationale was that the effectiveness of the military would be reduced if mothers were permitted to serve, although paternalism certainly had an influence, as demonstrated by a letter to a Marine Corps captain who married a man with two teenage children. Her request for a waiver of the rule requiring her discharge was denied because "a woman who is the parent of a child should devote herself to the responsibilities of her household and children" (York, 1978).

The Air Force's prohibition against the accession of women who were married or mothers was abandoned in 1971, followed by the Navy and Army a few years later. A May 1973 Supreme Court decision in a discrimination suit filed by an Air Force woman officer (*Frontiero v. Richardson*, 1973) decreed that women are entitled to the same benefits for their dependents as are military men.

Recruiting practices regarding applicants who were mothers, particularly if they were not married, were more restrictive than the regulations required. To test reality, in 1978 we asked a graduate assistant to approach each of the services' recruiting stations and attempt to enlist. She described her marital status in various ways and said that she had a young child. When she was "single," the Army recruiter refused her application on the grounds of "character disorder," the Navy recruiter provided such strong discouragement that few would venture to breach the system, and the Air Force recruiter required that she assign permanent custody of her child to a civilian and said he would seek a waiver so that she could enlist. When she was "married," the practices of the services differed according to whether her husband was a civilian, in the same military service, or in another military service (P. J. Thomas, 1981).

Service regulations concerning women who become pregnant have been revised many times in the past 20 years. In the early 1970s, the Air Force was faced by three suits challenging the constitutionality of its regulation (*Guiterrez v. Laird*, 1972; *Robinson v. Rand*, 1972; *Struck v. Secretary of Defense*, 1971). In each case it was argued that the plaintiffs were being deprived of equal protection under the law, guaranteed in the Fifth and Fourteenth amendments. The Air Force prevailed in these cases based on "permissive rationality," that is, the regulation promoting the ability of USAF personnel to be immediately available to serve worldwide (Beans, 1975). Apparently, the services realized that their mandatory discharge policies for pregnancy were becoming difficult to defend in a political era when discrimination was suspect and ratification of the Equal Rights Amendment seemed assured. All branches modified their policies in 1972 to allow for a waiver to be granted in individual cases, but the impact varied by service (York, 1978). A Navy woman who wanted a waiver had to prove she could care for her child and work full-time. If the pregnancy terminated (spontaneous or elective abortion) prior to a Navy woman's discharge, she still was separated unless the waiver had been approved. Army women had to be married to obtain a waiver or, if unmarried when the pregnancy aborted, to prove themselves of good moral character. The Air Force instituted the most lenient regulation: marital status played no part in the waiver decision, and women who lost their babies reverted to nonpregnant status. The Air Force also reinstated the officers who had brought suit.

The retention-by-exception policies prevailed until April 1975. At that time the Department of Defense (DoD) directed that all of the services discontinue discharging women involuntarily for pregnancy and institute an optional separation policy based on the woman's request. Since that time, military policies regarding pregnant women have fluctuated between separation on request to no separation unless conditions warrant and obligations are met. All of the services still separate women who are found to be pregnant in basic training as an "erroneous enlistment," and some discharge them during the initial skill training that occurs soon after. After the first few months of the enlistment, however, it becomes more difficult for a pregnant woman who wants to be separated to obtain an honorable discharge. Navy policy, for example, states that "servicewomen should be advised that requests for separation will not normally be approved" (Department of the Navy, 1989).

York (1978) has argued that the objection of the armed forces to pregnant women was not pregnancy per se, since that condition is a temporary disability, but rather resistance to having mothers in their ranks. In her view, the services were really concerned about performance and assignability, a view that we feel is only a partial explanation. As will be demonstrated in a later section, ambivalence about women in the military extends beyond the issues of pregnancy and motherhood.

MANAGEMENT ISSUES

Biology requires that motherhood and fatherhood be addressed as two separate phenomena by employers, despite calls for equal treatment. Within the military, there are special policies applying solely to mothers (or mothers-to-be), support services to minimize the impact of children upon the military mission, and continuing efforts to manage pregnancy. Nevertheless, concerns are often expressed that readiness and productivity are affected by motherhood (but not fatherhood). Female and male parents without a civilian spouse must have a plan providing for their children in an emergency. Stiehm (1989) makes an interesting observation: "Many commanders are dubious about those plans, believing that they are 'just a paper,' and that in an emergency deployment, servicewomen would not show up. There is also, we suspect, a belief that service women who are mothers *should not* show up—that, as women, their first responsibility is to their children" (p. 21).

Personnel Policies

The military services do not treat mothers and fathers in the same way as personnel who have no dependents living with them. Parents with more than one child are not permitted to enlist in the Air Force or Navy, while the Army will accept an applicant with two children.[1] Neither the Army nor the Navy accepts for enlistment a single parent who has custody of a child, though the Air Force will seek a waiver for the applicant if there is only one child. Assignments, while still gender-controlled in all of the services due to combat restrictions on women, do not take parental status into account unless a hardship is involved; that is, a military parent with a child who requires specialized medical care will not be assigned to an area where the care is unavailable. In addition, extraordinary circumstances involving a dependent will result in a humanitarian reassignment for a deployed parent.

While separation policies make no mention of gender, in practice mothers appear to be discharged more frequently than do fathers for reasons associated with their dependents. A review of all fiscal year (FY) 1990 separations of Navy enlisted personnel for parenthood revealed that 0.91% of female parents were discharged for parenthood and 0.05% of male parents (Thomas & Thomas, 1992). This finding may be a reflection of the unequal frequency of dual military marriages (25% of enlisted women and 3% of enlisted men) and the tendency for the woman rather than the man to leave the military when faced with a geographic separation.

Absenteeism

Military women, like other women in the work force, are believed to incur more absences than do military men, primarily because of their parenting responsibilities. Ever since the DoD policy of discharging women who became pregnant was abolished, complaints about the impact of pregnancy and motherhood on lost time have been voiced. The Navy has conducted three research studies to investigate gender differences in the absences of its sailors. The first study, which analyzed medical and personnel data tapes, concluded that women have fewer days of absenteeism than do men, even when pregnancy is taken into account (Olson & Stumpf, 1978). The second research effort relied upon work diaries as a data source and found no difference in the nonavailable time of women and men (P. J. Thomas, 1987). The most recent project compared the absences of parents to nonparents by marital status and gender (Thomas & Thomas, 1993). Work diaries maintained by supervisors on their subordinates at 11 types of commands (ships, squadrons, and shore stations) in the United States and overseas were analyzed for a sample of over 5,000 personnel. Gender had no effect on lost time in ships, squadrons, and half of the shore command types. Bases where women did lose more time than men were catchment commands for pregnant women who must be transferred off ships. Prenatal medical care or convalescent leave following childbirth were the cause for the higher number of female absences.

An Army study of the absenteeism of women and men also reported no sex difference in overall lost time. Women did lose more time than did men for home/family reasons; men lost more time than did women for disciplinary reasons; but neither of these gender differences was statistically significant (Savell, Rigby, & Zbikowski, 1982).

Need for Support Services

The dramatic increase in the number of married enlisted personnel since the advent of the all-volunteer force has been responsible for the growth in support services in the armed forces. Facilities such as commissaries and exchanges, medical services for dependents, family housing, child development centers, family service centers, after-school and youth programs are now found on almost all bases and posts. Mothers in uniform, who make up less than 5% of the total active force, have greatly benefited from these facilities. While it is difficult to assess the degree to which mothers, as compared to fathers, are responsible for the growth in these services, few would argue that female parents almost always shoulder more of the day-to-day responsibility for a family's well-being than do male parents.

The recognition that child care is an appropriate and necessary function for the military to provide resulted from changes in the demographics of the male military population, but it has also benefited women. Twenty-five years ago, few married enlisted men had a working spouse, and even fewer had both children and a spouse who worked. Child care was the responsibility of the nonworking mother. At that time, male single parents were not prevalent enough to be counted. By 1990, 55% of the married male sailors with children had wives who worked outside the home ($N = 94,000$), and approximately 10,000 Navy enlisted men were single parents whose children were living with them. Thus, today over 100,000 *male* Navy personnel potentially need child care or after-school youth programs. Numerically fewer but proportionately more female military personnel need these services.

Pregnancy

The subject of pregnancy, as the antecedent to motherhood, is important to consider. The military would prefer to "manage" pregnancy in terms of preventing unwanted pregnancies, reducing the number of very junior personnel who become pregnant, minimizing the impact of pregnancy upon day-to-day activities in the workplace, and reducing the number of discharges due to pregnancy. Pregnancy is often used as one of the most powerful arguments against utilizing more women in the military or in support of retaining the restrictions on women in combat. It continues to be perceived as a "way out" for women that is not available to men—a way out of the service, out of a less desirable environment, or out of a physically strenuous job. Thus, some see pregnancy as a manipulative tool. Pregnancy is the "only 'temporary disability' that service members can inflict upon themselves without fear of punishment. It is also the only temporary disability that earns a service member the right to decide for herself whether to stay in the service or get out, notwithstanding the desires of her commander or the needs of the service" (Mitchell, 1989, p. 168).

Pregnancy prevention is encouraged through educational efforts and the provision of contraceptive devices, on request. Prior to the influx of women, birth control was not a training topic for men, although instruction on the prevention of sexually transmitted diseases often achieved the same result. Early efforts to deliver sex education to women met with objections from members of religious groups that either did not subscribe to the prevention of conception or felt that sex education promoted sexual activity. AIDS, however, made teaching the dangers of unprotected sexual encounters a life-and-death issue that overrode religious sensitivities in the eyes of the military. Today all enlistees are exposed to lectures regarding safe sex. In addition, condoms are free and easily available, and women can obtain contraceptive counseling and devices as part of their medical care.

Junior military personnel who become parents have a particularly difficult burden to bear. They usually are not eligible for family housing and must rent more expensive units in the community. They often are not well enough socialized into the military to be knowledgeable about the services available to them, and their income is inadequate to support a family. For women, there is the additional stress of becoming new mothers at a time when they are first learning their jobs. Thus, efforts to reduce the number of unplanned pregnancies focus on personnel in their first enlistment. Within Navy commands, these efforts include videotapes on the responsibilities of parenthood and workshops to discourage early parenthood led by teams of medical, legal, and supervisory personnel.

To reduce the impact of pregnancy and early motherhood on the workplace, support services for mothers have been improved, and new policies have been enacted. Prenatal care makes use of both of these approaches. Not only has the number of military obstetricians and base clinics grown, but most clinics established a policy of treating women in uniform first so that they can return quickly to their units. Disruption to work centers aboard ships was reduced when the time that a woman would be transferred ashore changed from "immediately" to the 20th week of pregnancy. Deploying Navy aviation squadrons now trade a pregnant member for a nonpregnant one who has the same occupational specialty so that they leave the United States with a full complement of personnel.

Policy changes and improved support services have also served to reduce the number of women discharged from the military due to impending motherhood. When on-base child care was very scarce, facilities for newborns were often nonexistent, even though military women had to return to work 6 weeks after giving birth. As a consequence, women without a co-located husband often would choose to leave the military and move "back home" prior to childbirth. New regulations make it more difficult to obtain a separation before completion of the current enlistment, and military child development centers now accommodate infants. Both of these changes have had the desired effect in the Navy. Forty-four percent of all women who were discharged during the first 2 years of their enlistment in the 1975–1977 period were separated for pregnancy; 24% of those discharged in 1985–1987 were discharged for pregnancy. It is anticipated that the 1989 revision in the policy, Management of Pregnant Service Women (Chief of Naval Operations Instruction 6000.1A), will reduce the percentage even further.

Abortion, which could reduce the number of pregnancies, has been removed from military control. Ever since passage of the FY79 Defense Appropriations Act, with its attached antiabortion amendment, the military has been prohibited from performing or paying for the abortions of active-duty women or dependents, except in very limited circumstances. The DoD opposed this amendment—officially because of its adverse impact on women living overseas and unofficially because it would result in more births to women in uniform. It is difficult to ascertain the extent to which this bill has caused financial hardship for women who paid for their abortions, has resulted in a higher military birthrate than prior to its passage, or has had adverse effects on the health of women who obtained abortions in foreign lands.

Hospitalization data for Navy women for several years preceding the FY79 Defense Appropriations Act showed that induced abortions consistently outnumbered births in Navy hospitals (Hoiberg & Ernst, 1980). By 1988, however, less than 15% of all pregnancies experienced by Navy enlisted women were terminated through an elective abortion (Thomas & Edwards, 1989). Thus, it is likely that the prohibition against military-paid abortions has resulted in more mothers in uniform than would have occurred if all options had been available to pregnant women at no cost.

The belief that pregnancy has a negative effect on the morale of the work group is widespread. While probably true in isolated cases, research conducted by the authors (e.g., Thomas, Thomas, & McClintock, 1991) does not support the validity of this belief. Stiehm (1989) raises an interesting question about whether pregnancy is any different in this regard from other factors that remove people from their work spaces:

> The "morale" factor (the supposed hostility of those who are not parents and who take up the slack when a mother requires a particular schedule or when a pregnant woman must use half a day for a prenatal checkup) is hard to estimate. . . . Still, military schedules are adjusted for people who hold second jobs, for people who have especially dependent dependents (such as a wife who cannot speak English or drive), and

for others. Thus, it is not clear that adjustments made for parents are especially hard on morale. (p. 221)

Part of the belief that women "use" pregnancy may actually be derived from general attitudes about pregnancy. Walton, Sachs, Ellington, Hazlewood, Griffin, and Bass (1988) demonstrated that pregnant women are often cast in a dependency role. They receive special courtesies and assistance in physical tasks that others would not receive. However, pregnant military women frequently argue that they are not as dependent as others believe.

Is pregnancy important because of the problem it creates, or does it serve as an unwanted reminder of women's sexuality? In this regard, unwed pregnant women are especially problematic. Stiehm (1989) relates the experience of a single woman who had been involuntarily discharged due to pregnancy. "She later miscarried, but the Navy insisted on discharging her because it could not 'condone' an unwed pregnancy or a 'dilution of the moral standards set for women in the Navy'" (p. 116). For those who believe in sexual abstinence before marriage, pregnant servicewomen are a reminder of immorality.

WHO ARE THESE MOTHERS?

Do military mothers differ from military women without children? From military fathers? The descriptive information typically reported by the armed forces does not shed much light on these questions, and the somewhat fluid nature of parenthood introduces error into whatever data do exist. Personnel acquire natural, step- and adoptive children; they divorce and lose custody of their children; they obtain custody of a child who has been living with the other parent. Although service and pay records are supposed to be modified promptly whenever the number of dependents changes, at each step (individual, command, and headquarters) delays occur. Moreover, a child of a single parent or dual military parent is attributed to the parent who claims her or him for pay purposes. The end result is that the military does not know how many of their single parents actually have custody, as opposed to financial responsibility only; which of their military-married-to-military personnel are nonsupporting parents; or who has changed parental status recently.

In an effort to develop an estimate of the number of single parents with custody and to anticipate military child care needs, the Navy is conducting large-scale surveys of its personnel on a biennial basis.

Table 2.2   Background Variables of Navy Mothers as Compared to Several Groups

VARIABLE	MOTHERS	NONMOTHERS	FATHERS
Mean age	28.17	24.54	30.98
Mean Years in Navy	7.17	4.16	10.59
Marital status			
Single	32%	71%	6%
Civilian spouse	32%	10%	91%
Military spouse	37%	19%	3%
Military intention			
Undecided	26%	37%	18%
20-year career	53%	25%	69%
Mean number of children	1.60	—	1.93
Mean age of children	5.05	—	6.69

Since data are obtained from all respondents, regardless of marital or parental status, comparisons can be made between parents and non-parents, women and men, on the background questions that are asked. Table 2.2 presents some comparative statistics on these groups.

Navy mothers are older, have served longer, and are more career-oriented than are nonmothers. Among married women, 54% of the mothers have a military spouse, compared to 65% of the nonmothers, suggesting that juggling two military careers and parenthood may be more responsibility than these couples are willing to assume.

Navy women have fewer children than do men, and their children are younger. Being a wage earner and the primary caregiver undoubtedly serves to limit family size. Navy fathers are older, have spent more years in the Navy, and, as a consequence, are more apt to remain in the service until eligible for retirement (20 years) than are mothers. These findings reflect differences between women and men in the military and are not unique to parents; that is, the proportion of men in senior pay grades is higher than the proportion of women in high pay grades, and these senior people are older and have already decided to make a career of the military. As Figure 2.1 shows, the proportion of women and men who are parents is very similar up to the second class petty officer level (E-5). From first class through master chief petty officer, the discrepancy between percentage of mothers and fathers grows. This difference is partially a function of the relative recency of

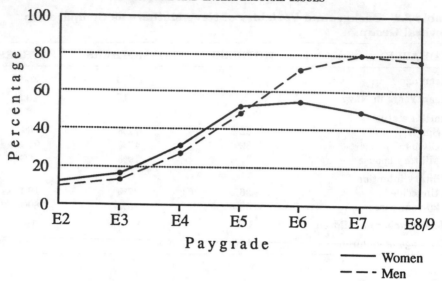

Figure 2.1   Paygrades for women and men.

the policy permitting women to have children and remain in the service. It also may reflect the difficulty senior enlisted women experience in combining parenthood with a Navy career.

MILITARY MOTHERS IN WARTIME

"The killing spirit and motherly love are necessarily inimical to each other and where the two are combined the one is weakened and the other perverted" (Mitchell, 1989, p. 170)

Operation Desert Storm impacted upon mothers in uniform with a force never experienced by fathers. We do not wish to imply that fathers do not feel the pain of separation and fear of the future when their units deploy to a war zone, only that the media have never burdened them with guilt for performing their military duty.

Newsweek (Beck, Wilkinson, Turque, & Bingham, 1990) called it the "Mom's War." *Time* focused on dual military couples assigned to the Persian Gulf (Sanders, 1991). Syndicated columnists, including Jack Anderson, Ellen Goodman, and Sally Quinn, wrote about the plight of military children when both parents or single moms were sent overseas in the line of duty. Pictures of tearful partings between mothers and infants tugged at the heartstrings of the nation. Editorials questioned what kind of a country sends its mothers to war. No event brought home the changed demographics of the military so forcefully as did Operation Desert Storm. A statement from a *People Weekly* story, titled "A Mother's Duty" (1990), captured the mood: "Until their country called, the working mothers of America's armed forces were struggling to balance the demands of home and career. Now they face danger, loneliness—and the fear that some of them might not live to see their children again" (p. 43).

According to the Pentagon, 35,000 of the 541,000 troops in the Gulf War were women, even though women still are excluded from combat. Among those troops were over 16,300 single parents with custody of their children, about one-third of whom were women, and about 1,200 dual military parents, both of whom had been deployed. Uncounted were the mothers with civilian husbands—men who were left behind to cope as "Mr. Moms." If the parental status of women in the other services parallels that of the Navy, approximately 12,000 mothers served in Operation Desert Storm.[2]

Public opinion was divided. A February 1991 poll conducted by the Associated Press revealed that 56% of the 1,007 respondents endorsed the participation of military women in the war against Iraq. Only one third, however, felt that mothers of young children should be sent to the war zone. Service regulations regarding single parents are unequivocal—they must be deployable worldwide or leave the military; regulations affecting new mothers, however, vary. Army and Air Force rulings exempt mothers from deploying for 6 weeks after childbirth, whereas the Navy does not deploy a woman until 4 months after birth. Congress brought pressure on the DoD, which agreed to consider a uniform policy that would defer for 6 months any woman who gave birth and a single parent who acquired custody; also, one member of a dual-military couple with children was to be permanently deferred. After the war ended, a policy was enacted to defer new mothers and single parents for 4 months.

In January 1991, two separate bills were introduced into the Senate and two into the House of Representatives[3] that would have had a profound effect on mothers in uniform. Dubbed the "Military Orphan's Bills," their intent was to exclude from combat single parents and one member of a dual military couple with children or to give these parents the option of turning down an assignment to a hostile area. In introducing his bill, Senator John Heinz said, "It is not for the convenience of the individual that I propose this, but to protect our posterity, our children, from being orphaned by an outdated policy that does not take into account the dramatic changes in American society and in the American armed forces" (January 31, 1991). The Pentagon's objection to these bills, which would have affected 5% of the active force

(66,000 single parents and 47,000 dual-military parents) was couched in terms of reduced effectiveness,[4] lack of fairness to personnel who are not single parents, and the voluntary nature of military service.

Each of the services requires that single and dual military parents have a dependent care certificate on file. These forms represent contingency plans for evacuating children from an overseas hostile area to a guardian in the United States and for caretakers if the parent is (or parents are) called to war. The forms are renewed at every new duty station and must be signed by the designated care provider. According to the Pentagon, the system worked during Operation Desert Storm. The Navy, for example, reported that only 4 of the more than 21,000 female and male reservists called to active duty were unable to serve because of child care problems. Another four reservists were returned early from the Gulf region for humanitarian and dependency reasons. Among the 82,600 active-duty personnel who were in the Gulf War, 157 were returned early for problems involving adult dependents, close relatives, and children (Department of the Navy, 1991). These statistics are rather remarkable. Navy leaders believe that the reason so few problems were experienced is that Navy personnel regularly deploy. The Army claimed that less than 0.1% of its single and dual military parents were unable to deploy because of inadequate plans for the care of their children.

Immediately following the ceasefire, Congress began to hear testimony on abolishing the combat restrictions on women or at least permitting women to fly in combat aircraft. One of the arguments leveled against moves to amend the law was the very nature of women. To quote General Robert H. Barrow, USMC (retired), "Women give life. Women sustain life, nurture life, but they can't take life. If you want to make a combat unit ineffective, assign women to it" (testimony before the Senate Armed Services Subcommittee of 18 June 1991). Opponents of the legislation argued that unless the military is able to mandate birth control, pregnancy will occur and women will have a way to leave the combat zone.

A bill co-sponsored by Representative Pat Schroeder (D-CO) and Representative Beverly Byron (D-MD) to permit Air Force women to fly combat planes and to repeal combat restrictions on Navy women quickly passed the House in May. Senators opposed to the legislation, however, introduced an amendment that would form a presidential commission to "study the issues" further before any change in the law was made. Among the issues the commission was charged to study were pregnancy and child care. On 31 July 1991, the Senate voted in favor of overturning the laws that bar Air Force and Navy women from flying combat missions *and* created a 15-member commission that reported out its recommendations on women in combat to Congress in November 1992. The legislation was written into the 1992 defense authorization bill, which was signed by President Bush in December 1991.

In some respects, the Gulf War was an extraordinary example of the dilemma faced by many working mothers daily—the conflict between work and family. Women who fulfilled their duty to country were alternately praised for honoring their commitment and castigated for abandoning their children to relatives or friends. Journalistic debates over whether they were doing something wrong added to their sense of guilt. Children's rights advocates and child development experts warned of the deep trauma the children would suffer—the emotional turmoil from knowing that they might never see their mother again, diminished belief in the existence of a just world, and anger toward a parent who left them. Perhaps these predictions were valid. In no other war were children exposed to cockpit views of smart bombs homing in on their targets, tanks moving across the desert, and graphic closeups of corpses in the sand. Just like the adults around them, they were obsessed with around-the-clock TV news channels. But why wouldn't a child be equally concerned when the parent in the war zone was a daddy?

Women were accused of denying the damage being done to their children because, as mothers, they would be unable to function in a war zone if they acknowledged it. Even homecoming for these mothers was not treated by reporters as a joyous reunion. On Mother's Day, a major daily newspaper in a city that is home to over 140,000 military personnel, ran a feature article titled "Even While Their Country Called, So Did Their Children" (Gaines, 1991). The article described the anguish of a young Navy mother whose 13-month-old daughter had forgotten her and how to say "mama"; it spoke of recementing relationships and trying to reestablish trust with older children.

SHOULD WOMEN BE IN THE MILITARY?

The ambivalence that exists about the role of mothers in the military begs the more basic question: should women be in the military at all? Pragmatists argue that the military needs women because of a declining pool of suitable young men. This is not a universal belief, however. Brian Mitchell, in *Weak Link: The Feminization of the American Military* (1989), feels that he speaks for the silenced majority who are convinced that women have weakened, rather than augmented, the military. His arguments are hardly new but reflect images of women that have existed for thousands of years. Arguments that insist upon the differences between women and men reinforce the notion of woman as "other." Some images demonstrate ambivalence about women's sexuality; women are seen as whores, sex objects, seductresses, or lesbians. Other images focus on women's capacity to bear children, viewing women as madonnas, earth mothers, or fertility goddesses. These images all serve to set women apart from men, and each is integral to beliefs about women in the military.

Simone de Beauvoir (1952) created the notion of woman as the "other" to describe the fact that, because the world is the work of men, they see themselves as the Subject and women as something else. The sense of being the other is experienced by all women who live or work in androcentric settings.

The military is the ultimate male-centered institution. In reality, many of the arguments against women in combat (or women in the military, for those who are even more conservative), center around the fact that women are *not* men. Women are seen as other because, on the average, they are not as physically strong as men or because they are not the same shape. According to Mitchell (1989), "the smaller size and different shape of women has caused innumerable problems solved only by a boom in the development and procurement of special clothing and equipment" (p. 161). Yet De Pauw (1988) points out that the military has never had difficulty providing uniforms for allies whose average male is smaller than the average American woman. The physical strength argument, long used to oppose women in combat, is now viewed as less credible since the Gulf War. One of the lessons learned, documented by the Center for Strategic and International Studies, was that the nature of war had been changed by the effect of high technology (Blackwell, Snider, & Mazarr, 1991).

Another common argument involves the effect of women's presence on male bonding; women are other, and men cannot be expected to bond with them. "The presence of women inhibits male bonding, corrupts allegiance to the hierarchy, and diminishes the desire of men to compete for anything but the attentions of women" (Mitchell, 1989, p. 190). Roush (1991), a retired Marine Corps colonel, finds Mitchell's assertions strange, given the bonding that occurs in mixed-gender revolutionary groups. He provides as examples the Eritrean rebels (35% women among front-line troops), municipal police and firefighting teams, and his experiences against women fighting with the Viet Cong. Bonding, he states, "requires three elements: organization for a common goal, the presence of (or potential for) danger, and a willingness to sacrifice. Not one of these elements is gender-specific" (p. 5).

A corollary of the male bonding argument is that combat effectiveness would be reduced in integrated units because men's natural protectiveness of women could cloud their judgement (Hart, 1990). Captain Carol Barkalow, USA (1991), aptly pointed out that different standards are applied to male/male selflessness than to male/female: "Then there's the argument that men will be overprotective of women. When men are overprotective of men, we give them awards for valor" (p. 30).

The ultimate argument, however, is that women should not be in combat because they are women and *not men*. Combat has been considered a man's job (Devilbiss, 1990), perhaps because some believe that testosterone gives men an edge on aggressiveness (Hart, 1990). Buckley (1991) states that women should not be in combat because it is against their nature. And finally, Gilder (1986) feels that breaking the tie between mother and child leads to disintegration of the human community.

Not surprisingly, some military women perceive themselves as other. Dunivin's (1988) study of women Air Force officers found that assimilation required adapting their roles to conform to male standards. However, they recognized and accepted that they were not men, at the same time knowing that they were not "typical" women. Therefore, they became "the exception" or other. This behavior extends to their reproductive function. These women forgo motherhood and sometimes even marriage to devote their energies to the military. They decry women who become pregnant as irresponsible or lacking in commitment. An extreme example of this behavior is the Air Force captain who agreed to submit to biweekly pregnancy tests in return for a job piloting a TR-1 spy plane (Hackworth, 1991).

Women's sexuality has been a prominent theme in myths and history (Hyde, 1985). This image of women is ambivalent—women's sexuality is at once attractive and arousing but also threatening and a source of fear.

Sexualization of work relationships, a common reaction to women in nontraditional jobs (Swerdlow, 1989), is apparent in the widespread sexual harassment experienced by military women. A 1989 survey of 38,000 military personnel revealed that 71% of the women had experienced three or more forms of sexual harassment (Martindale, 1990). Rustad (1982) described the sexual abuse of enlisted women in his study of an Army base in Germany that he called Khaki Town. Reports during 1990 of rapes at the Navy Training Center in Orlando, Florida, and sexual harassment at the U. S. Naval Academy prompted, in part, the convening of a high-level Navy study group to investigate the assimilation of women into the Navy (Moore, 1991).

Fraternization has been used as an argument against women in the military for many years, implying that the sexual allure of women is too difficult for most men to resist. Mitchell (1989) feels that women are dangerous even if relationships with men are not romantic or sexual: "Because men like women, men have difficulty treating women as they treat other men. . . . Comely and confident women who perform well will almost always win exaggerated praise. Some are more successful at their jobs because they can easily elicit the cooperation of charmed men" (p. 191).

Male obsession with female sexuality has forced military women of all generations to endure classification as whores or lesbians. (What could be worse than a whore? Someone who is not interested in men at all!) Treadwell (1954) documented the smear campaign directed against the Women's Army Auxiliary Corps (WAACs) and, later, the Women's Army Corps. Among the rumors circulating about women who joined the Army were that they solicited men and engaged in sex acts in public; that they were recruited to serve as sexual outlets for frustrated military men, that many had sexually transmitted diseases that were then passed on to their male partners, and that they joined the service to meet other lesbians and to engage in orgies. It was not surprising that recruitment was difficult when the general public believed that WAACs had to have large breasts and other anatomical specifications to be accepted into the Army. What originally was thought to be an Axis plot to make the military unattractive to American women turned out to be the result of rumors spread by Army males, soldier's wives, jealous civilian women, fanatics, and unhappy WAACs (Rustad, 1982). It should be noted, however, that such charges against women were not unusual; similar attacks were made upon nurses in World War I and British and Canadian women in the military (Hart, 1990).

To some, women must take complete responsibility for the temptations they present. Mitchell (1989), commenting on the pamphlet *Feminine Hygiene in the Field Setting*, which advises women to pack extra birth control pills, says, "It might have been more in the interest of the service to advise women that sex does not *just happen* anywhere and that they have no business making it happen while on maneuvers" (p. 171).

These attitudes about military women were echoed in the publicity surrounding women's participation in Desert Storm. The destroyer tender USS *Acadia* was dubbed the "Love Boat" when 36 out of approximately 380 women were found to be pregnant during the deployment and returned to the United States early. Most press accounts ignored the fact that some of the women were pregnant when they reported to the ship. Also ignored was concern over the sexual behavior of men aboard the ship. As Barkalow (1991) notes, "too often, the women are the only ones held responsible for pregnancy, not the men who helped get them that way" (p. 30).

Rumors of women soldiers "turning tricks" in the Persian Gulf also fed the imaginations of those back home (Kantrowitz, 1991). According to Colonel D. H. Hackworth (1991), "There is no question that pregnancy soared during the war. Three Pentagon sources report that as of mid-February of 1991, more than 1,200 pregnant women had been evacuated from the gulf—the equivalent of two infantry battalions. 'Nineteen ninety-two will be a baby-boomer year,' predicts one doctor at Andrews Air Force Base in Maryland" (p. 29). The Navy, however, found that the pregnancy rate dropped more than 50% among women in the Persian Gulf conflict. None of the female reservists and only 4.8% of the active-duty women were returned to the United States due to pregnancy (Department of the Navy, 1991). Hackworth also met women who became pregnant but who told no one so that they would not disappoint their comrades. He reported that many women complained that exacting statistics were kept on pregnancy but not on men's sports injuries, which were the biggest casualty producer during the war.

Single mothers in uniform pose a problem because of the moral overtones associated with those who have never been married. As an institution that still internalizes traditional values, the armed forces' acceptance of members who have borne children outside of marriage has been difficult. At least some portion of this conflict is due to the fact that many of the biological fathers of the babies are military men. Despite the sexual revolution, the military does not want to project an image of "loose" morals to the public or to the spouses of its service members. Often overlooked are the facts that two-thirds of the single parents with custody of their children are men and that most single parenthood results from divorce, not single women giving birth. Moreover, most single parents are in their second or subsequent enlistment.[5] Such personnel do not generate negative reactions. The occasional recommendation to separate all single parents from the military meets with little support because of the effect it would have on men and on careerists.

CONCLUSIONS

To Gilder (1986), motherhood is the glue that holds society together. The central position of the woman "in the home parallels her central position in all civilized society. Both derive from her role in procreation and from the primary and most inviolable of human ties, the one between mother and child. . . . She is the vessel of the ultimate values of the nation. The community is largely what she is and what she demands in men" (p. 31). Russo (1976) coined the phrase "Motherhood

Mandate" to describe the general belief that motherhood is central to the definition of the adult female.

This chapter has dealt, in depth, with the image of woman as mother. Those who oppose mothers in the military wish to see women as venerated madonnas: valued and revered for their fertility, self-sacrificing, pure, content with their role in life (Hunter College Women's Study Collective, 1983). Not surprisingly, women who made the military their career in the past were likely to remain childless. In the 1970s, the feminist movement raised women's expectations and led them to believe that they could have a career *and* a family. However, as Tetreault (1988) pointed out, "military women who are mothers fly in the face of the traditional military self-image as an elite organization that protects women and children" (p. 64). Being an iconoclast carries with it certain penalties. For military mothers, these penalties are derived from beliefs concerning their value to the institution, exaggerated attention to their sexuality, moralizing about their misplaced loyalties (whether to the family or to the military), and constant comparisons to the male "norm."

The armed forces are in an awkward position with regard to motherhood. While liberal and conservative alike are willing to acknowledge that the psychosocial dynamics of motherhood and fatherhood are not the same, differential treatment of parents in uniform is difficult to support. Most gender-specific policies have been rescinded over the past 20 years, and the effect of those remaining is gradually being weakened (e.g., the combat restrictions). In addition, as the demographics of men in the military have become more reflective of civilian society, policies and practices that impact negatively on the family are meeting with resistance. The accommodations that have had to be made to retain men have greatly benefited women and have enabled military mothers to better meet their many commitments.

Operation Desert Storm answered a question the military had often asked itself—would women with children be able to respond to a call-up and rapid deployment? The answer was a resounding yes. Now the services need to impress upon the news media the unfairness of burdening these women with guilt—a guilt that has never been imposed by journalists upon fathers going off to war.

NOTES

1. Phone conversation with Air Force, Army, and Navy recruiters at the San Diego Military Entrance Processing Station, 12 July 1991.

2. Thirty-four percent of Navy women are mothers whose minor children live with them, which, when applied to the 35,000 women deployed to the Persian Gulf, yields an estimate of 11,900.

3. By John Heinz, R-PA (S 325); Herb Kohl, D-WI (S 283); Jill Long, D-IN (HR 738); and Barbara Boxer, D-CA (HR 537).

4. In a 14 February 1991 letter to the Senate, Secretary of Defense Cheney and Joint Chiefs of Staff chairman General Powell said that enactment of the bill "would weaken our combat capability by removing key personnel from our deployed units and by undermining unit cohesion and esprit de corps."

5. A 1990 Navy survey of a representative sample of enlisted personnel revealed that 83% of single parenthood resulted from divorce or death of spouse. Eighty-eight percent of the single parents were petty officers or chief petty officers, and 73% were E-5 or above.

REFERENCES

Barkalow, C. (1991, August 5). Women have what it takes. *Newsweek*, p. 30.

Beans, H. C. (1975). Sex discrimination in the military. *Military Law Review*, 67, 19–83.

Beauvoir, Simone de. (1952). *The second sex*. New York: Vintage Books.

Beck, M., Wilkinson, R., Turque, B., & Bingham, C. (1990, September 10). Our women in the desert. *Newsweek*, pp. 22–25.

Blackwell, J., Snider, D., & Mazarr, M. (1991, July 28). The seven military lessons taught by Desert Storm. *The San Diego Union*, p. C-5.

Buckley, W. F. (1991, August 8). Whether to militarize women is not just a question of equality. *The San Diego Union*, p. B-13.

Department of the Navy. (1989). *Management of pregnant servicewomen*. (OPNAVINST 6000.1A). Washington, DC: Office of the Chief of Naval Operations.

Department of the Navy. (1991). *Role of women in the Persian Gulf conflict* (Memorandum 5300 Ser 2WW/1U580235 of 5 August 1991). Washington, DC: Bureau of Naval Personnel.

De Pauw, L. G. (1988). Gender as stigma: Probing some sensitive issues. *Minerva: Quarterly Report on Women and the Military*, 6, 29–43.

Devilbiss, M. C. (1990). Women in combat: A quick summary of the arguments on both sides. *Minerva: Quarterly Report on Women and the Military*, 8, 29–31.

Dunivin, K. O. (1988). There's men, there's women, and there's me: The role and status of military women. *Minerva: Quarterly Report on Women in the Military*, 6, 43–68.

Frontiero v. Richardson, 411 U.S. 677 (1973).

Gaines, J. (1991, May 12). Even while their country called, so did their children. *The San Diego Union*, pp. B-1, B-7.

Gilder, G. (1986, October 10). The sexual revolution at home. *National Review*, pp. 30–34.

Guiterrez v. Laird, 346 F. Supp. 289 (D.D.C. 1972).

Hackworth, D. H. (1991, August 5). War and the second sex. *Newsweek,* pp. 24–29.

Hart, R. C. (1990, April–May). *Women in combat.* Report prepared for the Topical Research Intern Program at the Defense Equal Opportunity Management Institute. Satellite Beach, FL: Patrick Air Force Base.

Hoiberg, A., & Ernst, J. (1980). Motherhood in the military: Conflicting roles for Navy women? *International Journal of Sociology of the Family, 10,* 265–280.

Hunter College Women's Studies Collective. (1983). *Women's realities, women's choices.* New York: Oxford University Press.

Hyde, J. S. (1985). *Half the human experience: The psychology of women,* 3rd ed. Lexington, MA: D. C. Heath.

Kantrowitz, B. (1991, August 5). The right to fight. *Newsweek,* pp. 22–23.

Martindale, M. (1990). *Sexual harassment in the military: 1988.* Alexandria, VA: Defense Manpower Data Center.

Mitchell, B. (1989). *Weak link: The feminization of the American military.* Washington, DC: Regnery Gateway.

Moore, M. (1991, April 4). Sex harassment called pervasive in Navy. *The Washington Post,* p. A4.

A mother's duty. (1990, September 10). *People Weekly,* pp. 42–49.

Office of the Assistant Secretary of Defense. (1992, October). *Population representation in the military services: Fiscal year 1991.* Washington, DC: Author.

Olson, M. S., & Stumpf, S. S. (1978). *Pregnancy in the Navy: Impact on absenteeism, attriting, and work group morale* (NPRDC Tech. Rep. 78-35). San Diego, CA: Navy Personnel Research and Development Center.

Robinson v. Rand, 340 F. Supp. 37 (D. Colo. 1972).

Roush, P. E. (1991, April). *Rethinking who fights our wars—and why.* Paper presented at the Harvard Law School Symposium on Women in the Military, Cambridge, MA.

Russo, N. F. (1976). The motherhood mandate. *Journal of Social Issues, 32,* 143–153.

Rustad, M. (1982). *Women in khaki: The American enlisted woman.* New York: Praeger.

Sanders, A. L. (1991, February 18). When Dad and Mom go to war. *Time,* p. 69.

Savell, J. M., Rigby, C. K., & Zbikowski, A. A. (1982). *An investigation of lost time and utilization of a sample of first-term male and female soldiers* (Tech. Rep. 607). Alexandria, VA: U.S. Army Research Institute for the Behavioral and Social Sciences.

Stiehm, J. H. (1989). *Arms and the enlisted woman.* Philadelphia: Temple University Press.

Struck v. Secretary of Defense, 460 F.2d 1372 (9th Cir. 1971).

Swerdlow, M. (1989). Men's accommodations to women entering a nontraditional occupation: A case of rapid transit operatives. *Gender and Society, 3,* 373–387.

Tetreault, M. A. (1988). Gender belief systems and the integration of women in the U.S. military. *Minerva: Quarterly Report on Women in the Military, 6,* 44–70.

Thomas, M. D., & Thomas, P. J. (1990, 25 October). *Survey of pregnancy and single parenthood.* Briefing given to RADM J. M. Boorda (Chief of Naval Personnel) Washington, DC.

Thomas, M. D., Thomas, P. J., & McClintock, V. (1991). *Pregnant enlisted women in Navy work centers* (NPRDC TN-91-5). San Diego, CA: Navy Personnel Research and Development Center.

Thomas, P. J. (1981). Role of women in the military: Australia, Canada, the United Kingdom and the United States. *JSAS Catalog of Selected Documents in Psychology, 11, 32.*

Thomas, P. J. (1987). *The Navy workweek at selected commands in the United States and overseas* (NPRDC Tech. Note 88-9). San Diego, CA: Navy Personnel Research and Development Center.

Thomas, P. J., & Edwards, J. E. (1989). *Incidence of pregnancy and single parenthood among enlisted personnel in the Navy* (NPRDC Tech. Report 90-1). San Diego, CA: Navy Personnel Research and Development Center.

Thomas, P. J., & Thomas, M. D. (1992). *Impact of pregnancy and single parents upon Navy personnel systems* (NPRDC Tech. Note 92-8). San Diego, CA: Navy Personnel Research and Development Center.

Thomas, P. J., & Thomas, M. D. (1993). *Absences of Navy enlisted personnel: A search for gender difference* (NPRDC Tech. Report 93-3). San Diego, CA: Navy Personnel Research and Development Center.

Treadwell, M. E. (1954). *The Women's Army Corps: United States in World War II. Special Studies.* Washington, DC: Department of the Army, Office of the Chief of Military History.

Walton, M. D., Sachs, D., Ellington, R., Hazlewood, A., Griffin, S., & Bass, D. (1988). Physical stigma and the pregnancy role: Receiving help from strangers. *Sex Roles, 18,* 323–331.

York, N. K. (1978). The legal struggle for a military woman's right to have children. In E. J. Hunter & D. S. Nice (Eds.), *Military families: Adaptation to change.* New York: Praeger.

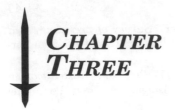

CHAPTER THREE

Long-Term Effects on Children of a Parent Missing in Wartime

Edna J. Hunter-King, PhD

No words [can] comfort someone in one of the most painful, heart-tearing situations imaginable. Nothing can take away the pain, hurt, and tears—nothing. But it is ironic that the most painful event in my life has also brought about the most changes of a positive nature. I have learned to value and appreciate relationships and life itself, for it can be so very short. I have pondered the existential questions of life at an early age, and in so doing [have been] enriched with wisdom to help me through life's ups and downs. I have learned the importance of being honest with myself and others, for my life may be short and I may not have a second chance to make things right.

—A 24-year-old daughter of a serviceman still missing in action

This chapter focuses on a special group of adult children who have suffered from a particular type of unresolved bereavement, *prolonged ambiguous grieving*. These are the children of servicemen who were declared missing in action (MIA) during the Vietnam conflict, a war that began over two decades ago (1964) and ended in 1973. For many of these individuals that war has never really ended. Final resolution of their grieving remains unattainable. Since the end of the Vietnam

War, 280 Americans previously missing in Southeast Asia have been accounted for (243 in Vietnam, 34 in Laos, 1 in Cambodia [returned by Vietnam], and 2 in the Peoples Republic of China). These figures, released in April 1990, reduced the number of those still prisoner, missing, and unaccounted for to 2,303. Also, as of that date, 1,362 firsthand live sighting reports in Vietnam had been received since 1975; 1,248 of those reports were resolved: 940 pertained to individuals who had since left Vietnam (returned prisoners of war [POWs], known missionaries or civilians detained after Saigon fell, and later released); 328 were believed to be fabrications. The remaining 114 sightings are as yet unresolved and under investigation (National League of Families, 1990).

Although this chapter focuses primarily on Vietnam-era children of MIA service personnel, the lessons learned generalize far beyond that conflict to many other situations where a loved one is missing. Only recently the daughter of former Congressman Hale Boggs, who disappeared while flying in Alaska in 1972, remarked on the similarities and differences between her situation as an "MIA child" and that of Vietnam-era family members:

> My family's experience could not have been more different, but it gives
> some small glimmer of how these families must feel. . . . While focusing
> on whether some MIAs might still be alive, we fail to understand why
> it's crucial to solve the mystery of the missing. . . . Their families are
> entitled to the peace of certainty; they deserve to mourn without fear
> that their mourning somehow implies they have abandoned hope; they
> are due the dignity of burying their dead. (Roberts, 1991)

CHILDREN CAUGHT IN THE WEB OF WAR— VIETNAM AND AFTERWARD

At the close of the Vietnam conflict, 566 American POWs were released and returned to the United States and their loved ones. However, at the time of Operation Homecoming, many other American servicemen remained in an official MIA status (McCubbin, Dahl, Metres, Hunter, & Plag, 1974). In 1973 doubt remained in the minds of many MIA family members as to whether or not all POWs held in Southeast Asia had been released. The doubts continue today, and to some extent they are justified. In the cases of over 60 of the MIAs who did not come back, there was strong evidence that they had indeed been captured. Nonetheless, they were not among the 566 men who returned. Today, over 20 years later, some of their children remain certain in their own minds that their fathers continue to languish in POW camps somewhere in

Southeast Asia, as reflected in the recent comments of the 22-year-old daughter of Vietnam-era MIA: "Don't accept anything [you hear] if you're not satisfied. Don't give up hope or faith. . . . Fight for those who are still alive and can't fight" (personal communication, 1988).

As part of a 7-year Department of Defense longitudinal study of Vietnam-era POW/MIA families, carried out at the now-defunct Army–Navy–Marine Corps Center for POW Studies[1] (CPWS) in San Diego from 1971 to 1978, children from these war-torn families were personally interviewed either by this author or by another of the center's professional staff members. Within the study sample, 378 of these Army, Navy, and Marine Corps families included children. U.S. Air Force policy did not mandate family members to be part of its follow-up of Air Force POWs. Other service branches, however, viewed the families as both potential *stress producers* and *stress alleviators* for the returning POWs, and the decision was made to include all family members in the center's longitudinal follow-up. The rationale was that if the families were functioning well at the time of release, they were more likely to be stress alleviators, rather than stress producers, for the returning men.

In a 1988 discussion of family stress management, Boss (1988, 1990) cogently pointed out that the family's coping resources are its individual and collective *strengths* at the time the stressor event occurs; for example, economic security, health, intelligence, job skills, proximity of support, spirit of cooperation in the family, relationship skills, and network and social supports. She cautioned that too often the term *coping* is used in family stress theory to represent a homeostatic, status quo model of the family, that is, no change, rather than the active managing of stress that leads to a new level of organization. Too often in family stress theory, the meaning given to the term *coping* has "not allowed for the possibility of change, either through evolution or revolution" (Boss, 1988, p. 63). Thus, it may not always be advantageous to cope, because if the family works too hard at being strong and keeping on an even keel in the face of what is happening to them, they maintain the status quo at all costs, and those costs become cumulative. This situation appears to have occurred for some of the MIA children of the Vietnam era.

Within the center's POW/MIA sample of families interviewed prior to homecoming, there were 298 children of men listed as POWs and 576 children of MIAs, making a total research sample of 874 POW/MIA children (Hunter & Phelan, 1974; McCubbin, Hunter, & Metres, 1974). When their fathers disappeared from their lives, the majority of these children were between the ages of 8 and 15 years, and their ages ranged from less than 1 year to 25 years of age. At the time of the initial interviews in 1972 (prior to the POWs' release), some children did not know for certain whether their fathers were held as POWs or were still MIA. They found out only when the war ended in the spring of 1973 and the actual release of POWs occurred (Benson, McCubbin, Dahl, & Hunter, 1974; Metres, McCubbin, & Hunter, 1974).

IMMEDIATE EFFECTS OF HAVING AN MIA FATHER

Before addressing the long-term effects on children of having had a missing parent, a review of known immediate effects on children, based on these earlier studies, is in order. The CPWS was established originally under the umbrella of "preventive medicine." However, from a research perspective, the Vietnam War also provided a unique opportunity to study the effects of prolonged wartime parental absence upon children, one that could never have been duplicated in a laboratory setting (Hunter, 1986a, 1988a) Conclusions from the center's findings were used during the Iranian hostage incident (Figley, 1980) and more recently in planning for the families of potential POW/MIAs during Operation Desert Storm in the Middle East (Hunter, 1990).

Results of the CPWS studies indicated that the impact of wartime father absence on children during the first few years after the men became listed as POW or MIA was determined to a large extent by three major factors, all relating to the mothers' adjustments: (a) mothers' attitudes toward the separation, (b) mothers' satisfaction with their marriages prior to the separation, and (c) mothers' abilities to cope with the separation period (Hunter, 1980; Hunter & Nice, 1978; McCubbin, Dahl, Hunter, 1976; McCubbin, Hunter, & Metres, 1974; Nice, McDonald, & McMillian, 1981).

Based on the mothers' reports, the physical health of the children was a major issue for them during the absence of the military fathers. Common childhood diseases were the most frequent concern, followed by accidental injuries and surgeries. Initial 1972 interviews (before release of the POWs) indicated that almost 20% of the children were judged by their mothers to have had significant emotional problems during the period of father absence. For families with children, the average number of emotional or behavioral problems was 4.3 problems per family. The most frequently reported symptoms were unwarranted and frequent crying, nightmares, rebelliousness, shyness, nail biting, and fear of the dark. Of those children judged by their mothers to have had significant problems, only about half had actually received professional counseling. Thus, even where the need for counseling was recognized, these children often did not receive it (McCubbin et al., 1974), possibly because within military families, seeking professional assistance to cope with family disruptions was still viewed by many as bearing a stigma.

Data were obtained both at 2 years after the Vietnam War ended (McCubbin, Dahl, Lester, & Ross, 1975) and again at 5 years postwar (Nice et al., 1981) in an attempt to find an answer to the question addressed in this chapter, *How does parental wartime captivity affect childrens' later adjustment?* Unfortunately, the answer remains unclear.

Initial, pre-1973 CPWS studies merely made comparisons between POW/MIA children and general population norms. Other studies during the first 2 years postrelease were within-sample comparisons of the adjustment of children from families who were eventually reunited (POWs) with (a) those who had not been reunited (MIAs) and in which mothers remained unmarried and (b) families in which the MIA mothers had remarried quickly after their husbands failed to return. Comparisons of between-group differences among the three types of POW/ MIA children found no significant differences among them with respect to overall social and personal adjustment 2 years postrelease. Also, there were no significant differences between the MIA families where the mothers had remarried and those who had not remarried within 2 years after the Vietnam War ended. However, *all subgroups of POW/ MIA children showed significantly poorer adjustment when compared with general population norms* for the instruments used (Hunter, 1983b, McCubbin et al., 1975).

Reports on fifth-year (1978) postrelease data from the CPWS studies were not focused specifically on the MIA group but solely on children of ex-POWs (Nice et al., 1981). Data from that study showed that when children in *intact* navy POW families were compared with children from a carefully matched comparison group of non-POW military families, no significant differences were found between these two groups of Vietnam-era military children. The investigators (Nice et al., 1981) noted that both groups (POW children and matched controls) exhibited relatively high standard scores on cohesion, moral-religious emphasis, and organization and relatively low standard scores on conflict, which placed these children in the "Structure-Oriented" typology derived by the authors from the *Family Environment Scale* (Moos & Moos, 1976). They concluded that emphasis on structured activities, role clarity, and intrafamily support was perhaps a reflection of an adaptation of the family system to stabilize the effects of disruptions, such as family separation and frequent geographic mobility associated with the military life-style.

Although the study by Nice and colleagues may shed light on what type of military family is best able to cope with *any highly stressful situation*, their conclusions are perhaps misleading if one attempts to use them to delineate long-term effects of MIA parental absence, which has been not only more prolonged but highly ambiguous as well. Indeed, there may be effects that are much *greater* for MIA children than for POW children because of this ambiguity and the lack of resolution that prevents them from ever completely finalizing their grieving for the lost parent (Boss, 1988).

VIETNAM-ERA MIA CHILDREN 5 TO 10 YEARS AFTER

Although, as previously mentioned, the mothers' adjustment to loss was a key factor in how well their children coped, another important factor in children's adjustment to the MIA situation was the age of the child when the father left. As an example, in 1978 a young teenage daughter who had been very close to her MIA father prior to his disappearance explained the long vigil for her missing father as follows:

> Nobody wants their own parent to die. And when you're in a situation where you're given a choice you're going to choose the one which is easier to accept . . . it appears easier . . . except when you draw it out over 7, 8, or 9 years. . . . You hope, or want somebody to be withholding information from you. (Smith, 1978)

As the years passed, this young woman continued to try to resolve her grief without success. Because of the unpopularity of the Vietnam War, some teenage children hid from their peers the fact that their fathers were POWs or MIAs and were puzzled by ambivalent feelings of shame they could not verbalize. The teenager further commented:

> The real conflict for me on campus came when my friends were actively marching and actively participating in the antiwar movement . . . something I wanted to do, but yet I couldn't perceive the war in the simple "black and white" terms that my friends were talking about at that time. . . . I don't think I ever resolved that conflict. (Smith, 1978)

During the Vietnam War, because the government had been unable to identify all POWs who appeared in propaganda films and foreign press releases, these photographs were routinely presented to the families in the hope they might be able to make further identifications of missing family members. The young woman mentioned previously explained her dilemma:

> When you're looking for something to cling onto . . . and I mean anything, and then the Department of Defense shows you POW propaganda files . . . and we sat there and stared at them frame by frame. . . . That photograph that appeared in the newspapers in 1971 was one frame out of those files. . . . I was positive that little face in the lower left-hand corner was my father. You don't even see that face immediately, but when I saw it, I gasped, because I knew. . . . It was all I needed. . . . I knew my father was alive . . . [but] my family was one of 25 families that each claimed that tiny little face to be their missing man! (Smith, 1978)

When the POWs were released in 1973, some of the wives of the missing were able at that time to accept the fact that their loved ones would probably never come home. They proceeded with their lives; some remarried. Ten years after the Vietnam POWs were released, a few families who had taken part in the earlier CPWS studies were reinterviewed (Hunter, 1983b). As part of the 1983 study, an interview was conducted by this author with a former MIA wife whose son was born after the father was listed as missing. The boy never knew his natural father. A few years subsequent to the POWs' release, when the boy was 9 years old, the mother was remarried to a former Vietnam-era POW. Although the loss of the boy's own father certainly affected his life course, according to his mother, he did not appear to ruminate and worry about his father's fate as his mother had. Her son had empathized with his mother's sadness, but "it was his *mother* he was feeling sorry for, *not* the father he never knew" (Hunter, 1983b).

The remarks by the teenage girl quoted above and those of the boy who was not born until after his father became MIA illustrate the importance of age in predicting adjustment to parental loss in the years immediately following the event. Older children are more likely to feel the loss of the missing parent than are very young children. Still another decade has passed since the 1983 study, and we again ask the question, *Have the Vietnam children of MIA men as yet been able to accept fully the loss of their fathers?*

VIETNAM MIA CHILDREN TODAY

Reports continue filtering in that some Vietnam-era missing men may still be alive and held captive. Thus, even today, over 20 years after the beginning of the war in Southeast Asia, many of the Vietnam-era children continue in an emotional limbo. The generic stressor these children have been called upon to face on a daily basis is *unresolved grieving due to the continuing ambiguity of the missing parents' status* (Boss, 1990). Thus, it becomes clear that being the child of a missing parent is not a single traumatic event; it is a chronic stressor. As Boss (1988) pointed out:

> . . . a chronic stressor should be defined as a stressful situation (rather than an event) that is characterized by (a) long duration, (b) the probability of pileup with other events, especially normal developmental transitions, and (c) the potential of high ambiguity in its origin (etiology), progression, and conclusion. (p. 45)

A small pilot survey was carried out recently by this author, focusing on that issue and others pertaining to this group of Vietnam-era MIA children.[2] Preliminary findings from that study are presented for the first time in this chapter. In 1988, over 15 years after the Vietnam conflict ended, a survey of a group of now-adult children of Vietnam-era MIA servicemen (N = 82) was carried out to explore the following question: *What are the long-term effects on children of a prolonged, ambiguous stressor such as an MIA situation?* It was presumed that responses on the survey would reflect present perceptions of how the entire MIA experience had affected the lives of this group of children over the years.

The sample of MIA children for the 1988 survey was obtained through a mailing to all sons and daughters on the mailing list of the National League of Families of American Prisoners and Servicemen Missing in Southeast Asia.[3] Eighty-two individuals completed and returned the questionnaire, a 33% return rate. Recall that the total population of 874 Army, Navy, and Marine Corps Vietnam-era POW/ MIA children in the CPWS study 16 years earlier ranged in age from less than 1 year to 25 years of age when their fathers were taken prisoner or reported missing. At the time of the most recent study, this group ranged in age from 20 to 45 years, with a mean age of 29.9 years. Thus, they were now all adults. Unfortunately, it cannot be assumed that the 1988 sample is representative of the total population of Vietnam-era MIA children. Although a few of the respondents had been in the group of children interviewed many years earlier for the CPWS studies, most had not. In fact, 73% of the 1988 participants were children of missing Air Force personnel. As mentioned earlier, children of Air Force personnel were not included in the longitudinal CPWS studies.

THE 1988 FOLLOW-UP OF
VIETNAM-ERA MIA CHILDREN

Data were collected through a mailed survey, *The 1988 Survey of Vietnam-Era MIA Children* (Hunter, 1988a). The survey was a two-page, 32-item, paper-and-pencil questionnaire. In addition to requesting basic demographic information, it included items concerning events surrounding the father's status as POW/MIA, whether or not the mother had remarried, and the family's past participation in the National League of Families and related POW/MIA activities. Subjects were asked to rate themselves on the degree to which they believed the entire situation (i.e., the loss/capture of their fathers and the intervening years of father absence) had affected their lives, compared with what it would have been had that loss not occurred. A rating of "Not at all" to "Very much" on a 4-point Likert-type scale was obtained for each of the following areas of personal functioning/adjustment: economic, physical, emotional/psychological, occupational, friendships, family relationships, marital/love relationships, and relationships with their own children.

Respondents were also asked to provide comments on (a) the most difficult aspects of having been an MIA child, (b) whether there were any advantages for them specifically because of their status as a son or daughter of an MIA father, (c) if there were any current problems or issues with which they were dealing that they believed were directly related to being the child of an MIA father and (d) what advice they might give to any children who might suddenly find a parent missing in action in future conflicts, based on their own experiences as children of MIAs.

Preliminary Findings

Results from the 1988 study now-adult children of Vietnam-era MIA fathers showed that most of the MIA fathers became casualties during the years from 1964 through 1967. Since that time, approximately half (48.8%) of the mothers had remarried; slightly over half (51.2%) had not remarried at the time of data collection. These MIA children had ranged in age from less than 1 year to 20 years of age at the time their fathers were first listed as missing, with the majority between the ages of 5 and 9 years. Of those who completed the 1988 survey, half (50.6%) were daughters and half (49.4%) were sons. Almost two-thirds were married at the time of data collection, and over 40% had children of their own.

Although these adult children reported that they believed the MIA experience had affected them in all areas of functioning addressed by this study, the degree and direction of the effects could not be determined from their responses. Further in-depth research is necessary, perhaps through personal interviews. Most of those who returned the completed questionnaires indicated their willingness to be interviewed at some future time. Personal in-depth interviews could supply answers to still unanswered questions and provide a fuller understanding of the full impact on children of a missing parent. This second phase of the study has not yet been undertaken because of a lack of funding.

When asked to rate themselves as to the degree to which overall MIA experience had affected them in various aspects of adjustment or functioning, the greatest effects were assigned to emotional or psychological adjustment, followed in decreasing order of degree of effect: family relationships, relationships with own children, occupational adjustment, and marital relationships. Friendships, according to their ratings, had been affected the least. Unfortunately, as mentioned earlier, from the survey it could not be determined whether these effects were for better or worse. However, from the comments that accompanied their responses, the author assumes that in certain areas (e.g., emotional and psychological) the effects were usually negative. In other areas, such as family relationships and relationships with their own children, the greater effects perceived appeared to be in a more positive direction. For example, many respondents mentioned closeness between family members, which they believed resulted from having had to cope with their loss and the resulting valuing of other close relatives.

As mentioned earlier, over half (51.2%) of the mothers of these MIA children had never remarried. Further analysis indicated that if the respondents' mothers had never remarried, the children themselves were less likely to have ever married. Also, if mothers had not remarried, their children were more likely to report higher perceived effects in every area of adjustment. Comparing MIA children whose mothers had never remarried with children whose mothers had remarried, the highest differences were in relationships with their own children.

Several participants commented on their opposition to their mother's remarriages. Others had encouraged their mothers to make new lives for themselves. The following remarks are examples of the comments made by these children about their mothers' remarriage or failure to remarry.

> My mother remarried three years after my father was missing and then was divorced after 11 years of marriage. I did not feel a part of her decision; I didn't feel we were a family or would be one.

I can remember mixed feelings [about mother's remarriage] because we were by ourselves with our mother so long, just us girls. . . . Now that I'm older I'm really glad!

I wish she had remarried [but] she never felt right about remarrying.

Although the majority of the mothers (61.8%) had been active in the National League of Families since the founding of the League in 1969, most of the children (69.1%) had become active only recently. In cases where mothers had never been active in League activities, the children were more likely to rate their relationships with mothers as having been more affected by the MIA experience than were those respondents who reported their mothers had been involved. Again, the direction of these greater effects (positive vs. negative) could not be determined.

Long-Term Effects

Participants' comments in the 1988 survey regarding how these now-adult MIA children believed wartime father absence had affected them over the years showed several common themes, many of which appear interrelated, such as (a) persistent fears of abandonment; (b) problems with intimate relationships; (c) feelings of isolation, alienation, and depression; (d) lack of basic trust in others (and the U.S. government); (e) feelings of resentment and hostility; and (f) a fatalistic attitude toward life in general. Comments below, taken from the survey, reflect these feelings, issues that persist in some MIA children after many years.

I believe I've developed an overly fatalistic attitude towards life and sometimes have trouble becoming close to people—perhaps for fear they will disappear and not return.

I am resentful of traditional families that have not had to deal with [the MIA tragedy], and because of that I'm very discreet about my personal life and past and am not able to discuss these things at all. I feel like I'm hiding a deep dark secret that no one could understand. The bitterness and hostility toward the war especially aggravate this.

[My mother and other relatives] put [my father] on a pedestal, and by the time I grew up [I found that] no mate could ever compare to the "god" [my father] had become.

Now that I am starting my own family, I have a fear of losing my husband.

Thus far the focus has been primarily on problems some of these MIA children experienced. There were also benefits accruing from the MIA situation, according to participants' responses. Advantages mentioned by participants included such rewards as financial benefits, closer family relationships, deeper relationships, increased personal strengths, persistence, higher self-confidence, earlier and greater maturity, openmindedness, the ability to view crises as opportunities for growth, and the increased valuing of human life. The comments presented below illustrate a variety of perceived benefits of having been MIA children.

> I learned to face things head-on and to value life; [to know] that it can be very short and to appreciate what you have.

> I feel I have made closer, deeper relationships because of what I learned.

> I can handle a lot in life now, no matter how bad it gets.

Although 25% of the subjects saw no advantage whatsoever in having been children of MIAs; 75% reported some advantage, principally financial or educational. Most of them had received Veterans Administration or Social Security benefits to pursue higher education. Many respondents were quick to point out, however, that they believed financial benefits in no way compensated for the absence of their fathers during their developing years. The continuing ambiguity, accompanied by persistent feelings of loss, is apparent in many comments made by participants.

> One of the most difficult aspects that I've had to deal with is the feeling of frustration and depression of not knowing where my dad is or if he is alive, and the inability to do anything about it.

> I really do want to know more about him and could easily become obsessed with finding out every detail about him. Around holidays I get very sentimental and am often thinking of my dad.

> I've gone on with my life, but every day I wonder about him. Every success, every accomplishment makes me realize how much I miss his being there.

> I still miss Dad terribly; sometimes I feel overwhelming loss. It's like being in prison. It would be better if my father's body were returned. At least there would be an end.

Recognition of the Need for Assistance in Coping

Even for those MIA children who appeared to have managed quite adequately, there was recognition that assistance from others often helped. Their comments often validated the seeking of professional counseling or support groups composed of individuals facing similar issues.

> The quality of your life is up to you. The process of talking about it, especially in support groups or counseling, and expressing the emotions is beneficial. To hold them inside, to let them go unexpressed is crippling.

> Get professional counseling, regardless of how strong you are; you will need it.

> Learn to accept that when one door closes, another one opens. Find a quiet place to be alone and cry. Let it out—for yourself. And try to bring humor into your life, from the smaller things to the large. And last but not least, be a sponge for your mom and brothers and sisters. Learn to listen!"

Advice for MIA Children in Future Wars

As to what advice these adult MIA children would give to any future MIA child, their responses reflected deep feelings and the increased maturity levels that were attained while managing the prolonged ambiguous grieving that seemed never to find resolution.

> It's difficult to have your life revolve around someone who may not even be alive. As much as possible, try to deal with the past and go on with your own life. You have to set your own goals and not center your life around the uncertainty, as difficult as that is.

> You must not let [your father's] plight affect your relationship with other people. You must try not to feel guilty if you are happy or joyful. Such guilt is inevitable: yet it must be channeled to positive action, not self-inflicted punishment. You will eventually begin to see the joy in living and the meaning of how much freedom costs and that we will always have to pay dearly for our freedom.

> Understand that your father gave you the greatest gift of all, his life for yours. Try to direct your anxieties and emotions in a positive way instead of a destructive way. Don't be so consumed with grief and anger that that's all you think about. It will consume you from the inside out if you let it. Instead, realize that your father was doing something he believed in largely to preserve the freedoms he had, for you. Honor him by enjoying these freedoms as much as you can and by working up to your potential. Work to become the kind of person you know he would be proud of.

CONCLUSIONS AND DISCUSSION

For more than 20 years children of U.S. servicemen reported as MIA during the Vietnam War have experienced a prolonged ambiguous grieving process for which there is still no final resolution (Boss, 1990). In this chapter, a 7-year study of this group of MIA children carried out from 1971 to 1978 at the CPWS in San Diego has been reviewed. Also, results from a 1988 follow-up are reported for the first time. The major purpose of both studies was to attempt to answer the question *What are the long-term effects of having been the child of a serviceman reported as MIA during the Vietnam conflict?* In this chapter the generic stressor was viewed as the unresolved grief and the continuing ambiguity of having a parent missing during the Vietnam War. These children also grew up lacking a father as a role model, and this loss appears to have led to difficulty in dealing with their own parental role later, perhaps resulting in second-generation effects. The question concerning possible second-generation effects in children who suffer prolonged parental absence or loss during wartime has been raised during the past few decades (see, e.g., Danieli, 1988; Hunter, 1986b).

Although not all MIA children reported unmanaged stress as adults, the major long-term effects for many of them appear to be feelings of alienation accompanied by chronic depression. For some children, the unresolved loss resulted in fears concerning further loss of loved ones, causing them either to (a) become very closed emotionally in order to avoid intimate relationships or (b) to become overly independent to the point of being alienated from society. Others became overly protective or overly solicitous of both their loved ones and themselves, evidenced by tendencies toward hypochondriasis. For some there appeared to be an intense need for attention, lack of self-confidence, persistent procrastination for fear of failure, irrational fears, fascination with death, and/or an obsessive desire to stay alive, manifested by overcautiousness.

Although there were expressions of feeling deserted, fears of abandonment, problems with intimate relationships, distrust of government, and tendencies to view themselves as loners, simultaneously some of these adult MIA children also believed they had benefited from the experience in many ways. Among the advantages they mentioned were (a) financial assistance they received as MIA children, which allowed them to attain a higher education; (b) earlier and greater maturity; (c) closer relationships with other members of their nuclear families; (d) greater personal strengths; and (e) increased awareness of the value of human life.

In discussing how families manage stress from a theoretical viewpoint, Boss (1988) emphasized the critical importance of the family's *perception* of an event or situation (i.e., the *meaning* they give to it) in determining how effectively the family and its individual members are able to manage stress. Boss chose to use the term *manage* rather than *cope* since she believes functional families will manage stress rather than merely cope with it or adjust to it. The inability of many in this group of Vietnam-era MIA children to manage their ambiguous stressor effectively, even after 20 years or more, was apparent. Others appeared to have coped with their situations admirably in past years and continue to manage their stresses effectively. The meaning given to the MIA experience by each child (i.e., his or her *perception* of the stressor) seemed to be the key variable in how these children had dealt with the MIA experience over the years, which, in turn, determined the scope and degree of long-term effects for them as adults.

Although there were definite limitations to both the 7-year CPWS effort and the 1988 follow-up of Vietnam-era MIA children, most of what is currently known concerning how families cope with a prolonged ambiguous situation such as a captivity or a hostage situation derives from those studies. Although the samples were era-specific, much of what was learned can be generalized across a much broader spectrum, as pointed out in a Department of Veterans Affairs conference on "lessons learned" during and after Vietnam concerning the long-term health care of POWs, their families, and the families of MIAs (Hunter, 1985).

For example, the support-group concept that was found so helpful for POW/MIA families also can be applied to families of cancer patients, patients with chronic neurological disease, and patients with other long-term care needs. Knowledge derived from the POW/MIA experience during Vietnam can also transfer to other victim experiences: spouse abuse, child abuse, sexual assault, rape, terrorist acts, and the indoctrination of young adults into cults, as well as to certain cultic child-rearing practices (Hunter & Hestand, 1984). Significant developments to help military families generally also stemmed from CPWS studies during the 1970s. For example, an innovative social work program was proposed and implemented for the Navy in 1972 by the center's staff (Hunter & Plag, 1973). Moreover, family service or support centers were established throughout all service branches as a direct result of the early research findings and recommendations emanating from CPWS (Hunter, 1977). Nonetheless, further research is indicated. Future studies of MIA children could perhaps result in comparable advances in caregiving programs and in knowledge concerning the long-term effects on families caught in the web of hostage and captive situations, in which resolution of their loss remains forever elusive.

NOTES

1. The Center for Prisoner of War Studies (CPWS) was organized in 1971 and officially funded in 1972. Although CPWS was a joint U.S. Army, U.S. Navy, and U.S. Marine Corps activity, it was located at the Naval Health Research Center (NHRC) in San Diego, California. For almost 20 years, NHRC had been studying how men (and more recently, women) cope with stressful environments. It was logical, then, when CPWS was established to prepare for the return of the 241 Army, Navy, and Marine POWs, to place it under the auspices of NHRC. Unlike other branches of NHRC, the CPWS was jointly funded by the Navy Bureau of Medicine and Surgery and the Office of the Army Surgeon General. Although the U.S. Air Force also followed their 325 returned POWs medically, the decision made by Air Force operational planners prior to the men's release was *not* to include families in their research planning. Although the family study segment ended in 1978, at that time a decision was made to continue the medical follow-up of the Navy POWs, together with a carefully matched comparison group, for an additional 5 years. This was eventually extended even beyond that time frame. Physical examinations of the Navy Vietnam-era ex-POWs continue to be conducted annually at the Navy Aerospace Medical Institute, Pensacola, Florida.

2. *The 1988 Survey of Vietnam-Era MIA Children* was developed by Dr Edna J. Hunter, under the sponsorship of STAR Network, Inc., of Alexandria, Virginia, and was endorsed by the board of trustees of the National League of Families of American Prisoners and Servicemen Missing in Southeast Asia for distribution to all children of MIAs on its mailing list.

3. The National League of Families of American Prisoners and Servicemen Missing in Southeast Asia was informally organized in 1969 and officially incorporated in the District of Columbia on May 28, 1970. The League is composed of the wives, children, parents, and other close relatives of American POWs, MIAs, killed in action/body not recovered, and returned Vietnam POWs. It is a nonprofit, nonpolitical, tax-exempt organization, financed by contributions from concerned citizens and the families themselves. The organization's objectives are to obtain the release of all POWs, the fullest possible accounting for the MIAs, and the return of remains of those Americans who died serving their country during the Vietnam War.

REFERENCES

Benson, D., McCubbin, H., Dahl, B., & Hunter, E. (1974). Waiting: The dilemma of the MIA wife. In H. McCubbin, B. Dahl, P. Metres, Jr., E. Hunter, & J. Plag (Eds.), *Family separation and reunion* (pp. 157-167). Cat. No. D-206.21:74-70). Washington, DC: U.S. Government Printing Office.

Boss, P. (1988). *Family stress management.* Newbury Park, CA: Sage.

Boss, P. (1990). Family therapy and family research: Intertwined parts of the whole. In F. Kaslow (Ed.), *Voices in family psychology* (Vol. 2, pp. 17–32). Newbury Park, CA: Sage.

Danieli, Y (1988). Treating survivors and children of survivors of the Nazi Holocaust. In F. M. Ochberg (Ed.), *Post-traumatic therapy and victims of violence* (pp. 278–294). New York: Brunner/Mazel.

Figley, C. (Ed.). (1980). *Final report of the Task Force on Families of Catastrophe, Mobilization: I. The Iranian crisis.* West Lafayette, IN: Purdue University, Family Research Institute.

Hunter, E. J. (1977). Conference on military family research: Current trends and directions. *U.S. Navy Medicine, 69,* 10–13.

Hunter, E. J. (1980). Combat casualties who remain at home. *Military Review, 1,* 28–36.

Hunter, E. J. (1983a). Let no war put asunder: Families are holding together 10 years after Vietnam. *LADYCOM, 15,* 35–36, 60–61.

Hunter, E. J. (1983b). Treating the military captive's family. In F. W. Kaslow & R. I. Ridenour (Eds.), *The military family: Dynamics and treatment* (pp. 167–216). New York: Guilford.

Hunter, E. J. (1985). Reunion preparation of POW families. In *Proceedings: Conference on Follow-up Care for Returning Prisoners of War, March 12–14, 1985, San Diego, California.* Washington, DC: Veterans Administration, Department of Medicine and Surgery.

Hunter, E. J. (1986a). Families of prisoners of war held in Vietnam: A seven-year study. *Evaluation and Program Planning, 9,* 243–251.

Hunter, E. J. (1986b). Missing in action. In T. Rando (Ed.), *Parental loss of a child* (pp. 277–289). Champaign, IL: Research Press Co.

Hunter, E. J. (1988a). Longterm effects of parental wartime captivity on children: Children of POWs and MIA servicemen. *Journal of Contemporary Psychotherapy, 18,* 312–328.

Hunter, E. J. (1988b). *Research instrument: The 1988 Survey of Vietnam-Era MIA Children.* Washington, DC: STAR Network.

Hunter, E. J. (1990). Persian Gulf veterans: Position paper on anticipated adjustment problems, types of post-return services needed, and relevant literature. In *War zone stress among returning Persian Gulf troops: A preliminary report* (pp. D-15–D-32). West Haven, CT: Department of Veterans Affairs.

Hunter, E. J., & Hestand, R. (1984, April). Thought control: From parenting, to behavior mod, to cults, to "brainwashing." In *Proceedings of the Ninth Biennial Psychology in the DoD Symposium.* Colorado Springs, CO: USAFA.

Hunter, E. J., & Nice, S. D. (Eds.). (1978). *Children of military families: A part and yet apart.* Cat. No. 008-040-00181-4). Washington, DC: U.S. Government Printing Office.

Hunter, E. J., & Phelan, J. D. (1974). Army, Navy, and Marine Corps returned prisoners of war: A demographic profile. In H. McCubbin, B. Dahl, P. Metres, Jr., E. J. Hunter, & J. A. Plag (Eds.), *Family separation and reunion* (pp. 11–20). Cat. No. D-206.21:74-70. Washington, DC: U.S. Government Printing Office.

Hunter, E. J., & Plag, J. A. (1973). *An assessment of the needs of POW/MIA wives residing in the San Diego metropolitan area: A proposal for the establishment of family services* (Technical Report No. 78-18). San Diego, CA: Naval Health Research Center, Center for POW Studies.

McCubbin, H., Dahl, B., & Hunter, E. J. (Eds.). (1976). *Families in the military system.* Beverly Hills, CA: Sage.

McCubbin, H., Dahl, B., Lester, G., & Ross, B. (1975). The returned prisoner of war: Factors in family reintegration. *Journal of Marriage and the Family, 37,* 471–478.

McCubbin, H., Dahl, B., Metres, P., Jr., Hunter, E., & Plag, J. (Eds.). (1974). *Family separation and reunion: Families of prisoners of war and servicemen missing in action.* Cat. No. D-21:74-70. Washington, DC: U.S. Government Printing Office.

McCubbin, H. I., Hunter, E. J., & Metres, P. J., Jr. (1974). In H. McCubbin, B. Dahl, P. Metres, Jr., E. Hunter, & J. Plag (Eds.), *Family separation and reunion: Families of prisoners of war and servicemen missing in action* (pp. 65–76). Cat. No. D-21:74-70. Washington, DC: U.S. Government Printing Office.

Metres, P., Jr., McCubbin, H., & Hunter E. (1974). Families of returned prisoners of war: Some impressions of their initial reintegration. In H. McCubbin, B. Dahl, P. Metres, Jr., E. Hunter, & J. Plag (Eds.), *Family separation and reunion: Families of prisoners of war and servicemen missing in action* (pp. 147–155). Cat. No. D-206.21:74-70. Washington, DC: U.S. Government Printing Office.

Moos, R., & Moos, B. (1976). A typology of family social environments. *Family Process, 15,* 357–372.

National League of Families of American Prisoners and Missing in Southeast Asia. (1990, April). *Newsletter.* Washington, DC: Author.

Nice, D., McDonald, B., & McMillian, T. (1981). The families of U.S. Navy prisoners of war five years after reunion. *Journal of Marriage and the Family, 43,* 431–437.

Roberts, C. (1991, September 25). Why MIAs live on: How it feels when one of the family is missing. *San Diego Union,* p. B-7.

Smith, R. (Producer). (1978). *He's only missing* [Video film]. Boston: Boston University.

CHAPTER FOUR

Psychosexual Scars of Recent Wars

Jose Florante J. Leyson, MD

It [war] is hell.
—William T. Sherman, U.S. Civil War general (1880)

It TOOK ALMOST 800 YEARS TO ESTABLISH THE CURRENT ETHICS OF SOLDIERING and warfare. In ancient times, tribal wars or conflicts had no particular rules of engagement. The victors did not take prisoners, but the vanquished were either enslaved (women were raped) or eaten. During the period of the Roman Empire, the Roman conquerors sometimes used their female slaves as mistresses. In A.D. 631, Muhammed (the Islamic prophet/leader) focused on the holy war (*jihad*) and instructed his followers to respect human rights. He considered rape a serious crime (Noss, 1982). During the Middle Ages, in the War of the Crusaders (Christianity vs. Islam, 1096–1291), knighthood was born. Most of the knights were gentleman warriors, the forerunners of modern (soldier) officers (U.S. Army, 1989). Because of long-drawn-out battles or foreign campaigns, combat stress seemed to creep in, especially in inexperienced soldiers. In the Napoleonic wars (1796–1815), Emperor Napolean refined the rules of warfare and the conduct of soldiers (Noss, 1982). However, anecdotal stories revealed that Josephine (his wife) had a soldier lover to ease sexual boredom and deprivation. The duration of major wars in the 18th century was 10 years or longer, and the

66

psychosexual consequences may have been ignored or not reported even though participants suffered enormous psychosexual trauma.

Some military historians believe that during the U.S. Civil War (1861–65) some soldiers who lived through the bloodier battles reported nightmares and marital difficulties upon return to civilian life. In a 1928 novel, *Lady Chatterley's Lover*, D. H. Lawrence cautioned readers that it was not proper to discuss the sexual concerns of a World War I paraplegic veteran who had been labeled impotent. In World War I, "shell shock" was superficially dealt with. During World War II the treatment of "war neurosis" or "combat exhaustion" was vigorously pursued. However, it was not until the late 1950s that intense research on "stress response syndromes" (war neurosis and psychosexual dysfunctions) was conducted ("Treating the Trauma," 1992).

The purpose of this chapter is to examine the chronic psychological maladjustment syndromes that may be associated with or result in psychosexual scars from recent wars and to reevaluate their innovative management.

Extreme behavioral and emotional reactions to the stress of combat have been recognized for centuries and variously labeled "battle fatigue" (combat neurasthenia) in World War II, "battle shock" during the Korean conflict and "traumatic war neurosis" in the Vietnam War. In the 1973 Yom Kippur War (Middle East) this psychological trauma was called "combat stress reaction" (Hazen & Llewellyn, 1991). Furthermore, in the early 1980s this condition was relabeled stress response syndrome or posttraumatic stress disorder (PTSD) in DSM III-R (APA, 1987). Many researchers believed that an individual's response to serious events in life may be due in part to preexisting personality features (Elliot & Eisderfer, 1981). In addition, emotional responses may be influenced in part by society and the culture in which a person lives (sociobiological theory) (Horowitz, 1990). In order to understand the various factors involved in stress-response pattern, which may result in psychosexual trauma or scarring, a historical perspective and an overview of different conflicts/wars will be presented.

KOREAN WAR (1950–53)

The Korean War (high-intensity conflict) began on June 25, 1950, when the army of North Korea (a Russian satellite) drove tanks across the 38th parallel and invaded South Korea. U.S. President Truman ordered American armed forces to aid in South Korea's defense, and later the United Nations for the first time authorized a multinational (20-nation) force participation. This was the first time America was involved in an armed effort to contain global communism (Fehrenback, 1991).

During the first year of the conflict, most of the soldiers and their officers were older, experienced, married, and veterans of World War II. A majority of the soldiers had a common idea, that containing communism was the right thing to do, and their vision was clear. These factors may have reduced the psychological trauma and psychosexual scars reported. Korean War veterans were welcomed home and honored in local parades; they blended well into the American society and economy. Furthermore, this conflict was not opposed, as the later Vietnam War was (U.S. Army, 1989).

During the years following the Korean experience, U.S. troops and UN multinational forces performed as "border police." The majority of the replacement U.S. forces were young, single, and inexperienced in combat. When the Korean War era ended, January 31, 1955, there were 33,629 Americans dead from combat, the rest (20,000) died from medical illnesses and drug abuse (617); total dead: 54,246 (U.S. Army, 1989). Prostitution and drug smuggling were rampant in and around the demilitarized zone. Some American veterans who married their Korean girlfriends manifested symptoms of PTSD. Others continued to exhibit PTSD and/or alcohol and chemical abuse behavioral patterns. Some of the psychosexual scars became deep psychological wounds (psychogenic impotence and desire disorders) (Kaplan, 1979).

Today there are 4.7 million veterans, of whom 108,600 are women. It is estimated that about 2% to 5% of the nondisabled veterans (male and female) are suffering from organic (2%) and psychogenic (5%) (desire, erectile, and orgasmic) sexual dysfunctions ("Treating the Trauma," 1992). Those who sustained some form of neurological or spinal cord trauma (disabled men) have 75% to 80% organic impotence and 15% to 20% psychogenic impotence. (See Table 4.1.)

VIETNAM WAR (1963–73)

The Vietnam War was the legacy of France's failure to suppress nationalist forces evolving in Indochina. The government of the Republic of South Vietnam was formed on 7 July 1954, with Ngo Dinh Diem as prime minister. Ho Chi-Minh formed the Viet Minh (a Communist revolutionary government) of North Vietnam, north of the 17th parallel. The United States pledged to support the Republic of Vietnam through the U.S. Military Assistance and Advisory Group Vietnam (MAAG-V) in November 1955. In November 1963, Diem's administra-

Table 4.1 Comparative Data Regarding the Psychosexual Scars of Recent Wars

WAR	DURATION	SEX	AGE	EDUCATIONAL LEVEL	TYPES OF CONFLICTS	STATUS OF DUTY	SOCIETY'S ATTITUDE	LEVEL OF TRAINING	POSTWAR PTSD THERAPY	SEXUAL SCAR
Korean War	1,095 days	Male	Older	High school	High-intensity	Drafted/volunteer	Warm	Average to poor	Late	Organic dysfunction[a] and PTSD[b]
Vietnam War	3,650 days	Male	Young (20 yrs.)	High school	High-intensity	Dafted	Cool	Average	Late	Organic dysfunction[a] and PTSD[b]
Grenada/Panama	8–12 days	Mixed	Middle age	High school/college	Low-intensity	Drafted/active	Lukewarm	Better	Delayed	PTSD[b]
Gulf War	43 days	Mixed; more women	Middle age	College	High/medium-intensity	Volunteer	Warmest	Best	Early	PTSD[b]

[a]Organic dysfunctions = sexual problems due to injuries/associated medical illness.
[b]PTSD = psychogenic sexual dysfunctions.

tion was overthrown in a military coup; the United States later realized that it was difficult to replace a solid Vietnamese democratic leadership. When the war ended on 29 April 1975 (U.S. political support was terminated on 29 March 1973), American military deaths exceeded 58,000. There were another 75,000 severely disabled and 303,704 wounded, out of the almost 1 million who saw combat. The majority of the soldiers were young men (average age, 20 years), single, with a high school education and a minority group background. The 10,000-day war seemed a tactical victory but a strategic defeat for the U.S. government.

Because of the U.S. Army's policy of limiting the tour of duty to 12 months (it was 13 months for marines), there was no unit cohesion, continuity or esprit de corps. The DEROS (date of expected return from overseas) system promised the combatant a way out of the war (i.e., going home regardless of the progress of the conflict itself) (Williams, 1980). Furthermore, the ineffective chain-of-command arrangements, unclear military objectives, difficulty of identifying the enemy (Viet Cong, who looked, acted, and lived like the regular civilian Vietnamese), unfamiliar terrain, and unconventional (guerrilla) warfare led to indecision, anger, and distrust of authority. The combination of these factors may have resulted in suspicion, which later led to marital/relationship dysfunctions (Figley, 1978; Peterson, 1991; Scurfield, in press).

The *drafted* young and inexperienced soldiers were exposed to massive battle casualties too early in life. The perception that the soldier was treated like a number, not as a person, led him/her to believe that he/she would go home in a body bag (dead) instead of becoming a live war veteran. These morbid experiences precipitated feelings of depression, anxiety, isolation, boredom, and recurring nightmares. The psychological trauma, which may have led to alcoholism and chemical abuse, then combined with these and often resulted in psychological and mixed (organic and psychogenic) erectile dysfunctions.

Prostitution, either the result of war or of the Communists' biological and psychological warfare, was responsible for the high incidence of sexually transmitted diseases (STDs) and the resurgence of resistant strains of gonorrhea. These STDs led to chronic prostatitis (men) and salpingitis (women), resulting in chronic mixed (organic and psychogenic) impotence and infertility problems for both sexes.

The majority of Americans resisted the Vietnam War. Upon returning home, Vietnam veterans did not easily blend into the mainstream. The ungrateful and resentful attitudes of much of the public made the Vietnam veterans feel isolated and rejected. The psychosocial stigma of an immoral war and returning as drug addicts resulted in many cases of PTSD and/or chronic depression with libido and relationship disorders (Goodwin, 1980).

IRANIAN AND LEBANON CRISES (1980–83)

Both of these low-intensity conflicts were geared for limited military missions and possibly were strategic adventurism for some diplomats. The psychological trauma of the Iranian hostage crisis was one of shame, rage, and inadequacy due to the helicopter rescue (Operation Desert One) debacle. The American-Iranian veterans suffered possibly short-lived sexual performance anxiety problems due to anger and poor self-esteem. However, in Lebanon (U.S. Marines suicide car bombing) the psychosexual dysfunctions were more deep-rooted because of the combination of the physical (massive body injuries) and psychological traumas of betrayal and of rage directed toward the terrorists. For example, I treated a U.S. Marine veteran of the Lebanon crisis who was suffering from mixed type of impotence, which included poor self-image and organic pelvic neuropathy due to partial spinal cord trauma from shrapnel injuries. As in other conflicts or terrorist attacks, the ex-serviceperson also occasionally experiences PTSD, which includes feeling guilty and having gruesome nightmares.

GRENADA INVASION
(OCTOBER 25–NOVEMBER 2, 1983)

"Operation Urgent Fury" was launched by the United States to deter dictatorship and Communist expansionism in the Caribbean island nation of Grenada. When the Organization of East Caribbean States (OECS) requested U.S. president Ronald Reagan to assist the small national army in defending against the Cuban-backed Communist rebels, U.S. military retaliation was swift but a little chaotic. The lines of communication (LOC) between different armed services (army, navy, and marines) were not well established. Most of the ground troops used portable radios and commercial mobile telephone hookups to report and receive orders from higher-command headquarters. The unity of Joint Task Force command was not in place; thus, the execution of the battle plan was not ideal. Intelligence gathering and reporting were inadequate and inaccurate. There were casualties from friendly fire. Because the Grenada invasion was a low-intensity conflict and a limited engagement, postwar psychosexual scars were few in those who participated;

that is, psychogenic impotence from inadequacy and loss of control of emotional upheaval were minimal.

PANAMA INVASION
(DECEMBER 20, 1989–JANUARY 31, 1990)

"Operation Just Cause" was also a low-intensity conflict. This military operation had dual purposes: (1) to extricate a drug baron (trafficker) and (2) to put an end to military dictatorship. As in other recent engagements, there were still dilemmas, confusions, and frustrations faced by U.S. soldiers in Panama. In a fluid battle environment, the sudden change of a commercial district into a battlefield posed difficult situations for determining who was or was not the enemy (Briggs, 1990). There were deplorable behaviors by some soldiers, who were accused of sexual harassment and raping civilians. Because the American soldiers sensed that they were helping a longtime ally in destroying one of South America's drug smuggler collaborators and in snuffing out military one-man rule, a mission considered valid by many, the postwar emotional trauma and sexual dysfunctions were mostly temporary or fleeting. After both of these conflicts, the returning veterans could blend back into society as champions of democracy and the oppressed.

PERSIAN GULF WAR
(JANUARY 17–FEBRUARY 27, 1991)

On August 2, 1990, the Iraqi tank army overran Kuwait because of unresolved disputes over oil-pricing policies and underground oil territorial rights. Five days later, U.S. President Bush ordered the execution of Operation Desert Shield, deploying U.S. combat troops, warplanes, and a naval task force to Saudi Arabia and the Persian Gulf region. On January 17, 1991, Operation Desert Storm (ODS) commenced, with air attacks against the aggressor and the Iraqi positions in the conquered Kuwait (Leyson, 1991). The United States led multicoalition forces (30 allied countries and 18 supporting nations) in warfare that was violent, decisive, and finally victorious (Scurfield & Tice, 1991; Thurman, 1992). On February 27, 1991, the 43-day war (100-hour ground war) was over, and Kuwait was liberated by the coalition forces.

The Gulf War was somewhat unique compared to the other recent wars or low-intensity conflicts (Grenada/Panama) for several reasons. The 1990s war plans of the Department of Defense (DoD) have been streamlined through responsive leadership, with better personnel/

equipment training and enhanced psychophysical programs for the individual soldier. As a veteran of ODS (Gulf War) and a reservist myself, I have seen enormous changes, including a better caliber of soldier in all units. However, there are still issues that need to be addressed postwar, such as better pay, job security, postwar financial rescue for the self-employed reservist and physician; racial discrimination; sexual harassment; and homosexuality (Leyson, 1991). Another difference is that most of the soldiers (537,000) were volunteer (reservists), middle-aged, professional, and highly specialized (see Table 4.1). However, there were specific populations of ODS, that were at high risk of psychotrauma (Scurfield, in press). One such subgroup is women on active duty, who were mobilized and deployed in numbers unprecedented in U.S. military history. The participation of women in direct combat support caused tension and ethnoreligious conflict between Muslim and Western customs and attitudes.

The second subgroup was the "weekend warriors" (reservists), who were rapidly activated. Many did not feel themselves adequately prepared either attitudinally or in training and equipment to feel confident for battle. They left behind disrupted families and in some cases disrupted careers. Some spouses felt abandoned and faced the unanticipated problems and challenges of single parenthood.

A third special population included the ethnic minority troops, who were estimated to represent 40% to 60% of U.S. troops in ODS. Americans of Arabic and other Middle Eastern descent (Jews, Syrians, Southwestern Asians) faced extraordinary pressures and ethnic conflicts. During ODS, there was considerable mixing of service personnel of both sexes. The soldiers could socialize and even sexually interact with each other. These activities lessened the effects of boredom and minimized alcohol and drug abuse. Medical care was the finest in U.S. military history, including the placement of pre- and intramobilization "combat stress reaction programs." Because of the short duration of the engagement, clear political and military objectives, utilization of air-land battle doctrine, the wholehearted commitment and support of the American people and the world, the postwar social support and welcoming reception given to returning desert warriors, cases of PTSD and psychosexual scars were minimized (Scurfield & Tice, 1991; Thurman, 1992).

Furthermore, 2½ months after ODS, Congress (through Public Law 102-25, Section 335) directed the DoD and the Department of Veterans Affairs (formerly the Veterans Administration) to submit a plan for assessment, identification, and rehabilitative therapeutic management for soldiers with PTSD ("Medicine in the Gulf, 1991; "Mental and

Emotional Problems," 1991). Conversely, the Vietnam veteran had to wait 5–10 years before there was a solid implementation of a similar plan. Most of the noncombat casualties were due to food poisoning, thermal injuries, multiple chemical environmental sensitivity syndromes (allergic reactions to fine "desert" sands), other combat stress reactions and chronic fatigue syndrome (Leyson, 1991).

INCIDENCE, ETIOLOGY, AND CLINICAL DIAGNOSIS

The overall incidence of combat stress reaction, or PTSD, in modern warfare ranges from 10% to 25% of all combat casualties. During the Korean War, psychiatric evacuation dropped to 6%, compared to 23% in World War II. On the other hand, the Vietnam experience resulted in 15.2% men and 8.5% women who manifested PTSD, while 11.1% male and 7.8% female (of a total of 350,000 soldiers) showed signs of partial PTSD. Data from the Department of Veterans Affairs revealed that of the 10,000 Gulf War veterans screened there were 328 psychiatric cases, 55 acute stress cases, 10 PTSDs, and 16 with related psychological disorders ("Medicine in the Gulf," 1991).

The main clinical criteria in diagnosing PTSD (APA, 1987) are the persistence of the following symptoms: (1) reexperiencing of the traumatic event, (2) avoidance of stimuli associated with the trauma, and (3) increased arousal phenomena/symptoms. The *reexperiencing phenomena,* including recurring intrusive memories (flashback), may precipitate chronic depression leading to libido (desire) disorders, ejaculatory/erectile dysfunctions, and orgasmic difficulties (Kaplan, 1979). *Avoidance of stimuli* may lead to alienation and disinterest in pleasurable activities or the feeling of decreased capacity for intimacy/tenderness, resulting in "spectatoring" (nonparticipatory sexual activity), libido disorders, and relationship dysfunctions for members of both sexes (Williams, 1980). *Increased arousal symptoms* include hypervigilance, exaggerated startle response (ODS veterans), irritability, and sudden outbursts of anger and even anxiety. These symptoms can precipitate all types of libido disorders and psychogenic sexual dysfunctions.

Vietnam veterans who were exposed to Agent Orange (dioxin) may experience peripheral neuropathy, resulting in organic neurogenic impotence and liver diseases (testosterone-hormonal imbalance) and leading to libido disorders in both male and female. Veterans who are polydrug abusers and chronic alcoholics are subject to libido disorders and organic neurogenic impotence. Veterans of all wars who are physically disabled from spinal cord injury (SCI) and other vascular pelvic injuries/trauma may experience both neurogenic and vascular impotence with orgasmic difficulties (Leyson, Francouer, & Skowsky, 1991). Those who are amputees without associated pelvic trauma usually suffer from psychogenic sexual dysfunctions due to poor self-image or maladjustment syndromes.

Helplessness (a sense of not having done enough to assist a wounded soldier, rather than the survivor guilt felt by most combatants) was a major symptom of female nurses during the recent Gulf War ("Mental and Emotional Problems," 1991). This symptom can lead to spectatoring because one is preoccupied with nonsexual thoughts during a sexual activity. When I was reassigned (cross-leveled) at Walson Army Hospital, Fort Dix, New Jersey, after the ground war, at the Sex Clinic I diagnosed women with orgasmic dysfunctions due to spectatoring resulting from the feeling of helplessness. Some women had dyspareunia due to nonneurogenic (anxiety-reaction) urinary bladder retention and genitalia pains from "desert sand dermatitis" in the pelvic area. A majority of ODS veterans experienced libido disorders and/or impotence of psychogenic causes ranging from financial to emotional bankruptcy and plain physical exhaustion. Some recent war veterans with PTSD manifested stress-related chronic muscle pain/fatigue psychosomatic genital pains, which resulted in their avoiding sexual activity or led to dyspareunia in women (Leyson, 1991).

DIAGNOSTIC WORKUP

Like any medical diagnostic testing, the first step is taking a medical history, then conducting a sexological history. In PTSD it is crucial to check for a premorbid medical history in order to delineate the presence or absence of a personality disorder, classify the types of martial/relationship dysfunctions, and determine the kind of sex therapy to be used in the future (APA, 1987, Leyson et al., 1991; Williams, 1980). Premorbid medical history should include an assessment of the following: (1) presence, type, and duration of substance abuse; (2) family background, psychosexual trauma in childhood, and behavioral patterns in dealing with parents and civilian and other authorities; (3) the veteran's combat experiences and reactions to death and the killing/destruction; (4) coping skills after the war and the individual's role in the present society; and 5) interpersonal relationships within the family and their social status. One concern is the presence and frequency of explosive behavior.

To facilitate the sexual history taking, one is advised to utilize the mnemonic SEXUALITY (Leyson, 1991).

*S*enses: Check for abnormalities of the sexually associated senses; touch, sight (color blindness), hearing, and smell, including anesthetic areas in the genitals.

*E*ndocrine: Elicit history of endocrine problems (e.g., diabetes mellitus).

X-ray: Check for prior diagnostic radiographic procedures (e.g., myelogram) causing myelitis and/or nerve damage.

*U*rinary: Ask for history of genitourinary problems (e.g., chronic prostatitis and renal failure).

*A*ttitude: Evaluate the sexual attitudes and types of sexual and relationship preferences (e.g., oral sex can be stimulating but disgusting to some people).

*L*ibido: Check for for sexual desire and frequency of sexual activity. Any sexual problems occurring at least three times should be considered for therapeutic intervention.

*I*nterpersonal: Elicit the status of the couple's marital/personal relationship.

*T*reatments: Determine what kind of treatment was used in the past. Diuretics are notorious as iatrogenic causes of impotence and libido disorder in women.

*Y*esterday: Check for past illness, trauma, and/or surgery that may have a bearing on the present health of the person.

A sexological physical examination should consist of a routine medical examination and blood pressure with vital signs to rule out organic causes. To expedite such sexological evaluation, another mnemonic, SEXUAL, can be utilized (Leyson, 1991).

*S*enses: Check for smell, perception, and color blindness. Those with organic brain syndrome have communication problems and delayed response to sensual stimuli.

*E*ndocrine: Feel for thyroid masses. Palpate for breast, liver, or abdominal masses.

*EX*ternal: Abnormal hair distribution, skin/genital lesions, and masses in pelvic and genital organs.

*A*nesthesia: (arterial) and presence of numbness or absence of sensation in the pelvic and genital areas. Check for arterial femoral pulses.

*L*imbs: Check for amputation and paralysis, which not only compromise normal sexual responses but also negatively alter one's self-image.

LABORATORY AND PSYCHIATRIC EVALUATIONS

Routine lab work should include complete blood count (CBC), liver and renal function studies, urinalysis, and urine culture. This is an adequate screening procedure for young veterans. In older patients (60-plus years) and those complaining of loss of libido, testosterone level (both sexes), LH (luteinizing hormone), and FSH (follicle stimulating hormone) should be determined. In patients with head trauma and neurological disorders who complain of impotence and ejaculatory dysfunction, the above hormonal tests plus prolactin determination should be ordered (Leyson et al., 1991).

Psychological evaluation will determine the presence of "performance/sexual anxiety," depression, marital discord, and/or distorted or poor body image (Kaplan, 1983). Psychometric testing should consist of Derogatis and Sexual Interaction Inventory, Male Impotence/Female Dysorgasmic Test, MMPI, and body image testing when there is evidence of depression and psychogenic impotence (Schiavi, Derogatis, Kuriansky, O'Connor, & Sharpe, 1979). It has been shown that MMPI profiles of PTSD patients indicate the severity of delayed response to stress in Vietnam veterans, especially those from urban and disadvantaged environments. This means that veterans from inner cities who come from underprivileged families are vulnerable to relationship problems and may have difficulties of sexual response to pleasuring techniques due to built-in anxieties (Burke & Mayer, 1985). Psychiatric evaluation is usually indicated when there is overt psychotic behavior, and it is necessary to rule out psychological aberrations in covert psychiatric problems for patients who are candidates for penile implants or penile vascular surgery (Leyson et. al., 1991).

SPECIAL DIAGNOSTIC PROCEDURES

Veterans who are not chemical abusers and are generally healthy still often suffer from psychogenic sexual dysfunctions. However, those with polydrug abuse and associated medical illness or postcombat trauma will need several sophisticated diagnostic tests to clearly delineate the organicity of the sexual dysfunctions. To be considered are the following:

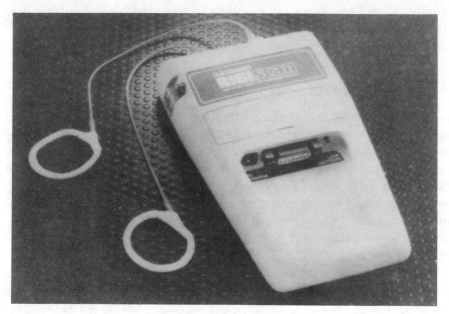

Figure 4.1   RIGISCAN is a semi-portable NPTR monitor for patient's home use for three (3) test nights. The two ring electrodes are placed—one around the base and the other around the groove of penile head (coronal sulcus). (Courtesy of Dacomed Corp., Minneapolis, MN 55420)

1. Penile tumescence/rigidity monitoring (NPTR) (Figure 4.1). Normal soldiers have three to five nocturnal erections during sleep. However, those with psychological and emotional problems showed normal erections and rigidity (Figure 4.2). Those with organic etiologies will demonstrate flat tracing (no or weak erections and poor rigidity).

2. In females, vaginal plethysmography (Figure 4.3) and perineometry are diagnostic tests designed to diagnose weak/poor vaginal muscle orgasmic contraction and decreased lubrication at sleep or during erotic stimulations.

3. For younger patients with a history of pelvic or vascular trauma, color duplex penile arterial ultrasonography and selective pudendal arteriography to rule out vascular insufficiency or obstruction. Venography and cavernosometry are used, and nuclear washout penograms are indicated for patients with suspicious penile venous leaks or penile fibrosis (compartment pathology) (Leyson, 1991). There is no specific diagnostic procedure that yields 100% accuracy. The different testing

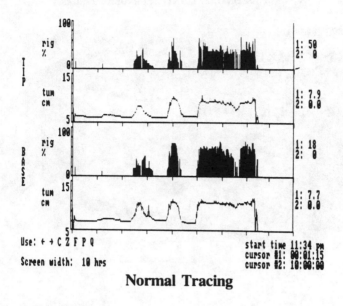

Normal Tracing

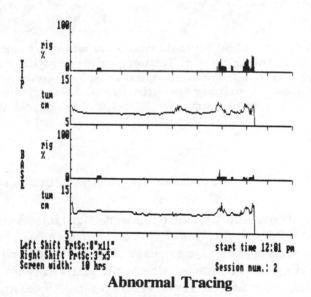

Abnormal Tracing

Figure 4.2 Nocturnal Penile Tumescence Rigidity (NPTR) recordings showing normal erection and poor (abnormal) erection. Top tracings represent rigidity and bottom tracings are tumescences (expansion).

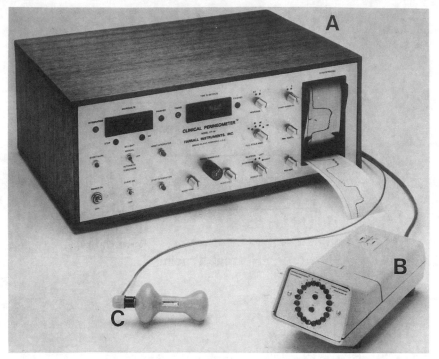

Figure 4.3   (A) Modified vaginal bruximeter which measures nocturnal vaginal contraction(s). (B) Trainer periometer with vaginal plug
(C) used to monitor pelvic and vaginal muscles activity during peri-
neal exercises (for urinary incontinence and sexual dysfunction).
(Courtesy of Farrel Instruments, INC. Grand Island, NE 68802)

methods will be corroborated according to the patient's clinical complaints.

    4. The papaverine intrapenile (chemoerection) injection test is both
diagnostic and therapeutic; it is simple and quick and can be performed
in an office setting. The test consists of injecting 0.5 ml (15 mg) of
papaverine (Figure 4.4) into one side of the penis (corpora cavernosa),
and if normal, there will be a good erection after 15–20 minutes lapse
time. A normal test means the cause of impotence is psychogenic, indicating normal penile vascular supply. No or soft erection indicates that
there is a penile vascular insufficiency or obstruction. Patients should
be cautioned that if the chemoerection lasts for more than 2½ hours,
they should call the urologist/sexologist for treatment (detumescence)
to avoid penile necrosis or priapism.

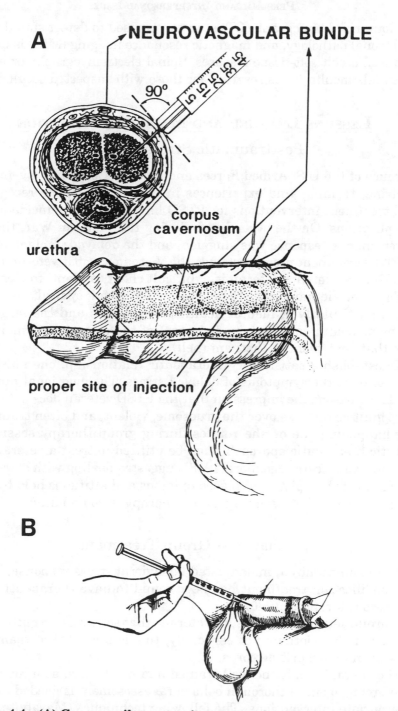

A

NEUROVASCULAR BUNDLE

90°

corpus cavernosum

urethra

proper site of injection

B

Figure 4.4   (A) Gross penile anatomic topography. (B) Proper technique for intrapenile chemoinjection (Papaverine can be mixed with other vaso-active (vasodilator) drugs for longer and firmer erection.

Computerized tomograph (CT) scan can be used to detect spinal verte-
bral (bone) pathology, and magnetic resonance imaging (MRI) is utilized
to unveil occult soft-tissue diseases. Spinal electromyography or evoked
potentials monitoring is reserved for those with suspected occult SCI.

LESSONS LEARNED AND MANAGEMENT OPTIONS

Posttraumatic Stress Therapy

Because of the U.S. Armed Forces and Medical Corps improvement in
doctrine, training, and experiences in the Gulf War, the recognition
and treatment interventions for PTSD have reduced its incidence and
complications. On the other hand, during the Vietnam War, the U.S.
government's response was sluggish, and the delayed implementation
of PTSD treatment programs made the Vietnam combat veteran resentful. Thus, a Vietnam veteran is a difficult client (patient) to treat. The
majority of Vietnam vets are generally distrustful, cynical, and suspicious, particularly of mental health professionals and the large government health care system. It is part of the same government system that sent them to Vietnam (hell).

To establish a satisfactory therapeutic relationship, one must take
into account the symptoms of delayed stress. The emotional numbing
tends to give one the impression that the PTSD veteran does not experience guilt or remorse over the gruesome, violent, and often traumatizing happenings he or she relates during group therapy sessions. A
holistic therapeutic approach must be utilized to treat a veteran with
psychosexual scars. Egendorf (1978) suggested dealing with stereotypical views of therapists and biased opinions and attitudes held by some
veterans before behavioral or group therapy is commenced.

Behavioral Group Treatment

PTSD is an acquired, maladjusted behavioral stress response; behavior modification treatment has been found to have therapeutic effectiveness (Marafiote, 1980).

A group setting will reassure veterans that society is accepting them
back. For the Vietnam vet especially, this is a symbol of team/troop
cohesiveness—esprit de corps.

The therapist must be well trained and must serve as a model and
reinforcing agent. A thorough behavioral assessment is needed to select
appropriate interventions. The following techniques (Marafiote, 1980)
are among those that are being utilized:

1. Relaxation training and biofeedback. Biofeedback will reinforce future sex therapy training to tighten loose vaginal muscles or delay response to stimuli to avoid premature ejaculation.
2. Thought stopping.
3. Modeling, behavioral rehearsal, and role reversal.
4. Assertiveness training.
5. Covenant control—replacing cognitions that typically lead to the undesirable behavior with alternative competing cognitions. The chain is likely to be disrupted and the negative consequences avoided.
6. Cognitive restructuring,
7. Cognitive rehearsal—reenactment of how a husband-veteran demonstrates his love for his wife or family.
8. Contracting.
9. Homework.
10. Charts and graphs—these measures give a visual demonstration of the group's investment and progress.
11. Refunding fees—a cash incentive or emotional financial motivation to solve one's own problems.
12. Bibliotherapy—this technique serves as an important stimuli for self-change and motivation. Clients can read books or articles that may interest them particularly.

For more in-depth discussion of these behavioral techniques and philosophy, one can read: *Post-traumatic Stress Disorders of the Vietnam Veteran* (Williams, 1980).

Therapeutic Interventions for Women Partners

For the behavioral therapy to be effective, it should be reinforced by the significant other. The female partner should be guided on the following interventions:

1. Cope and learn problem-solving techniques.
2. Receive sharing and support from a peer group.
3. Attempt better understanding of the veteran's problems.
4. Develop greater skills and more self-confidence.
5. Offer alternatives to reduce tension and some release from the daily stresses of life.
6. Give better attention to one's spouse.

7. Provide techniques for enhancing mutual trust and honesty in the relationship.

8. Provide options for creating or seeking better opportunities to pursue one's own goals and needs.

9. Be more appreciative of one's partner.

10. Provide financial and emotional security and stability through utilizing services of Veterans Affairs, the U.S. armed forces, and other veteran or corporate support groups and community and family life education and support group programs (Williams, 1980).

Psychopharmacologic Treatment

In cases where behavior strategies are not sufficiently effective or the psychiatric illness is severe, pharmacologic intervention becomes necessary. Before any drug therapy is started, however, it is advisable to treat alcoholism and polydrug abuse. Then the following drugs can be used:

1. *Antianxiety agents:* hydroxyzine hydrochloride, (Atarax®, Vistaril®, Benadryl®).

Benzodiazepine group: (Valium®, Tranxene®, Serax®, Librium®, Ativan®, Centrax®) Suggested doses are as follows: Valium, 40 mg/day; Tranxene, 7.5 mg four times a day; Serax, 10 mg four times a day (ideal for elderly patients); and Librium, 25 mg four times a day. Valium should not be used at more than 40 mg/day because it can cause urinary retention and decrease libido. For amphetamine abuse, Mellaril® (up to 800 mg/day) is advised; for short-term sleep disturbances, Dalmane® or Restorial®, 30–60 mg at bedtime; for alcoholism, an adjunctive therapy of Antabuse® is suggested (Yost, 1980).

2. *Depression: tricyclic antidepressants:* Tofranil, 75–150 mg to 300 mg/day, which can also help improve urinary incontinence that may be embarrassing during sexual activity. Other antidepressants include Elavil®, Norpramin®, Sinequan®, and Vivactil®. For a patient whose depression is associated with libido disorders, the use of Prozac®, Wellbutrin®, or Zoloft® is recommended. Although the public media have claimed that Prozac increases suicidal tendencies, most medical literature has discounted that claim (Leyson, 1991). Zoloft is ideal for elderly veterans because it has fewer anticholinergic side effects (Ayd, 1992).

3. For *persistent psychotic symptoms* associated with PTSD that may lead to bizarre sexual behavior, neuroleptic agents such as Haldol®, Navane®, and Loxitane® (5–40 mg/day) are suggested.

Some Vietnam veterans reported the use of marijuana as an anti-anxiety medication. Others claimed it eliminated their nightmares and flashbacks. However, I do not advocate the use of marijuana because it can depress the memory brain centers, resulting in suppression of dream activity. Furthermore, chronic marijuana abuse can lead to male infertility and impotence due to cerebral, peripheral nerve, and testicular (Sertoli cell) damage (Leyson et al., 1991).

Psychospiritual Counseling

Since most sexual scars of nondisabled veterans are of psychogenic etiology and some patients are not at ease with mental health professionals in their initial entry to psychotherapy, I suggest the following steps from McEver (1972) and others for pastoral (psychospiritual) therapeutic counseling.

1. Evaluation. A brief and simplified psychological assessment and review of the patient's diagnosis, such as psychogenic or organic sexual dysfunctions, PTSD only or in combination with substance abuse, with or without physical disabilities.

2. Listening and comforting. The pastor/chaplain lends a sympathetic ear to the patient's problems or concerns and communicates to the patient that God accepts his/her mistakes (Helminiak, 1989).

3. Catharis (catalysis). The chaplain functions as a catalyst to let the patient ventilate his/her guilt feelings of anger and project such anger onto God. The counselor also tries to help patients become aware of their responsibilities and capabilities, using reflection to focus patients' attention on what they can be or do in the future.

4. Relaxation and meditation. The psychospiritual therapist can teach the patient the basic techniques of physical relaxation (i.e., deep breathing exercises, thinking calming thoughts, and using music in conjunction with each or separately). Furthermore, meditation can supplement relaxation exercises by verbal and nonverbal praying (Zanzig, 1990). Verbal praying can simply consist of reciting the standard "Our Father" or "Hail Mary." On the other hand, nonverbal prayer is described as "plain talking to God"—telling God all of one's complaints or problems and asking for help or forgiveness. For 10 minutes listen to the Lord and respond to him. Then thank the Lord and take a "word" with you.

The atheist patient is encouraged to find self-assurance and self-worth (McEver, 1972).

5. Challenge. Through this ministry, the counselor helps patients to regain their self-confidence and to commit themselves to positive values and goals. For the physically challenged (disabled), counselors can also help guide them to discover a vocational purpose and later reignite a psychoemotional flame to initiate a personal relationship.

6. Closure. This stage is usually the end of pastoral counseling (3–4 months). The patient at this point usually has finally "found" himself or herself. The counselor can provide the patient with a "reminder"— a code phrase such as "I am my friend," "I have self-worth," "I can do something about this problem."

For homeless patients, a referral to a social work agency, veterans' service, or charity organization is imperative. For patients with residual deep-rooted psychological problems, referral to a psychologist or psychiatrist for continued therapy and periodic follow-up is important.

Psychosexual Scars Management

Once the mind is clear of mental turmoil, the therapist can commence treatment for the aching and lonely soul. The management of psychosexual scars entails sex education and psychosexual counseling. In sex education, men should be informed that it takes an average 15–20 minutes to stimulate the female to orgasm, while it only takes an average 3–5 minutes to induce men to orgasm (Singer & Singer, 1978). Thus, the woman needs to be shown patience and prolonged foreplay, and the man must learn to delay his orgasm rupture. One can teach the engaged or married couple the 10 ways to make love lasting (Bessell, 1984):

1. Communicate effectively and lovingly.
2. Continually refresh the energy of love and romance in your relationship.
3. Keep finances/expenses under control.
4. Spend quality time together.
5. Keep outsiders out of your relationship.
6. Be sensitive to work-related stress.
7. Don't take your spouse for granted.
8. Don't take anger to bed.
9. Develop some separate interests so that each of you has a breathing space.

10. Don't expect your spouse to change after marriage, and learn the art of compromise and understanding.

For disabled veterans and for nondisabled individuals who may have problems in their relationships, a divorce-prevention strategy can be found in *Sexual Rehabilitation of the Spinal Cord Injury Patient* (Leyson et al., 1991).

Sex Therapy

Madonna–Prostitute Complex (M-P)

For those involved in short wars but whose physical absence was longer because they remained on active duty even after the conflict, the Madonna complex may occur (Leyson, 1991). The veteran is afraid to make love to his spouse for fear that he/she may hurt her or him (gay couple) due to prolonged sexual abstinence. Treatment is sexual reeducation. Patients are encouraged to resume sexual activity gradually until both can adjust to their previous sexual patterns or frequency. The prostitute component of the (M-P) complex is manifested by a veteran whose desire for sexual frequency has increased tremendously and who treats his/her spouse without respect or consideration (like a prostitute). Part of the remedy consists of using reorientation-to-reality techniques. Explain to the veteran that his wife or significant other needs to be respected as a person and that sexual activity is between consenting adults.

Hypersexuality and Cheating Spouses

Oversexuality is an attitudinal reaction of needing great frequency of sexual activity, with a hidden agenda to compensate for prolonged sexual deprivation. Treatment consists of psychological counseling to relax and be patient. Lovemaking will be more satisfying if done in an unhurried manner with one's partner's full consent and cooperation. For those with already "rocky" marital relationships, the following suggestions may help avoid extramarital affairs: (1) apply the 10 ways to make love endure; (2) engage in periodic physical pleasuring and spiritual enrichment; (3) take time and know how to play; have fun and laugh in and out of bed; (4) develop a better self-concept by overcoming the fear of emotional and physical inadequacies; (5) take time to plan lovemaking. The couple should remain lovers, even as parents, stepparents, or foster parents.

Abbreviated Sex Therapy for Psychogenic Impotence
and Orgasmic Dysfunction

1. Teach patients the normal male and female sexual response cycle.
   Older patients need longer foreplay; younger couples need training to prevent premature ejaculation.
2. Teach sensate-focus techniques (Kaplan, 1983). Define erotic and
   extragenital sensual zones. Suggest sensory stimulation—for
   example, sexy clothes and romantic environment.
3. Assign homework of sexual exercises for 1 hour twice a week.
4. Let the couple study the "genital map." Discuss possibilities of
   mutual masturbation. Indicate that communication is what makes
   your partner "tick" (i.e., feel important to you).
5. Encourage the couple to rekindle the romance they may have
   experienced during an earlier phase of the relationship. Teach
   them to avoid performance anxiety and "spectatoring" by being
   sexually competent.

Treatment for Premature Ejaculation

Pain trigger suppression techniques:

1. Kaplan's method: penile withdrawal and nonerotic thoughts (Kaplan, 1979)
2. Masters and Johnson's method: withdraw the penis and squeeze
   the glans penis until the man feels pain and the ejaculatory sensation is suppressed (Kaplan, 1979; Leyson et al, 1991).
3. Beatrice's technique: Squeeze the scrotum until it hurts.
4. Leyson's technique (ideal for obese persons): pinch the perineum
   at the median raphe until a pain sensation is triggered, substi-
   tuting discomfort for the erotic sensation.

Anesthesia. Apply 2% Xylocaine® ointment to one side of the penile
shaft before sex to reduce sudden crescendo of erotic sensations.
Alpha-2 blockage. Oral Dibenzyline® 10 mg or Minipress® 1 or 2 mg
an hour before sexual activity to prolong vas deferens contraction and
delay ejaculation.

Sexual Surrogation

The utilization of sexual surrogate therapy with married *nonparalyzed*
couples has been abandoned by Masters and Johnson due to its inef-

fectiveness (Rodriguez, 1983). However, for the *physically disabled* single veterans, Leyson et al. (1991) have suggested specially trained sexual surrogates as a therapeutic alternative. Their use must be monitored carefully by a sexologist and done in accordance with ethical guidelines. The malpractice issue that may arise for utilizing a certified sexual surrogate therapy option is most likely to be promotion of prostitution. However, because this kind of sex therapy is properly supervised and sanctioned by a sexologist, the chance of indictment will be rare (Leyson et al., 1991). Sexual surrogates for the disabled are also trained in techniques for safe sex.

Specific Medical and Surgical Treatments

The contemporary medical management therapy for impotence consists of the following:

External Assistive and Mechanical Erection Devices

1. Occlusive rings or ribbon bands and dildos (Figure 4.5).
2. Vacuum assistive erection devices from hand to battery-powered gadgets (Figures 4.6 and 4.7).

Pharmacological Therapy

1. Transdermal: apply on the penis a patch impregnated with glycerylnitrate (experimental).
2. Oral: yohimbine (1 tablet up to six times a day). For neurological impotence, dopamine (levodopa) at 500 mg four times a day for at least 3–4 weeks, plus sex therapy. Hormonal therapy with zinc or testosterone is indicated only if there is a demonstrable deficiency of the mineral and hormone.
3. Intrapenile injection: chemoerection with 30–45 mg of papaverine only or in combination with prostaglandin E_1 or vasoactive intestinal peptide (VIP). Alposterol (prostaglandin E_1) 10–30 µg is ideal because it produces less penile corporeal fibrosis or scarring.

Surgery

Surgical options are the last resort for impotence treatment. Selection of candidates must be thorough. Vascular penile surgery or implanta-

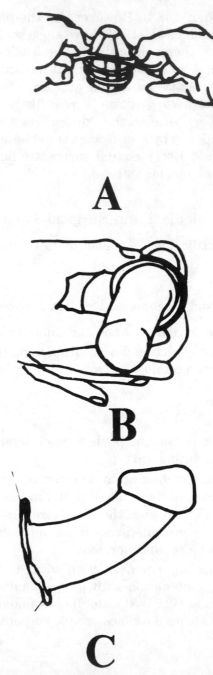

Figure 4.5 (A) Occlusive ring is applied around an introducer. (B) then the ring is slide from the introducer into position around the base of the penis. (C) The ring is in its proper position—used to maintain or convert a soft erection into a firmer one.

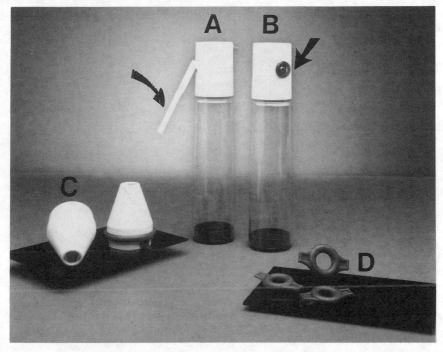

Figure 4.6   Vacuum erection assistive (A) manually operated and (B) battery powered devices (arrows—handle or button). (C) ring introducer. (D) constrictor (occlusive) ring(s) is applied around the penis (see Fig. 5C) once erection is induced, in order to maintain the erection. (Courtesy of Mentor Corp. Minneapolis, MN 55411)

tion of penile prostheses, which are divided into several types—solid, malleable, intrapenile (corporeal), inflatable—are some of the options (Figures 4.8 and 4.9).

Lesbian and Female Orgasmic Dysfunction

Sex therapy is the initial step in the management of orgasmic difficulties. Treatment can include consideration of masturbation, sensate-focus techniques, and hormonal replacement, if indicated. For pelvic anesthesia, oral dopamine-like drugs are suggested. Wellbutrin and Zoloft medication can be tried if orgasmic dysfunctions are accompanied by libido disorders and depression.

SUCTION DEVICE TREATMENT OF IMPOTENCE

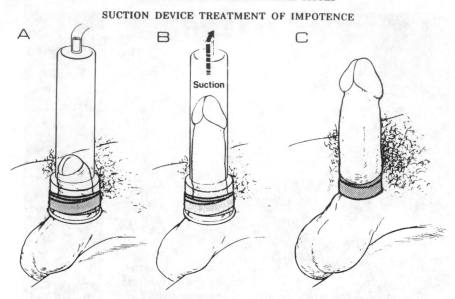

Figure 4.7   Sequence of events leading to erection and application of constrictor ring(s) (to be removed after two minutes limit).

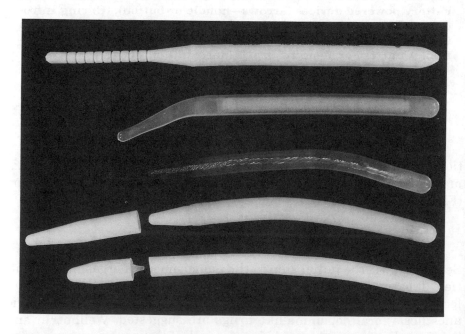

Figure 4.8   Five kinds of solid penile (sex) prostheses from flexible to malleable.

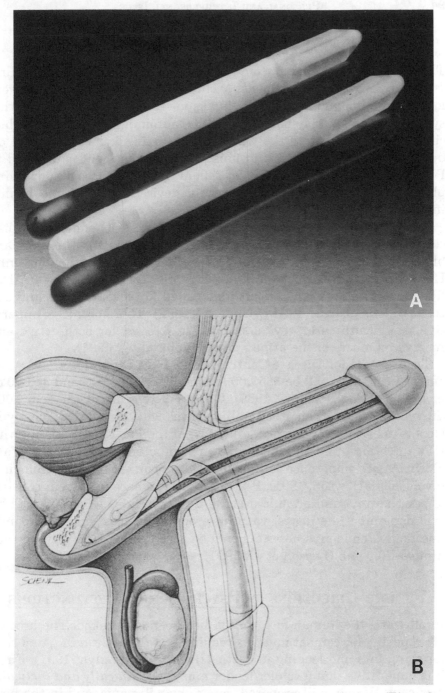

Figure 4.9 (A) A pair of intrapenile inflatable prostheses. (B) each prosthesis is inserted into one of the penile body, in an inflated and deflated state. (Hydroflex—Courtesy of American Medical Systems, Minnetoka, MN)

Acquired Immunedeficiency Syndrome (AIDS) and Other Diseases

There are recent reports from veterans of the Gulf War regarding "strange diseases," which consist of chronic headaches, not feeling well, loss of appetite, and even paralysis. Some researchers believe that this symptom complex may be due to PTSD, autoimmune response to bio-chemicals released into the war zone, or toxins from the oil and oil burning by-products. If this premise is true, treatment is directed to PTSD and neurological causes of sexual dysfunctions (i.e., dopamine plus vitamin B complex, vacuum erection devices, and/or chemo [penile] injection).

The Korean and Vietnam wars have produced drug addicts; this has contributed to their having a high incidence of AIDS. The standard blood test for AIDS types I and II can detect HIV antibodies only. However, the newly discovered non-HIV disease presenting as AIDS-like manifestations may be left undetected for several years and can cost millions of lives ("AIDS Update," 1992). Therefore, it is impera-tive that health care providers advocate *safe sex* for both active and reserve members of the armed forces (Volberding, 1991).

The Centers for Disease Control (CDC) have estimated that by the end of 1992 there will be 365,000 living victims of AIDS and 84,000 or more dead ("AIDS Today," 1989). It is predicted that by the year 2000 (if no cure is found) about 50 million cases will be recorded, mostly in North America, Africa, Brazi, and most of the Far East. Patients with HIV infection suffer from psychogenic impotence. However, in full-blown AIDS, impotence is due to organic causes from neurological involvement (Leyson, 1991). Psychogenic impotence treatment consists of sex therapy, and organic erectile dysfunction can be improved by oral dopamine-like drugs, vacuum erection devices, and intrapenile injections. Penile prostheses may not be practical for AIDS victims with limited life span (Leyson et al, 1991).

FUTURE DIRECTIONS IN PSYCHOSEXUAL DYSFUNCTIONS

In all wars, the human factor often has been overlooked. The process of preparing for combat involves readiness of the *body*, *mind*, and *soul* for going into and leading in battle (Hazen & Llewellyn, 1991). First, it is imperative that a soldier/leader must be *technically and tactically proficient*. If one is ill-prepared, he or she will panic, and in the heat of battle, confusion and fear may subdue the combatant before a bul-let or shrapnel will. The second consideration is *mental preparation* on what to expect, particularly the unexpected. A soldier must learn how to make the mental transition from peacetime and to decompress gradually to combat zone. Each soldier must learn to accept fear as a normal response for self-perservation and must acquire the mechanisms for coping with fear. Some soldiers turn to God and their comrades for support and comfort. Others choose to escape via denial or drugs and alcohol.

Physical preparation and conditioning for combat include regular exercise, adequate food, and sufficient sleep. Physical readiness hardens the body and mind and toughens the soul. Finally, the *spiritual aspect* of combat preparation includes a soldier's relationship with family, friends, and his/her God (Flynn, 1992). Religion provides a sense of comfort and peace to many soldiers in the chaotic and stressful environment of war. Spiritual readiness makes a soldier face death in a calmer and more peaceful manner.

On the management side we must convince our strategic and military planners to continually train future medical officers, physician's assistants, nurses, and psychologists in the identification and handling of battle fatigue. By properly understanding the principles of acute combat stress, this approach could be a "combat force multiplier" in the combat zone and a healing gesture for those who may have a propensity for PTSD (Hazen & Llewellyn, 1991). Reduction of PTSD may prevent the occurrence of psychosexual wounds or scars and lead to saving lives or rebuilding crumbling marital relationship.

The ultimate goal in the prevention of combat stress is to eliminate war. For many, peace is not merely the absence of conflict; it is a sense of well-being and security, and it may include a sense of the presence of a high power.

REFERENCES

AIDS today. (1989, January). *Infectious Disease Today*, pp. 1, 14.

AIDS Update: Non-HIV viruses. (1992, July). Paper presented at the Seventh International Conference on AIDS, Amsterdam, Netherlands.

American Psychiatric Association. (1987). *Diagnostic and statistical manual of mental disorders* (3rd ed., rev.). Washington, DC: Author.

Ayd, F. J., Jr. (1992). Sertraline (Zoloft): The latest FDA approved serotonin uptake inhibitor anti-depressant. *International Drug Therapy Newsletter, 27,* 9–12.

Bessell, H. (1984). *The love test.* New York: Morrow.

Briggs, C. E. III (1990). *Operation Just Cause—A soldier's eyewitness account.* New York: Stackpole Books.

Burke, H. R., & Mayer, S. (1985). The MMPI and the post-traumatic stress syndrome in Vietnam era veterans. *Journal of Clinical Psychology, 41*, 152–156.

Edgendorf, A. (1978). Psychotherapy and Vietnam veterans: Observations and suggestions. In C. R. Figley (Ed.), *Stress disorders in Army Vietnam veterans*. New York: Brunner/Mazel.

Elliot, G., & Eisderfer, C. (1982). *Stress and human health*. New York: Springer Publishing Co.

Fehrenbach, T. R. (1991). *This kind of war*. New York: Bantam Books.

Ferris, R. (1988). Brief sex therapy or the 15 minute hour: Brief guide to office practice. *Medical Aspects of Human Sexuality, 22*, 49–56.

Figley, C. R. (Ed.). (1978). *Stress disorders in Army Vietnam veterans*. New York: Brunner/Mazel.

Flynn, F. V. (1992). Preparing for combat. *The NCO Journal, 2*, 12–13.

Goodwin, J. (1980). The etiology of combat-related post-traumatic stress disorders. In T. Williams (Ed.), *Post-traumatic stress disorders of the Vietnam veteran* (pp. 1–24). Cincinnati, Ohio: Disabled American Veterans.

Hazen, S., & Llewellyn, C. (1991). Battle fatigue identification management for military medical students. *Military Medicine, 156*, 263–267.

Helminiak, D. A. (1989). Self-esteem, sexual self-acceptance and spirituality. *Journal of Sex Education and Therapy, 15*, 203–209.

Horowitz, M. J. (1990). Stress-response syndrome: Post-traumatic and adjustment disorders. In R. Michels (Ed.), *Psychiatry* (Vol. 1, pp. 1–10). Philadelphia: J. B. Lippincott.

Kaplan, H. S. (1979). *Disorders of sexual desire and other concepts and techniques in sex therapy*. New York: Brunner/Mazel.

Kaplan, H. S. (1983). *The evaluation of sexual disorders*. New York: Brunner/Mazel.

Leyson, J. F. (1991, August). *Psychosexual scars in Operation Desert Storm*. Paper presented at the "Lessons Learned—Operation Desert Storm" Medical Quarterly Conference, Fort Dix, New Jersey.

Leyson, J. F., Francoeur, R., & Skowsky, W. R. (1991). Controversies, research, evaluation and treatment of impotence, sexual surrogate for the spinal cord injury patients: In J. F. Leyson (Ed.), *Sexual rehabilitation of the spinal cord injury patient* (pp. 221–229, 251–264, 435–443, 483–530). Totowa, New Jersey: Humana Press.

Marafiote, R. (1980). Behavioral strategies in group treatment of Vietnam veterans. In T. Williams (Ed.), *Post-traumatic stress disorders of the Vietnam veteran* (pp. 49–72). Cincinnati, Ohio: Disabled American Veterans.

McEver, D. H. (1972). Pastoral care of the spinal cord injury patient. *Pastoral Psychology, 23*, 47–56.

Medicine in the Gulf. (1991, August). *U.S. Medicine Journal*, p. 91.

Mental and emotional problems of Gulf War veterans. (1991, November). *American Legion Magazine*, p. 30.

Noss, J. B. (1982). The world's religion; Major wars in history (pp. 1417). Funk & Wagnall's *New Comprehensive International Dictionary of the English Language-Encyclopedia Edition* (pp. 1417, 1634–1637).

Peterson, K. C. (1991). *Post-traumatic stress disorders: A clinician's guide*. New York: Plenum.

Rodriguez, R. (1983, March). Sex surrogate confidental. *Forum Magazine*, pp. 31–36.

Schiavi, R. C., Derogatis, L. R., Kuriansky, J., O'Connor, D., & Sharpe, L. (1979). The assessment of sexual function and marital interaction. *Journal of Sex and Marital Therapy, 5*, 169–224.

Scurfield, R. M. (in press). Post-traumatic stress disorders in Vietnam veterans. In J. P. Wilson & B. Raphael (Eds.), *The international handbook of traumatic stress syndrome* (Vol. I). New York: Plenum Press.

Scurfield, R. M., & Tice, S. N. (1991). Interventions with medical and psychiatric evacuees and their families. *Treatment program handbook*. Tacoma, WA: American Lake VA Medical Center.

Singer, J., & Singer, I. (1978). Types of female orgasms. In J. LoPiccolo & L. LoPiccolo (Eds.), *Handbook of sex therapy*. New York: Plenum Press.

Thurman, M. R. (1992). How we work and win (Operation Desert Shield/Desert Storm). *The NCO Journal, 2*, 8–9.

Treating the trauma of PTSD. (1992). *Disabled American Veterans Magazine, 34*, 8–13.

U.S. Army Center for Military History. (1989). The beginnings; Korean War; the US Army in Vietnam. In *American military history* (pp. 18–25, 545–569, 619–686). Washington, DC: Author.

Volberding, P. A. (1991). *Management of HIV infection: Handbook update*. New York: World Health Communications.

Williams, T. (1980). Therapeutic alliance and goal setting in the treatment of Vietnam veterans and a preferred model for development of interventions for psychological readjustment of Vietnam veterans: Group treatment. In T. Williams (Ed.), *Post-traumatic disorders of the Vietnam veteran: Observations and recommendations for the psychological treatment of the veteran and his family* (pp. 25–48). Cincinnati, Ohio: Disabled American Veterans.

Yost, J. (1980). Psychopharmacologic treatment of the delayed stress syndrome in Vietnam veterans. In. T. Williams (Ed.). *Post-traumatic disorders of the vietnam veteran* (pp. 125–132). Cincinnati, Ohio: Disabled American Veterans.

Zanzig, T. (1990). *Learning to meditate: A thirty day introduction to the practice of meditation*. Winona, MN: Mary's Press, Christian Brothers Publications.

A Reason to Believe:
The Sustenance of
Military Families

Richard W. Bloom, PhD

MILITARY FAMILIES PUT UP WITH THE DOWNSIDE OF MILITARY LIFE. OR TRY
to. They may experience separations from kith and kin. They may be
the brunt of envy, disdain, or hatred from civilians. They may face a
tide of arbitrary traditions, policies, and rituals. They may need to cope
with novel and alien societies, cultures, and climates. They may harbor dissonance when thoughts, feelings, motives, and behaviors are
quite different from military standards. At times they may be required
to act as if pain were pleasure, tension were relaxation, the impossible
were the mundane. Even when military families are society's elite and
have it all, the foreboding of sudden freefall may be as real as blood.

To put up with the downside, military families develop and maintain reasons to believe that pale before an upside. The upside may
comprise experiencing material well-being, professing desirable values,
living a preferred way of life, being sheltered from the storm. Some-

This chapter does not necessarily reflect the views of the United States Department of Defense,
the Ministry of Defense of the Republic of the Philippines, or any government, agency, organization, or official source of information. The author lived in the Republic of the Philippines
from September 1989 through August 1991. Written events without formal citations should
be attributed to author's own observations.

how, families must believe it's all been worth it. Reasons to believe are a military family's red badge of courage, its talisman, its very sustenance of life. But when beliefs crumble, the downside looms large.

Developing and maintaining reasons to believe may be the greatest challenge faced by military families—not just in the United States but in nation-states and power groups worldwide. These families face almost bizarre changes in the (a) nature of political and military force; (b) identity, capabilities, and intentions of adversaries; (c) concepts of security, war, conflict, coexistence, and peace; (d) role of the military in society; (e) encroachment of economic and technological threat, both domestic and international; and (f) ethnic, nationalist, and religious ferment (Freedman, 1992; Pfaff, 1991; Rubinstein, 1991).

In a "new world order" defined only as a shattering of the old, what worked as reasons to believe may not work anymore (Flynn & Scheffer, 1990). Developing and maintaining new ones pose significant obstacles and augur profound consequences. As reasons to believe go, so too will who will fight, when, how, and why, and what they will fight for. Whether victim of misfortune or soldier of fortune, reasons to believe will constitute the sea of the people in which they swim.

This chapter illustrates challenges to military families in farflung societies for reasons to believe. First, it details the experience of U.S. military families living in the Republic of the Philippines for several years prior to a sudden relocation in June 1991. Second, it identifies historical moments that confront families of several other military entities like the armed forces of the Commonwealth of Independent States, Peru, and Cambodia, as well as guerrilla groups in Somalia. For all military families, the chapter analyzes the centrality of reasons to believe for coping and adaptation strategies.

U.S. MILITARY FAMILIES IN THE REPUBLIC OF THE PHILIPPINES

The Context

From 1989 through June 1991, U.S. military families arriving in the Philippines were confronted with the complex, duplicative, and deindividuating requirements of administrative inprocessing. This led many military dependents to perceive that they were only anonymous extensions of their military sponsors, that they were left to haplessly face the vastly different Filipino microsocieties and microcultures as only appendages of people, bereft of unique identity (cf. Chapman, 1991; Prentice-Dunn, 1991). But this was not all. There was an ongoing terrorist threat by insurgents, separatists, and Philippine military rebels (U.S. exit from Manila, 1992). There were infrequent assassinations. There was recurrent theft of U.S. government and personal property by Philippine intruders who would "jump the wall" day or night and by some Philippine employees exploiting U.S. military passes as a license to steal. There were bogus legal actions brought by some Philippine citizens against U.S. citizens who happened to be in the wrong place at the wrong time. There was extreme familial and marital stress partially induced by the moral weaknesses and carnal proclivities of some U.S. citizens.

These malign traits interacted with the huge local prostitution industry, the plethora of cheap establishments purveying alcoholic beverages, and the vast pool of local men, women, and children who would do almost anything to escape appalling socioeconomic conditions ("For Americans and Filipinos," 1991). There was the almost all-pervasive heat and the ever-changing security restrictions hampering one's lifestyle. There was a severe earthquake and aftershocks, temblors, and several typhoons. There were unexpected family separations due to Operations Desert Shield and Desert Storm and expected though usually unwanted separations to support other mission requirements. There were the beginnings of military personnel reductions, decreases in tangible military benefits, slow-downs in military promotions and quality-of-life initiatives. There were prolonged government-to-government negotiations on whether U.S. rights to use Philippine territory for military purposes would be renewed and, if so, under what conditions. There were frequent, highly publicized statements by the Philippine political elite, international media representatives, even U.S. political figures, minimizing or castigating the very need for a U.S. military presence in the Philippines. The reasons to believe held by U.S. military families were under siege and in some cases had succumbed to free-floating anxiety, confusion, low morale, poor social cohesion, and anhedonia (cf. Bollen & Hoyle, 1990).

Then in March 1991 volcanic activity began to increase at Mount Pinatubo, about 9 miles from Clark AB. Pinatubo had been dormant for 600 years, but concern began to build among technical experts, political and military command authorities, people living near Pinatubo and their friends and relatives worldwide, and others with a need to monitor international events and their consequences. All of this, mixed with opinions of people who barely cared or understood, reverberated and were augmented and discounted through the infinite iteration of mass telecommunications, the "word on the street," and an incestuous insularity bred by antiterrorist security restrictions (cf. Walker &

Blaine, 1991). Conversations about Pinatubo usually revealed more about people than Mother Nature.

The pace quickened. On 7 June a crisis action team of military, political, and technical personnel began to formalize and finalize plans to evacuate Clark AB. On 10 June, all U.S. government nonessential personnel and all U.S. government-sponsored families were ordered by command authorities to relocate from Clark AB to Subic Naval Station (NS) about 30 miles away SSW. Over 8,000 people made the trip to Subic by private vehicle, a trip taking over 6 hours in a slow, winding caravan, through chaotic and congested local traffic, under a blazing sun. An indeterminate number left Clark for Manila or Philippine villages or were already at Subic on the basis of rumors that a command-directed relocation was imminent ("Air Force Finishes," 1991; U.S. evacuates, 1991).

On 12–14 June, increasingly significant volcanic activity led almost all essential personnel remaining at Clark to temporarily relocate on the far side of the base, at other times to stay well away from the base on the slopes of Mount Arayat ("As Philippine Volcano Erupts," 1991; "Filipinos Fleeing," 1991; "Volcano Explodes," 1991). Military families had partial awareness of their loved ones' movements back at Clark through military-sponsored television, radio, and newspapers; Philippine and civilian U.S. telecommunications and media; telephone conversations with friends and relatives worldwide who relayed information from their own sources; and face-to-face gossip ("Volcano Imperils," 1991).

Then on 15 June, a convergence of two severe volcanic eruptions, earth temblors, and a low-intensity typhoon caused major damage within a radius of 80 miles of the volcano. The two eruptions alone were three to five times more intense than those of Mount Saint Helens ("An Indicator," 1991). The convergence of natural disasters has been likened to one of the most awesome events in recorded climatic history. Property damage occurred without distinction as to rank among U.S. military families, other foreign nationals, and the Philippine people. Loss of life was limited almost totally to the Philippine people ("Clark Base," 1991; "Filipino Families," 1991; "Filipinos Assessing Cost," 1991).

From 16 June to 30 June all U.S. military nonessential personnel and all U.S. military families were relocated from the Philippines to the United States or to their next duty assignments ("Air Force to Cut," 1991). Over 4,000 people left on 17 June; the 2-week total, including all U.S. government agencies, was about 20,000 ("20,000 Ordered Back," 1991). Also, on 16 June, recovery and reconstitution operations began at Subic NS and Clark AB by a mission essential team (MET) ("Long Closing Seen," 1991, "Philippine Volcano Buried," 1991). The MET did not, unlike most crises, leave its families behind, but instead were left behind by its families.

The Loss of Self, Loved Ones, Friends, and Colleagues

With two exceptions, the lives of U.S. military families were spared throughout the Mount Pinatubo experience. Also spared were other U.S. citizens, loved ones, friends, and colleagues, although some local national friends, employees, and their relatives died as a result of the natural disaster. Fantasies of death were common, especially between the first major eruption of Pinatubo through the relocation of nonessential personnel and families out of the Philippines (cf. Kohn & Levan, 1990). There was some preoccupation with growing older and less attractive by the day. This preoccupation seemed to stem from anxiogenic cognitions that time was going by, the situation was unappealing, and the longer one remained in this situation, the more unappealing one would become (cf. Watson & Morris, 1990).

But loss is much broader than physical demise, injury, disease, decreasing attractiveness, and aging. There is the loss of being with those we want to be with. It was not an easy experience to stand on the flight line watching the Clark AB community depart for Subic on 10 June. Or watching loved ones leave for CONUS, as the MET stayed behind. Sure, departing families were now safe. But hearts still broke. Significant others were departing to unknown situations and circumstances, for an unknown amount of time. What would the future bring? One could only surmise, but to surmise was itself a preoccupation fraught with despair (cf. Balk, 1991).

People we have met, known, and loved become part of ourselves, our self-identity. As we lose them, we lose part of ourselves as well. Thus, with the relocation after the Mount Pinatubo eruptions, there was a huge psychological task to accomplish. One had to reconstruct or reconsolidate one's own life. Some MET members had done this frequently, others seldom. A consensus was that prior experience did not help much, at least in the beginning. One was hurting inside. One was faced with constructing a new community, creating new social roles and rules, reconstructing the fragments of many a heart. Déjà vu ineluctably arose, the images and sensations associated with others one had lost, either temporarily through previous separations or permanently through a relationships termination or through death (cf. Eisenbruch, 1990).

MET members who were on unaccompanied status (i.e., having left their families behind during their tour of duty in the Philippines) confronted even longer separations from their loved ones. One realized that the stay in the Philippines was becoming open-ended. Plans to tolerate a separation for just a definite period had to be modified. This applied as well to personnel without legally defined families but with families of significant others, close friends, and even desired environments and life-styles.

Some people had personal hopes that had to be put on hold for the unknown future. These included plans to be married or to get divorced. Plans for vacations and visits. Plans to try to fix relationships and put things back on track. For these people, there was darkness without light at the end of the tunnel. Others had personal hopes dashed as they received phone calls and letters ending marriages, affairs, and relationships. Some were both perpetrators and victims.

With so much loss, there was a need for respect and admiration from others to help counter feeling less than whole. Some tried to fill this need by exaggerating danger to those away from the scene. This occurred frequently during the relocation to Subic through the reconstitution and recovery efforts at Clark. Tremors became earthquakes, ash venting became a major eruption, light rain became a tropical storm or typhoon, dust raised by moving vehicles became a dust storm. Realistically, there was enough disaster and tragedy without having to embelish nonevents. But a psychological need was being met. (Using time-honored techniques of behavior sampling, I seldom noted the obverse of minimizing danger, unless those away from the scene themselves maximized it; cf. Cassel, 1990).

Putting loss out of mind and "pressing on" is an axiom that at times requires almost superhuman effort. MET members coped by looking out for each other's creature comforts, sharing assets, savoring gallows humor, trusting peers by expressing anxiogenic and depressogenic cognitions, and assuming professional roles. Competent leadership from the top down was a crucial element in effecting adaptive functioning.

It should be added that, even with the very real sense of loss, there were sighs of relief when nonessential personnel and families were relocated. They would soon be safe from the volcano and away from many of the dangers and inconveniences of any Third World country. There would be less of a demand on scarce resources and the fragile, support infrastructure (e.g., potable water and electrical power) in the wake of the Mount Pinatubo experience.

Radical Changes in Life-Style

Daily routines were cast aside during all or part of the Mount Pinatubo eruptions (cf. McFarlane, 1990). One experienced the sudden loss of running water, electric power, and easy access to food during the convergence of natural disasters on 15 June and on and off for weeks. No shaving, no showers, no washing clothes, the rationing of precious food and water, the smells of unflushed toilets and unwashed bodies. Besides one's own personal discomfort, many personnel were still with their families until the evacuation out of the country and had the latter's discomfort to handle as well. The temptation to feel that helping others would take away from helping one's own was marked. This was especially true immediately after 15 June, when batteries were at a premium, the unknown everywhere.

Real and perceived shortages affected social conventions (cf. Lima, Pai, Lozano, & Santacruz, 1990). Sometimes one wondered whether very thin veneers of civilization were being stripped away, baring an ugly narcissism. For example, a military officer arrived 10 minutes early at the one building providing food at Subic NS. He had been erroneously briefed by colleagues that the building was always open. His reaction to being told by the staff that there would be a 10-minute wait was "But I'm a MET member." When this did not produce some food, the member growled, "I hope you don't need emergency services while you're here," threw his tray and eating utensils on the floor, and stormed out. Military spouses and children who cried, threw tantrums, and even stole what did not belong to them did not always have stellar role models.

After relocating to Subic but before departing the Philippines, some military family members—active duty and dependents alike—became unable to nurture and care for others. They withdrew socioemotionally as they tried to deny the shortages and general lack of creature comforts. (Here I would like to add a comment on paradoxical effects of shortages. In actual shortages that are not severe and in assumed shortages that are not real, many people tend to hoard assets in case things get worse. Often they use more of these assets than they would ordinarily. Thus, we find that there are individuals who gain weight or are cleaner than usual during natural disasters through a hoarding mentality. In severe shortages, of course, there's nothing to hoard).

Living space also was at a premium. Most Clark families and single and unaccompanied individuals were doubling and tripling up with Subic families. Others were living in their vehicles, sleazy off-base motels, gymnasiums, other government buildings, and fields. A common experience was being holed up in one room with other adults and children for at least 36 hours on the eve of 14 June through the morning of 16 June. The sky was pitch-dark, black with ash, the sun totally blotted out. In extremely cramped quarters, many waited interminably, without power and water, sweating, listening to the wind howl and the rain of gravel and ash beat down, feeling earth tremors, attempting to comfort and control screaming children and panicking adults, adjusting to the foul smells of communal waste products, wondering whether the end of the world was at hand. Speaking with people the following week, I heard quite a few ascriptions and attributions to the New Testament book Revelation.

Even after most military dependents and nonessential personnel had been relocated out of the Philippines, space was limited. Not just one's own living space but the space to engage in desired out door activities was minimal. The amassed ash on the ground and in the atmosphere precluded safe jogging, extended walking, and recreational driving. Gymnasiums were being used to house people. The addictive pull of physical exercise was exemplified by military family members jogging and running on roads with huge potholes, drifting ash dunes, and near dust storm conditions. This, in turn, increased the probability of needless injuries that would have to be treated.

Without power, with a shortage of batteries, and with damage to broadcasting transmitters, a sizable minority could not listen to music or the news, watch television, use a computer, or even, at times, read.

Another life-style change comprised the new groups of people with whom one would be working, socializing, and meeting. Sometimes this involved despair, anger, or resignation. For long periods of time there would be close contact with people one detested, felt uneasy with, believed to be incompetent, or had absolutely no interest in. Sometimes one was pleasantly surprised that there were good-humored, stable individuals with plenty of common sense among one's new contacts. Regardless of what one confronted, there seemed to be a direct impact on mission performance and life satisfaction.

During the relocation to Subic, some single parents for the first time had to put infants, pets, and possessions into an automobile and head for an unknown future. Some of these vehicles broke down on the way. Single parents then had to temporarily entrust their automobiles, infants, or pets to others in the caravan they hoped were friends while logistical problems were worked out. Upon arriving at the Subic inprocessing center, these parents might be confronted with hordes of people, seemingly incomprehensible procedures, no way to break the code, and all of the usual responsibilities as night fell. Although interdisciplinary teams of human service and social service providers were set up to help, much more was needed.

In a significant sense, most of the above can be construed as loss of control over one's life (cf. Rosolack & Hampson, 1991; Steinglass & Gerrity, 1990). And unfortunately, U.S. citizens, most of whom appreciate the vast amount of personal latitude afforded by U.S. tradition, even in the military, are often vulnerable to behavioral constraints. Over and over again, personnel stated something like "It wouldn't be so bad if they would just tell us what's gonna happen, how long we're gonna be here, and what we're supposed to do. Then we could cope. But now things are 'expletive deleted.'"

Fatigue

Fatigue was experienced from a number of sources. One, but only one, was too little sleep. For the Clark community as a whole, too little sleep began in earnest on the night of 9 June. Armed Forces Television first broadcast that there would be a special announcement at 2000 hours on if, when, and how there would be a relocation and who would relocate. At 2000 hours the public affairs personnel broadcast that there *might* be a relocation and that a further announcement would come at 2200 hours. At 2200 hours there was no announcement. Instead there were several television shows with occasional captions at the bottom of the screen indicating that an important message was imminent. The announcement finally came at about 2335. Public affairs authorities described a relocation plan, announced that a final decision about whether to implement would be made at 0500 hours the next morning and wished us all a good night's sleep. How many people could possibly have a good night's sleep that night? At 0500, the authorities announced that there would be an evacuation. It began at 0600 hours.

The smells from poor sanitation and personal hygiene and the body heat from too many people in too little spaces also contributed to fatigue. This was exacerbated by the hot, humid climate in conjunction with loss of power, which ensured that one worked in a T-shirt soaked with sweat that would turn writing stationery into soaked tissue paper merely by brushing it with the underside of a forearm.

Fatigue increased without the "adrenalin" often provided by a well-backed sense of purpose capturing the imagination. For example, in Desert Shield, there eventually was a public consensus of a threat to U.S. security interests and numerous shows of support for the troops. In contrast, the Pinatubo ash warriors were placed in harm's way to protect equipment. They also were to project a presence until their leaders determined the fate of assets that many legislators and foreign policy experts claimed to be *not* vital and, in fact, insignificant ("The End of a Military Era," 1991; "U.S. Will Abandon," 1991; "Volcano Stills City," 1991). Reasons to believe were rare commodities in this context; there was only fatigue in the theater of the absurd (cf. Rochford & Blocker, 1991).

Communication

During the Mount Pinatubo experience, it was difficult getting information to people with a need to know (de la Fuente, 1990; Papadatos, Nokov, & Potamianos, 1990). For at least a week after 15 June, phones were down much of the time. This was true for operations, operational support, and medical organizations. Because of loss of power and power surges, computers often were down. This made it extremely difficult to manage projects such as identifying and returning relocatees' personal vehicles or updating lists of houses whose contents had been inventoried and packed out. Portable hand-held radios sometimes failed to work at the most inopportune times. Physical distances among military families precluded the easy use of runners or drivers for short-suspense actions. Fatigue exacerbated difficulties in hearing what people were saying and effectively speaking to them. The same was true for written messages, which seemed in retrospect to contain an inordinate amount of typographical errors, non sequiturs, irrationality, and illogic.

Difficulties in maintaining contact made it easy for personnel to avoid their military responsibilities and remain undetected with family and friends. While a small cadre of medical staff and personnel from other organizations worked virtually all of their waking hours, others remained with their families, drank alcoholic beverages, walked aimlessly, or slept.

Sometimes communication problems had paradoxical effects. For example, the lack of reliable phones and the extreme mobility of MET members led to the issuing of portable, hand-held radios for communication. Although the radios sometimes didn't work well, they seemed to foster camaraderie as personnel developed call signs. The call signs became part of the new identities MET members needed to construct after their loved ones had left. (See "The Loss of Self, Loved Ones, Friends, and Colleagues" above.) This phenomenon also was suggested by the amount and kind of patter on the radios, patter that almost always was mission-related, not mission-essential. The excess amount and extraneous content probably indicated that psychological needs—to be somebody, to be liked, to be respected—were being fulfilled.

Other communication problems, as perceived by military families, involved higher command levels outside the country. A significant one was unwittingly creating and being susceptible to a huge disparity between what was happening and what seemed to be happening. Many families perceived that command authorities elsewhere seemed to minimize the threat of disaster and the accompanying human implications.

They perceived that higher headquarters attempted to return medical patients who had been treated at facilities in the United States even as relocation plans for the military communities in the Philippines were primed for implementation and volcanic/tremor activity continued to increase. Routine permanent changes of station into the Philippines allegedly were being pressed during early portions of the disaster. Whether or not these events actually occurred, they were a reality via the perceptions of military families.

Still another communication-induced dysfunction was the "cry wolf" phenomenon. From April through June, bits and pieces of estimates and other information seemed to habituate many in the military community to any real, impending threat. Only several days before the relocation from Clark to Subic did most individuals begin to take things seriously. For command and support personnel, this meant that some time that could have been used to serve the community was spent largely looking out for one's own.

The biggest communication "horror story" probably is the one about the military head of family who apparently never got the word about the impending relocation to Subic. He showed up at Clark on the day after the relocation, became frightened at the almost total absence of people, returned to his home, stayed there for several days, rode out the 36 hours of blackness in his house, went foraging for food after his car had been stolen, fought off wild dogs, paid black marketeers premium prices for food, and finally made contact with his military unit 18 days after the initial relocation. He stated by way of explanation that he didn't socialize much and wasn't in the habit of watching television or listening to the radio.

Communication is tough enough because the same information often is perceived and interpreted differently by different people (cf. Simon, Francis, & Lombardo, 1990). As well, there is a continuous leveling and sharpening of reality dependent on social psychological and perceptual processes (cf. Rosnow, 1991). Crises bring an inexorable tendency to magnify the above (cf. Knight, 1990). Therefore, many complaints by military families that the "straight word" wasn't getting out were inevitable. Communication problems can be managed, but not extinguished.

Unknown Political Constraints

Military families were not "in the loop" on the politics of the volcano. Perhaps, they did not have a need to know. On the other hand, there was a natural tendency to ponder the alleged machinations behind the scenes (cf. Harris, 1990). When things went bad, some questioned whether this was because our leaders wanted them to go bad so that the financial price for keeping U.S. military units at Clark and Subic would decrease. There would then be an easily defended rationale for no longer maintaining a presence at Clark, Subic, and the other military facilities in the Philippines. Public statements on future eruptions, earth tremors, mudslides, flooding, and the future of the U.S. military in the Philippines could be either self-serving or the straight word. Aid for U.S. citizens could be diverted to Filipinos through some "back channel" agreement. Some military personnel began to feel like no more than chumps, guinea pigs, or hostages to the convolutions of corrupt and uncaring civilian and military leaders.

One nadir of morale was on 4 July, when statements by U.S. national leaders specifically mentioned Operations Desert Shield and Desert Storm with not a word about military personnel in the Philippines. In the absence of their families, MET members could have received a tremendous lift from being specially cited. Instead, feelings of emptiness increased, as MET members more easily believed that *no* one cared, that what they were doing was not important, not even worthy of comment. Could effective mission performance be consistently proffered when such depressogenic cognitions decreased self-esteem, self-worth, even self-identity?

Other political constraints were operating on an interagency and interservice level. On 23 June, many military families perceived that they received different "straight words" from the U.S. embassy in Manila and from public affairs sources at Subic on whether U.S. citizens in Manila were to remain in Manila or go to Subic for outprocessing. These families also perceived that the sources of information differed on using the terms "relocatees" instead of "evacuees" and "State Department–ordered evacuation" instead of "military relocation." Some military families perceived that this had to do with who would have to pay for what and how things would look to Filipinos with influence on base negotiations.

As another example, it seemed as if higher headquarters were communicating that nonessential personnel would *not* be relocated from the Philippines at the very time that the assistant secretary of defense for public affairs was saying otherwise before television cameras in Washington, DC. (I classify these last two problems as political rather than communicative because some military families perceived that all political players knew what the score was, but had axes to grind.)

As still another example of the impact of unknown political constraints, initial military policies for filing claims seemed almost ludicrous, especially to some officers' families. As explained at special briefings, one had to first contact one's insurance company, handle claims through it, and then approach the military for any claims not covered. Many officers received extremely speedy, caring, and generous service from their own insurance companies, perhaps an adjudicated sum of about $20,000. Then one turned to the military for claims on insurance deductibles, maybe of a few hundred dollars. Military representatives would not take an insurance company's adjudication as valid. To reimburse several hundred dollars for a deductible, the military needed to readjudicate the entire $20,000 claim. Whereas the insurance company had accepted the honor of the officer for how many and what kind of clothes had been lost or destroyed, the military needed to know when each item was purchased and what condition it had been in before the natural disaster. Military adjudicators stated that in this way they could ensure officers had gotten the full value for lost possessions. In practice, few officers were compensated for their full deductibles; their families often created tortuous and even bizarre political attributions to make sense out of the situation.

Perhaps the appropriate reaction is so what? Since officers have pledged to serve our country and give the supreme sacrifice if necessary, what's a few hundred dollars? Perhaps. But the bottom line was that some felt demeaned and bereft of far more than money, namely, honor and dignity. It became more difficult to give one's all for the mission and to handle family separation. One felt like a political pawn. Military families could have turned a deaf ear to all the above. Few did.

Vices

Some cynics might comment that the convergence of a volcanic eruption, a tropical storm, and earthquake tremors is not the best time to give up personal vices, if there are still ways to indulge. I can provide several observations that would support this.

Being drunk was a common form of recreation among some military personnel and family members during the evacuation and relocation efforts, as well as during the reconstitution and recovery operations. During the time one was drunk, one had less accurate perceptions of threat and comprehension of procedures to confront it. In a period when anything could happen at anytime, and frequently did, drinking removed an individual as an effective coper. It made individuals less formidable bulwarks against danger for their families and their colleagues.

Some people exhibited alcohol-influenced, inappropriate social and legal behavior. Off-duty examples (recognizing that off duty could become on duty at the drop of a hat) were having sex with prostitutes (e.g., female transvestites), picking fights with prostitutes and other local nationals, becoming involved in automobile accidents, cutting and bruising oneself and others while falling into potholed, stagnant water–filled streets, and bellowing obscene epithets at anyone who could be seen through an alcohol-induced fog. The Ugly American was alive and well courtesy of John Barleycorn and hindered efforts to improve U.S.-Philippine relations during a very sensitive time of base negotiations.

There also were examples of on-duty problems. An officer with significant responsibility was heard slurring, obviously intoxicated, over his portable radio. Several company-grade officers avoided detection by their military units for at least a week after the initial relocation from Clark AB. What should have been duty time was spent wrapped around cases of beer and local prostitutes.

A special comment on prostitution. Given the magnitude of the disaster, many of the local hostesses," "masseuses," and streetwalkers left the immediate area. However, some remained behind, usually those with the most desperate socioeconomic conditions and the least assets for adequate self-hygiene. As well, the local social hygiene capability had become virtually nonexistent. Concurrently, after all family members had been relocated, essential personnel found themselves alone with a cadre of local nationals in the most dire straits and extremely willing to meet any sexual need for a small fee—an invitation for a huge rise in the sexually transmitted disease (STD) rate. Military public affairs and medical personnel attempted to counter this with primary prevention information in the daily base newspaper and a free condom program. Military recreation specialists continued to develop more alternatives to going downtown on sexual shopping sprees. However, the STD rate continued to remain higher than before the relocation.

So why didn't the command authorities crack down and keep the troops on base away from the sex and alcohol establishments? Probably for the same reason given by command authorities throughout military history—to help maintain morale, task-related discipline, and mission performance while deployed in difficult situations.

The Mount Pinatubo experience confronted everyone with a moral calculus. Some were found wanting. Yet people are human, even exemplars of military rectitude. There must be a way to get away some of the time, at least mentally. For some, this will entail psychoactive substance abuse and sexual exploitation. For others, it may be reading the Good Book, engaging in group athletic competition, or relatively wholesome social events. Where there's a will there's a way. The fall-out on the military family can be managed but not extinguished.

The Red Badge of Courage

Being in a bad way can be good or bad. Military history is replete with examples of black sheep, lost battalions, Dirty Harrys, and groups of the misfit, the misplaced, and the misfortunate who have performed superhumanly. So being one of the MET members, one of the "ash warriors" who, bereft of kith and kin, daily faced the potential wrath of Mother Nature posed both a threat and an opportunity. Personnel could play up the negatives of the situation to make themselves special—the few, the proud, the ash warriors. The worse things would get, the more special one would feel, the more one could surmount, the better one would perform (cf. Lange, 1989). This is the essence of the special operations credo, and some commanders tried to play up this angle by selecting only the best of their troops to be MET members and publicly stating so: "Only the best to fight and win in the worst conditions."

Others seemed to attempt the obverse. As an example, there were at least several individuals who had been passed over for promotion and who had continued to receive weak performance reports. These individuals were told that they were deemed mission-essential because they were essentially unemployable anywhere else. In fact, they were told that their peers, obviously superior in every way, were being allowed to leave the Philippines to take on jobs of greater responsibility. Only in the most perverse way, by attempting to show "The System" that it was wrong, could these individuals perform as required by the mission (cf. Dowd & Seibel, 1990). Were their commanders banking on this rationale to get the job done? Were they merely looking for bodies to fill a required number of slots?

In any case, the bad—whether reality or rumor—should be viewed by leaders as an opportunity for motivation, not merely as a threat to some perfect and unattainable conception of what one should be thinking and feeling. And there were rumors. Personnel returning to the United States were being given the best choices of military assignments, while MET members would be left with the dregs. Higher headquarters authorities were participating in a golf tournament while MET members were mired in the ash and waiting for a decision on what would happen to them and the territory and equipment being protected. Ash from Mount Pinatubo was radioactive and very dangerous to one's health. Our national command authorities didn't care at all about us because the president, the secretary of the Air Force, and the Air Force chief of staff had more important things to worry about. The heart of the matter often was less important than how leaders chose to handle the red badge of courage. The military heart, temporarily bereft of family, easily succumbed to pain without a reason to believe.

THE FUTURE OF MILITARY FAMILIES
Research and Policy Development

There are at least several lessons to be learned from the above. First, the military mission and the welfare of the military family are inextricably entwined. Air force personnel, soldiers, and sailors harbor perceptions of their families. These perceptions affect concentration on the mission, memory for instructions, motivation to carry out orders, willingness to rise above the occasion when necessary. The perceptions vary through time in their causal salience for particular mission behaviors.

Unfortunately, the extant literature on social cognition suggests that retrospective analysis of which perceptions most affect or effect which behaviors is extremely difficult to determine. Contaminating factors include availability heuristics, contrast effects, cognitive schemata, nexi of cognitions and emotions, response styles, response sets, general approaches to impression management, and varying contexts, from the historical through the interpersonal (Nisbett & Ross, 1980).

Research dollars should be allocated to help accurately identify family perceptions that have the most robust impact on military performance. These perceptions will necessarily suggest specific family needs that should be satisfied.

Second, the number and kinds of stimuli that significantly impact on the military family are extremely large. Temporal relationships of these stimuli—a priori, concurrent, and a posteriori—are extraordinarily complex. Making valid, causal statements about which stimuli impact on what family parameter in a particular way is more difficult than suggested by many articles on stress and the military family (Tzeng & Jackson, 1991).

Third, while the challenge to reasons to believe can be huge, so too is the challenge to their reliable and valid measurement. The challenge comes from the same factors affecting family perceptions. Of these, impression management may be of greatest concern (cf. Diener, Sandvik, Pavot, & Gallagher, 1991). Asking a military family member why he or she puts up with the downside may be similar to asking citizens if they support their totalitarian leader or asking church leaders if they engage in proscribed sex practices. Accurate data can come back to haunt in unfortunate ways.

Support Programs

What can be done *now* to nurture the sustenance of military families, giving them a reason to believe? As seen above, the challenges to research and policy development are daunting. Yet only an ivory tower academic would counsel the luxury of waiting until the challenges are met and surmounted. The military family can't wait because it already exists. Its pleasures and pains, ethos and pathos, are real. As real are the support programs that already exist, bereft of adequate research. There is a moral necessity to do the best with what is available, even if this leaves only intuition, compassion, and a prayer.

Even now, the best we can is better than what we now have. The problem lies in the seeming premise of current support programs—that it is preferable to treat symptoms, not causes. Dissatisfaction with material status is countered with attempts to raise salaries, improve housing and recreation facilities, increase job opportunities for spouses and children, increase the easy availability of cheap domestic help and child care, decrease the cost of goods at "military and government only" shops, increase subsidies for other myriad military services. Dissatisfaction with psychological status is countered with advocating total trust in God, the government, and command authorities, providing mental health services directed toward a family's inner pathology, running community meetings and "rap" groups to air out differences (if not induce catharsis), initiating group activities and awards to increase self-esteem and a sense of collective identification.

The plain fact is that support programs based on treating symptoms are doomed to fail. This is because of the existence and consequences of social comparison processes (cf. Van Dyk & Nieuwoudt, 1990). In most parts of the world, for most military families, as perceived injustices and disparities are alleviated, new ones ineluctably appear. More important, family members often become more demanding and insistent, as if the more one obtains, the more one expects. This insidious process has been well explicated in theories of political revolution and suggest that those in power gratify those without only at their peril (Brinton, 1952).

Treating symptoms instead of causes returns us to a reason to believe. Comprehensive attempts at material and psychological sating, by their very existence, underlie and contribute to a void of belief and a lack of commitment. Such attempts are no different from entertaining the masses with circuses in ancient Rome as the empire was collapsing, and providing rewards for tasks fueled by intrinsic reinforcement thereby weakens the reinforcement.

What military families need are reasons to put up with the downside, reasons that will not be fragmented at the first material or psychological inconvenience. Such reasons to believe are based on knowledge and values that transcend daily occurrences, that cannot be taken away or terminated except in the most extreme circumstances. For military personnel and families alike, reasons to believe are reasons to live with the downside—ultimately, reasons worth dying for. Families with such beliefs will still be continuously challenged but will less often succumb.

An International Look

Developing and maintaining a reason to believe is becoming ever more difficult in many parts of the world. By no means are U.S. military families the ones with the challenge. Unless the challenge is met, dysphoria and dysfunctional behavior within families and decrements in the military mission will increase.

The Disestablished Soviet Union

The families of Soviet military officers, at least after Stalinist purges, could look inward to adequate material benefits and even prestige in the eyes of some others ("CIA Chief Says," 1992; "Yeltsin Deputy Calls," 1992). With the disestablishment of the Soviet Union, the advent of the Commonwealth of Independent States (CIS), and the real possibility of the CIS's demise, these same families face a topsy-turvy world ("Bush and Yeltsin Declare," 1992; "11 Soviet States," 1991; "Ukraine and Soviet Troops' Loyalty," 1992). Two mainstays of a reason to believe —material gain and love of motherland—are no more. Instead, the very quests for food, clothing, shelter, fuel, and a sense of collective identity have shattered reasons to believe ("5,000 Angry Military Men," 1992; "Rift over Military," 1992).

Peru

In Peru, reasons to believe are under tremendous pressure. Military families are being targeted for death by insurgent terrorists like the Sendero Luminoso and the Tupac Amaru and, at times, by narcoterrorists ("Strike by Peru Rebels," 1992). The recent suspension of constitutional government for the alleged aim of combatting terrorism, insurgency, corruption, and economic disaster has radically changed social relations with one's neighbors ("Peru Chief Orders," 1992; "Peru Suspends," 1992). Diplomatic and economic sanctions by regional governments have pierced self-esteem and hopes for a better life, even if material rewards may temporarily increase. The fragmentation within the military of insurgent agents, monarchists, fascists, democrats, dupes, sociopaths, the alienated, and those terrorized by not knowing which way to turn obviate coherent, long-term planning for a better life and contribute to the very shattering of social cohesion, let alone reasons to believe ("U.S. Will Assist," 1992).

Cambodia

The greatest threat to reasons to believe is the unknown, specifically the viability of the United Nations plan for the ceasefire, military demobilization, weapons collection, transition rule, and elections affecting Cambodian government military forces in their power struggle against three insurgent forces, including those of the Khmer Rouge ("Cambodia, bleak and fearful," 1992; "UN Gives Cambodia," 1992). Fears for one's very life, as well as economic concerns, are pitted against strong religious beliefs, which to some families make human experience but an evanescent illusion ("Rival Factions in Cambodia," 1992; "Sihanouk Says," 1992).

Somalia

Bloody killing, atrocities, and economic disaster are fragmenting reasons to believe for families of insurgent groups ("Clashes Go On," 1991; "Hundreds Slain," 1991; "Somali Refugees Find," 1992). Identification with a military entity or with one's ethnic, tribal, or clan roots is not necessarily a ticket to surviving chaos and maintaining even the most meager existence ("Foes Step Up," 1991; "Somali Capital," 1991; "Warring Somali Factions," 1992). Drought and lack of food have been attacking the very biological substrates from which reasons to believe, and coherent thought, arise ("Somali Hospitals Crowded," 1991; "UN and Somalis," 1992; "UN Sees Danger," 1992).

CONCLUSION

Change is the essence of nature, yet the human condition is inherently a quest for some stability. Reasons to believe are routes to manage this conflict, yet successful management is transient at best. Military families, then, are confronted with a continuous cognitive task. This task should be the focus of military family research, policy, and support programs. It should be addressed on a daily basis so that when crisis comes, military personnel and their families are ready for the challenge and can count on the entire military bureaucracy to support their mission. Symptomatic treatment through additional material and psychological support is not enough. Instead, causal treatment—developing and maintaining beliefs worth dying for—is necessary. Military families may not always have a reason to believe. Does the reader?

REFERENCES

Air Force finishes Clark evacuation. (1991, 11 June). *The New York Times*, p. 3.

Air Force to cut Philippines units. (1991, 21 June). *The New York Times*, p. 3.

An indicator of a volcano's ferocity. (1991, 30 July). *The New York Times*, p. 3.

As Philippine volcano erupts, experts warn of mudflow. (1991, 15 June). *The New York Times,* p. 4.

Balk, D. E. (1991). Death and adolescent bereavement: Current research and future directions. *Journal of Adolescent Research*, *6*, 7–27.

Bollen, K., & Hoyle, R. H. (1990). Perceived cohesion: A conceptual and empirical examination. *Social Forces*, *69*, 479–504.

Brinton, C. (1952). *The anatomy of revolution*. New York: Prentice-Hall.

Bush and Yeltsin declare formal end to cold war; agree to exchange visits. (1992, 2 February). *The New York Times*, p. 1.

Cambodia, bleak and fearful, yearns for UN peacekeepers. (1992, 5 March). *The New York Times*, p. 1.

Cassel, R. N. (1990). The quest for identity, drug abuse, and identity crises. *Journal of Instructional Psychology*, *17*, 155–158.

Chapman, J. G. (1991). The impact of socially projected group composition on behavior in a common dilemma: A self-attention perspective. *Current Psychology: Research and Reviews*, *10*, 183–198.

CIA chief says threat by ex-Soviets is small. (1992, 23 January). *The New York Times*, p. 8.

Clark base once vital to military. (1991, 16 July). *The New York Times*, p. 6.

Clashes go on in Somali capital. (1991, 20 November). *The New York Times*, p. 8.

de la Fuente, R. (1990). The mental health consequences of the 1985 earthquakes in Mexico. *International Journal of Mental Health*, *19*, 21–29.

Diener, E., Sandvik, E., Pavot, W., & Gallagher, D. (1991). Response artifacts in the measurement of subjective well-being. *Social Indicators Research*, *24*, 35–56.

Dowd, E. T., & Seibel, C. A. (1990). A cognitive theory of resistance and reactance: Implications for treatment. *Journal of Mental Health Counseling, 12,* 458–469.

Eisenbruch, M. (1990). The cultural bereavement interview: A new clinical research approach for refugees. *Psychiatric Clinics of North America, 13,* 715–735.

11 Soviet states form commonwealth without clearly defining its powers. (1991, 22 December). *The New York Times,* p. 1.

Filipino families feel smothered by the ash. (1991, 23 June). *The New York Times,* p. 6.

Filipinos assessing cost begin volcano cleanup. (1991, 19 June). *The New York Times,* p. 7.

Filipinos fleeing as volcano builds. (1991, 16 June). *The New York Times,* p. 1.

5,000 angry military men gather with complaints in the Kremlin. (1992, 18 January). *The New York Times,* p. 1.

Flynn, G., & Scheffer, D. J. (1990). Limited collective security. *Foreign Policy, 80,* 77–101.

Foes step up artillery duels in Somalia's capital. (1991, 24 November). *The New York Times,* p. 11.

For Americans and Filipinos, basics of life are at stake in fate of Navy base. (1991, 29 September). *The New York Times,* p. 21B.

Freedman, L. (1992). Order and disorder in the new world. *Foreign Affairs, 68,* 20–37.

Harris, M. J. (1990). Effect of interaction goals on expectancy confirmation in a problem-solving context. *Personality and Social Psychology Bulletin, 16,* 521–530.

Hundreds slain in 5th day of strife in Somalia. (1991, 22 November). *The New York Times,* p. 9.

Knight, E. A. (1990). Perceived control and actual outcomes of hassle situations on the job. *Psychological Reports, 67,* 891–898.

Kohn, R., & Levan, I. (1990). Bereavement in disaster: An overview of the research. *International Journal of Mental Health, 19,* 61–76.

Lange, A. (1989). The "help" paradigm in the treatment of severely depressed couples: A combination of paradoxical and problem-solving elements. *American Journal of Family Therapy, 17,* 3–13.

Lima, D. R., Pai, S., Lozano, J., & Santacruz, H. (1990). The stability of emotional symptoms among disaster victims in a developing country. *Journal of Traumatic Stress, 3,* 497–505.

Long closing seen at Philippine base. (1991, 14 June). *The New York Times,* p. 15.

McFarlane, A. C. (1990). An Australian disaster. The 1983 bushfires. *International Journal of Mental Health, 19,* 36–47.

Nisbett, R., & Ross, L. (1980). *Human inference: Strategies and shortcomings of social judgment.* Englewood Cliffs, NJ: Prentice Hall.

Papadatos, Y., Nokov, K., & Potamianos, G. (1990). Evaluation of psychiatric morbidity following an earthquake. *International Journal of Social Psychiatry, 36,* 131–136.

Pfaff, W. (1991). Redefining world power. *Foreign Affairs, 68,* 34–48.

Peru chief orders new mass arrests. (1992, 8 April). *The New York Times,* p. 12.

Peru suspends democracy, citing revolt. (1992, 7 April). *The New York Times,* p. 1.

Philippine volcano buried 40 people alive. (1991, 15 July). *The New York Times,* p. 12.

Prentice-Dunn, S. (1991). Half-baked idea: Deindividuation and the nonreactive assessment of self-awareness. *Contemporary Social Psychology, 15,* pp. 16–17.

Rift over military widens at meeting of ex-Soviet lands. (1992, 15 February). *The New York Times,* p. 1.

Rival factions in Cambodia pledge to uphold peace plan. (1992, 27 January). *The New York Times,* p. 6.

Rochford, E. B., & Blocker, T. J. (1991). Coping with "natural" hazards as stressors: The prediction of activism in a flood disaster. *Environment and Behavior, 23,* 173–194.

Rosnow, R. L. (1991). Inside rumor: A personal Journey. *American Psychologist, 46,* 484–496.

Rosolack, T. K., & Hampson, S. E. (1991). A new typology of health behaviors for personality-health predictions: The case of locus of control. *European Journal of Personality, 5,* 151–168.

Rubinstein, A. Z. (1991). New world order or hollow victory? *Foreign Affairs, 68,* 53–65.

Sihanouk says violence threatens peace. (1992, 30 January). *The New York Times,* p. 7.

Simon, L. J., Francis, P. L., & Lombardo, J. P. (1990). Sex, sex-role, and Machiavellianism as correlates of decoding ability. *Perceptual and Motor Skills, 71,* 243–247.

Somali capital a grisly battlefield as civilians die in clan warfare. (1991, 29 November). *The New York Times,* p. 12.

Somali refugees find little relief at Kenya camp. (1992, 16 February). *The New York Times,* p. 8.

Somalia hospitals crowded as rebels battle for control. (1991, 21 November). *The New York Times,* p. 12.

Steinglass, P., & Gerrity, E. (1990). Natural disasters and post-traumatic stress disorder: Short-term versus long-term recovery in two disaster-affected communities. *Journal of Applied Social Psychology, 20,* 1746–1765.

Strike by Peru rebels fails to disrupt Lima. (1992, 16 February). *The New York Times,* p. 20.

The end of a military era. (1991, 27 November). *The New York Times,* p. 3.

20,000 ordered back to the U.S., fleeing volcano. (1991, 17 June). *The New York Times,* p. 1.

Tzeng, O. C., & Jackson, J. W. (1991). Common methodological framework for theory construction and evaluation in the social and behavioral sciences. *Genetic Psychology Monographs, 117,* 49–76.

Ukraine and Soviet troops' loyalty. (1992, 10 January). *The New York Times,* p. 8.

UN and Somalis are said to agree on aid. (1992, 17 February). *The New York Times,* p. 3.

UN gives Cambodia troop proposal. (1992, 21 February). *The New York Times,* p. 3.

UN sees danger of Somali famine. (1992, 27 February). *The New York Times,* p. 3.

UN votes to send 22,000 to back peace in Cambodia. (1992, 29 February). *The New York Times,* p. 4.

U.S. evacuates Philippine base as volcano erupts. (1991, 10 June). *The New York Times,* p. 1.

U.S. exit from Manila: Making of a hasty retreat. (1992, 5 January). *The New York Times,* p. 12.

U.S. will abandon volcano-ravaged air base, Manila is told. (1991, 16 July). *The New York Times,* p. 6.

U.S. will assist Peru's army in fighting cocaine and rebels. (1992, 25 January). *The New York Times,* p. 4.

Van Dyk, A. C., & Nieuwoudt, J. M. (1990). The relationship between relative deprivation and the attitudes of rural Afrikaans-speaking women towards blacks. *Journal of Psychology, 124,* 513–521.

Volcano explodes in the Philippines. (1991, 12 June). *The New York Times,* p. 1.

Volcano imperils Philippines base. (1991, 13 June). *The New York Times,* p. 14.

Volcano is unforeseen third party in talks on bases in Philippines. (1991, 11 July). *The New York Times,* p. 12.

Volcano stills city by base in Philippines. (1991, 17 July). *The New York Times,* p. 7.

Volcano's ash dismays Filipinos and Americans. (1991, 20 June). *The New York Times,* p. 14.

Volcano's refugees describe hours of ash and mudslides. (1991, 18 June). *The New York Times,* p. 1.

Walker, C. J., & Blaine, B. (1991). The virulence of dread rumors: A field experiment. *Language and Communication, 11,* 291–297.

Warring Somali factions reach a truce. (1992, 15 February). *The New York Times,* p. 5.

Watson, P. J., & Morris, R. J. (1990). Irrational beliefs and the problem of narcissism. *Personality and Individual Differences, 11,* 1137–1140.

Yeltsin deputy calls reform economic genocide. (1992, 9 February). *The New York Times,* p. 10.

CHAPTER SIX

Special Warriors, Special Families, and Special Concerns

Thomas C. Mountz, PhD[1]

IN U.S. MILITARY HISTORY, "SPECIAL WARRIORS" HAVE BEEN AN ENIGMA TO THEIR enemies, senior commanders, and particularly, family members. The special warrior is a partisan, a guerrilla fighter living under a cloak of mystery and operating in utmost secrecy.

There are few journal articles or scientific papers written on the special warrior. Most of the information on him is from popular sources, some based in fact, other clearly folklore. Fact and folklore have produced Francis Marion of South Carolina, known as the Swamp Fox, who commanded troops that wreaked havoc on the British regulars during the War for Independence. Another is the Confederate raider John Singleton Mosby, leading a cavalry of undetermined numbers against federal forces in Northern Virginia during the Civil War. More recently there have been the highly fictionalized movies of Delta Force and Navy Seals.

Today's real-world operators are also found in law enforcement special weapons teams, in drug interdiction teams, as foreign counterintelligence officers, as well as U.S. Army Rangers and Special Forces, U.S. Navy Seals, U.S. Marine Corps Force Recon, and U.S. Air Force combat-control technicians. These raiders, guerrillas, partisans, and special operators all occupy a unique place in our ideal of heroism and glory; they have a special mystique. They are either loved or hated, respected or disdained. They hold a special place in the hearts of their countrymen—to some they represent terrorism in its most basic form; to others, salvation as freedom fighters. In fact, in many parts of the world these persons are engaged in rebellious, illegal, terrorist-like activities (Beckwith, 1985). An unknown source has stated "one country's (man) terrorists is another country's (man) hero." The special operator we shall explore is a hero. The comments, opinions, and feelings expressed in this chapter reflect my years of serving in these teams and being intimately involved in the work they are required to accomplish. Many of the situations have been experienced by the author and his family.

WHO ARE THEY?

All special operators have a set of unique traits in common (Wolfe, 1984). It is difficult to describe these characteristics as a personality constellation. These are the qualities within a people that drive them to accomplish their goals, even against overwhelming odds. These same characteristics may be seen as problematic in many people, but blended together and welded into an operator, guided by a mission and a commanding officer, they become a formidable personage, in some respects a human weapon.

The operator is bright intellectually, clever, resourceful, determined, wily, and above all, cautious in revealing a great deal about himself, his family, or his associates. He is seen as protective to the point of excessive devotion where his fellow operator is concerned; this total commitment that he demonstrates also encompasses his family. However, it is often difficult for his spouse to understand and accept the concept of family being equated with "work" on such a level. If one is a fellow operator, "all that is mine, is yours." This represents a dimension of wholehearted caring and sharing difficult for many spouses to comprehend.

The individual is just that: an individual, totally self-sufficient and case-hardened. There is no task or mission that will not be attempted. When the risks are high and the stakes higher, the inner drive kicks in and makes the operator a precision machine. This specific and almost automatic reaction to a tough assignment as a critical challenge to be accomplished is also hard to explain to the spouse. The potential dangers inherent in the mission are not perceived as a deterrent and are often not discussed. The operator expects the same type of effort and commitment to the task from his fellow operator and also from his partner and family. It is not an expectation of perfection, just an expectation of maximum support with no hesitation.

The special operator is challenged by the unknown. Uncertainty, ambiguous demands, ever-changing time factors, and delays are elements of daily life. To trust a schedule is to be constrained; to trust an outsider is to doom a mission to failure. The attitude of absolute self-confidence and self-reliance is ingrained in each operator from his earliest days in training. Any needs or dependencies upon another extend no further than the "buddy" next to you. The spouse often feels set aside or left out of planning. A family can plan, only to find their arrangements must be altered at the last moment if the operator's assignment interferes with them. Always flexible, "Semper Gumby" could be his motto.

An operator must restrict or contain his emotional sensitivity. His job demands performing virtually antisocial acts. His willingness to do so is supported by an unfailing devotion to the cause of freedom and the cohesive thinking he shares with other operators as part of their patriotism. While awaiting a high-altitude, high-opening jump on an aircraft, a long dive, or a difficult patrol, the operator becomes quiet, introspective, and encapsulated. Each operator is reflecting, thinking procedures, emergency contingencies, on-task thoughts. Certainly, thoughts of personal mortality or harm pass through consciousness but do not linger. Although there are thoughts of home, family, and friends, carrying out and surviving the mission is the foremost concern. If something goes awry, if an injury is sustained, or death takes a buddy, the first thought is, what did he (the victim) do wrong, what was forgotten, or what caused the malfunctioning of the equipment? There is little immediate expression of sorrow or grief. In time, the grief reaction sets in. It is a paced phenomenon on the path toward resolution. If one ruminates or obsesses about the incident he may be caught up in "Losing the bubble"—not compartmentalizing (concentrating maximum thoughts and effort)—and may end up being a hazard to himself or others because he was not fully focused on the all-important task.

In the United States and abroad it is recognized that these operators work extremely hard. Every day entails at least 12 hours of work. The only easy day was yesterday. Most working days are about 15 or 16 hours long. The remaining hours of the day are divided into sleep, family, friends, and play. Operators also play hard. The same energy and zeal devoted to work is put into play. Think of playing, for fun, with a herd of elephants; they are big, strong, yet gentle. Too often people forget that active play is a means of venting pent-up anger.

Competitive, aggressive, total impact is how they play. Some men in the special forces, when off duty, engage in extreme behaviors when drinking too much alcohol. But generally, the self-knowledge of personal limits and command or mission requirements have a very sobering effect. Work, play, and drinking behavior may appear to be excessive. But almost all special operators can be trusted to know their limits and apply restraint when required.

LIES—WHAT'S REAL? SECURITY/SECRECY

The second general area that presents significant problems for spouses and family members is that of secrecy. In the special operations arena, secrecy is a major factor in protecting the safety of the mission, unit, and each individual. This secrecy is called operational security (OPSEC). OPSEC is a way of life; it is a critical necessity for daily operations. The operator is schooled, trained, retrained, and constantly reminded of what is to be held as a secret, who may be told the secret, and identifying who needs to know this information. The operator often must keep all aspects of his work a secret from his closest confidant.

In marriage, where total and open communication is considered essential for closeness and intimacy, OPSEC may pose a barrier. Sometimes the wife feels excluded from a major portion of her husband's life. The operator may, out of personal needs, misinterpret what OPSEC is and use OPSEC to foster jealousy, mistrust, and poor communication. The wife has a need to know, a need to be able to feel secure in turning to her spouse to answer a question or help solve a problem. However, the operator may have told his spouse he is at one location and yet not be there or anywhere near when she calls him for information, support, solace, and/or affection. This necessity for OPSEC has kindled mistrust, and many spouses wonder "Where are you when I need you?" Carrying OPSEC one step further, many wives do not actually know what their husbands do. Because their work and whereabouts are shrouded in mystery, wives, children, and parents nurture fantasies around the role of an operator. Those fantasies are often larger than life and may serve both as protective covering and a distancing maneuver.

FINANCES

The area of finance is as unique as all other areas of these special operators' lives. Special operations services have enjoyed priority funding in the U.S. military. Their mission has required up-to-date, first-line equipment, upgraded travel capabilities, and the immediate ful-

filling of requests. This reality of the ability to receive immediate fulfillment causes problems when the same immediacy is expected at
home. Generally, it is suggested that the members have their earnings
direct-deposited in an at-home account, with the spouse having access
to and full authority over all financial accounts. It is recommended that
a power of attorney or other legal instrument giving the wife power to
act as a personal representative be arranged so that the wife may
handle issues arising during deployments or, ultimately, in the case
of the operator's death. This is a major concern and in many cases is
neglected or disregarded.

Operators often disregard what is happening in family finances
because of implicit trust in their partners and willingness to allocate
this responsibility to them. But often the operator's own impulsive
buying or other overspending puts him in debt. All too often, when
presents are purchased, the same mentality applies as in work; that
is, only the best and most expensive items will do. Frugality is not
expected at work and does not appear to be a principle applied at home.
The extravagant spending also supports the "play hard" concept, as it
permits one to rest hard when he can be making the surroundings
relaxing, pleasant, and comfortable.

Since the spouse is often required to be the financial planner, accoun-
tant, and enforcer, a jealousy may develop when the operator shows
up with money and personal gear for operational use that is far in
excess of what could be dreamed of for daily living needs. Furthermore,
the wife may not fully understand why the operator on temporary duty
is able to live in a first-rate hotel or eat at four-star restaurants because
of special funding appropriated just for this purpose, while she is just
making it on an E-6 salary. Sometimes reality is unfair. The operator
will exploit and use the benefits when and where he can because tomorrow he may have to jump into a jungle and survive in a hostile and
treacherous terrain for an extended period while carrying out an operation.

Upon his return from an extremely harsh and demanding environment, the operator may experience a much greater appreciation
of family time, warm showers, a good football game on TV or a multitude of other things that many people tend to take for granted. In
short, an appreciation for "the simple things in life" comes to the fore-
ground. At the opposite end of this spectrum, however, is the possibility that the operator's reality was such that it caused him to become
accustomed to a better life-style than his salary at home will permit.
Therefore, upon his return, he still desires to maintain the better life-
style provided by his work assignment world while simultaneously
meeting the responsibilities of family life. Unless the operator is able

to strike a balance between the two, the family will ultimately suffer.

Another problem area revolves around "personal" toys. Again, the operator likes the best, biggest, fastest, and loudest. Sometimes it appears that these toys (cars, stereos, guns, knives, etc.) are bought despite family needs. A compromise of or denial of the need for these costly adult toys is felt as a sign of personal weakness and loss of control. The spouse is often attempting to balance, adjust to, and accommodate these behaviors. Interestingly, there appears to be an overall acceptance of the toys because the wife also enjoys riding around in a new car or having expensive "things" at home.

CHILDREN

Absolute devotion, pride, and dedication are the most obvious characteristics shown toward the children when the operator is home. The child may be perceived as an extension of the operator. Often a son is seen as a "mini" operator; a daughter is placed in a position of a "little princess."

In many instances it seems that the father's role has, out of necessity, given way, and the mother performs in a single-parent capacity. She must often assume this position because of her warrior husband's extended absences, long workdays, and need for rest when off duty. When Dad is home, play activity and relaxation keep the family busy. The operator may be guilty of trying to force too much into too little time and space. But the love is there. It is obvious after a long deployment that there is emotional hurt when the child shies away from the father. It takes time to reconstitute after a deployment, come down to earth, or catch up with normal living. Frequently, children do not understand these changes; unfortunately, there are times when parents do not understand either. The frequent departures and reentries are taxing for all.

The mother assumes a great deal of responsibility in child rearing, discipline, and control. It appears that there is little sharing of responsibility. However, the operator seems to be aware of what is going on with the children at home and school. Apparently, there is adequate communication about the children between the mother and father in the special-warrior family (Marcinko, 1992).

Some couples have chosen to refrain from having children until the operator's special duties are over. Jokingly, one may hear that "the operator doesn't want competition." This appears to be a false impression. Most operators love to be with their children and can legitimately fulfill some of their own needs in the parenting role.

FIDELITY

Many wives state that their husbands are married to the team or the buddy. This may not be an inaccurate perception. The operator is away many more hours than he is at home, either on deployment or in carrying out his numerous responsibilities on normal work days. The bonding process that goes on from Day 1 of training is not well understood by many wives. In trying to explore personal allegiances, the couple may conflict over who is more important, "the team or me." A couple can overcome these problems through open acceptance on both sides that the job is an important part of life and that both home and work satisfy different aspects of the man's complex need system. There is little objective reason for jealousy.

A wife may express concern over whether there are other women and what behaviors her husband engages in while he is away. When present, this concern is generally based on an assumption that if the temptation is there, her husband will be a participant. Sometimes memories of premarital behavior, suspicion regarding single friends, and rumors support the reasons for suspicion or condemnation. Generally, the best predictor of future behavior is past behavior. However, in this case, it is safe to assume that the special operator has made a commitment and lives true to his character; from my observations and experience, the married operator generally is as faithful to the marriage as to his mission. It is interesting to note the number of years some operators have been married. Many operators have had lengthy marriages of 15 years or more. Also, there is a tendency of these men to marry at an older age and enter the relationship with a quite mature commitment.

How does a wife know if her husband is being unfaithful? Obviously, much of his behavior might point to infidelity, such as late hours, going to bars, being on the road away from home (when it is not essential for the job). Some of this is inherent in his work and therefore inconclusive. Since the special operator prides himself on being a master of deception, if he is confronted and denies that he is having an affair, is he lying? What are his true feelings about home, family, and spouse? Chances are he will not lie in an instance where the basic integrity of his family is concerned. He will guard operational security; but to his spouse, on matters of home and family, he is truthful. Recognizing the general nature of these statements and acknowledging a high degree of individuality and personal interests, it is still hypothesized that most operators are proud of and responsible to their family concerns. Certainly, there are exceptions, but faithfulness and commitment are major components in the special operator's character.

SUPPORT NETWORK

For the wife living with the circumstances of marriage to a special-warfare operator, there are numerous pluses and minuses. The pride gleaned in knowing the husband is not only involved in important missions but also is extremely dedicated gives a sense of being special in an ordinary world. The knowledge that when the operator is allegedly working he is engaged in important government service provides some relief from suspicious thoughts.

The hours of separation, loneliness, feelings of jealousy, anger about missed family outings and celebrations or commitments, broken-down cars, blown fuses he is not there to fix, and a host of other major and minor disasters are among the bad points. Not having someone to turn to to satisfy urges or special needs, watching CNN and wondering/waiting, fearing the *knock on the door* that bring news of a fatality or serious problem, rearing children alone, attending PTA meetings alone, missing proms, graduations, and many other such occasions marked by the operator's absence sometimes make the spouse want to "throw in the towel" and end the marriage.

Interestingly, there is an internal strength that keeps the spouse and family going. There are external aids, ombudsmen, wives' groups, informal team gatherings, neighbors, extended family and friends who offer excellent support. Professional counseling with the base chaplain and referral to family services, local mental health units, and self-help groups can be utilized also. Often the special operations unit will have a clinical psychologist assigned to assist on a full-time basis. However, most do not. The main resource is within the couple. Communications between the husband and wife are essential. Times and events may limit what can be shared, but talking about concerns, feelings, desires, and personal issues will sustain family survival and success. Nothing can ensure total success. To enable the family to keep functioning well, both partners need to commit to each other and establish a common goal of staying together regardless of external influences and pressures.

PROFESSIONAL THERAPY

Individual, marital, and family therapy help reduce barriers to communication and provide a nonthreatening forum in which to express concerns that normally end in conflict. A therapist with a knowledge of their special concerns and the intense, mission-driven, military context or ecosystem in which they live can usually be accepted rapidly as a caregiver. The thearpist must realize the strong inner commitment to self-sufficiency and the profound concern over disclosing personal information. The most successful therapist is a team member, such as the psychologist (the "doc"), assigned to the team full-time. The spouse may at first resist talking to the "doc" due to the assumed close relationship established in the team with the husband; however, in time, trust can be established and maintained.

Sharing in reading to children, trips to stores, playing ball or games, or any activity that puts the operator with the child is encouraged. Listening to the children, watching their play, and participating in the child's life should be stressed by the clinician.

Carefully selected self-help books and literature can offer useful suggestions on overcoming problems. Courses in stress management, family finances, child development, parenting, home appliance repair, and car maintenance are available through local schools and colleges. These might be useful adjuncts to therapy for one or both spouses.

Finally, trust, faith, and confidence in each other and in oneself will go far in eliminating fears and doubts. Maintaining a strong belief in personal capabilities to perform a task, under reasonable expectations and with a realistic outlook, is difficult. Remember, these two people met, selected one another, fell in love, and married. Most often they complement each other. It can generally be asserted that the special-warrior wife is competent and resourceful and in every way a fine match for her operator spouse.

REFERENCES

Beckwith, C. (1985). *Delta Force: The army elite counterterrorist unit*. New York: Dell.

Marcinko, D. (1992). *Rogue warrior*. New York: Pocket Books.

Wambaugh, J. (1973). *Blue knight*. New York: Dell.

Wolfe, T. (1984). *The right stuff*. New York: Bantam Books.

NOTE

[1]The author has served in various special units, including Seal Team Six, the Naval Investigative Service, and the Marine Security Guard Battalion. During the nearly one decade of service in and to these special units the author has screened candidates for duty, particpated in both training and actual operations, and provided mental health care and referral for the members and their families. The author and his family have experienced nearly all of the unique aspects of these most interesting assignments. He is married, has two adult daughters; one, a teacher and the other a doctoral candidate in biochemistry. His wife was able to complete an advanced degree as a reading specialist.

Attitudes, Knowledge Base, and Skills Essential to Treat Military Families: Core Elements in Training and Supervisory Endeavors

Florence W. Kaslow, PhD

THE BODY OF LITERATURE ON SUPERVISION AND TRAINING OF MENTAL HEALTH professionals expanded markedly during the 1970s and 1980s, in contrast to the paucity of material on this topic prior to that time (Satir, 1963), except in the field of social work (see, e.g., Austin, 1950, 1952, 1956, 1960, 1963). However, little of the material is focused on training and supervision of clinicians to treat military families. This chapter attempts to move from the general arena of training of mental health professionals to the specific arena of the essential ingredients for those treating military families (see Kaslow, 1984, pp. 269–305, for an earlier chapter on a related topic.)

Most of the books and articles pertinent to training and supervision that have appeared in the past two decades deal with tutelage of novices: graduate students in psychology, social work, or marital and family therapy or psychiatric residents during their clinical internships or residencies. Certainly books such as these (Hess, 1980a; Kaslow, 1977a, 1986b; Liddle, Breunlin, & Schwartz, 1988; Mead, 1990; Piercy, 1986) can be utilized as basic texts by senior military officers who serve as directors of residency training programs for psychologists and psychiatrists in all service branches. Separately or in combination they can provide the course material for discussion and critique and the springboard from which adaptations can be made for intervening with the specific service populations to be treated. A few articles have dealt almost exclusively with paraprofessionals receiving on-the-job training (Richan, 1972, 1977). These seem to be applicable to and modifiable for training medical corps personnel who have no prior background in mental health or the behavioral sciences and yet are assigned duties in departments of psychiatry, particularly in inpatient units as attendants or orderlies or in emergency teams near the front lines. In some ways such personnel are comparable to the indigenous workers Richan and Royster (1972) describe. For example, they share many background characteristics with their patients and are able to empathize with their problems and issues. They also need to learn how not to overidentify and impede their functioning as helping professionals.

Some more-recent publications analyze the nature and process of supervision and training of the intermediate- and advanced-level clinicians who may want to learn a new specialty like marital and family therapy or expand their depth and breadth of clinical acumen after a period of practice in individual and/or group therapy (Kaslow, 1986b). There is a developing body of material on peer supervision, which is a viable alternative to hierarchical supervision in some situations, particularly where senior clinicians seek each other out for reciprocal consultations (Cade, Speed, & Seligman, 1986; Roth, 1986). Some innovative models that combine peer and hierarchical supervision have been promulgated by Landau-Stanton and Stanton (1986) in their "Pick-A-Dali-Circus" model of systems supervision and by Brodsky and Myers (1986), who have evolved an "In Vivo Rotation" model. These exciting new additions to the armamentarium of supervisory methods provide for rotation of the role of therapist between numerous clinicians over a short span of time, with the other trainees and supervisors who are part of the treatment team serving as participant observers. The onlooker, who sometimes serves as therapist, learns to critique his or her own activity and receives on-the-spot feedback from other members of the rather large treatment team. This interesting format may prove quite compatible with training needs in the military, where cooperation within the system with various team members is of central import and where substitution of one therapist for another may be essential under emergency conditions brought about by a disaster or deployment.

This chapter attempts to provide an overview of the following aspects of supervision, training, and consultation as they are specifically applicable to understanding and treating the military family: accountability; history; kinds of training programs and approaches; supervisor/ supervisee match; process, content, and techniques; and goals and evaluation. The objective is to construct a training format that will prove of value for civilian as well as military mental health practitioners. For this to occur, training must be generated from a broad multicultural perspective rather than a provincial, ethnocentric one, since the armed forces are composed of a heterogeneous racial, religious, and ethnic population. Although the special competencies of members of each discipline, such as that of psychiatrists in psychopharmacology and psychologists in psychodiagnostic testing, need to be articulated and fostered, verbal and nonverbal psychotherapeutic methods should be taught and supervised utilizing a multidisciplinary perspective applicable to professionals from the various disciplines.

Given the rapidity with which orders may be received for someone to ship out, as was the case in U.S. involvement in the Kuwait/Iraqi action of 1990–1991, clinicians need to be adept in doing crisis intervention work. They also need to possess skills in brief therapy with families beset by a multitude of problems like chemical addiction, incest, violence, and relocation/separation/reunion. Time is often a reality limitation since the individual/family *must* move when reassigned and does not have the choice of remaining in a community until longer-term therapy is completed.

Therapists new to treating military personnel will need guidance regarding confidentiality, given that it is often military policy that the commanding officer can have access to the records of personnel under his command. Information acquired from such records at times may be used to block a promotion, thus offsetting the benefit of "free" treatment. If a person's problems are severe, their disclosure could lead to an unwanted transfer or diminish his or her chance of receiving a much wanted promotion. Military personnel can go to civilian agencies or private practitioners and invoke patient privilege, but services may be unaffordable if not covered by the Civilian Health and Medical Program of the Uniformed Services (CHAMPUS).

It behooves therapists in both civilian and military sectors to learn the routes for collaboration, the kinds of services available at base facilities and other special programs (see, e.g., Figley, chapter 9, this volume), the laws that regulate their practice, and the essential dicta of both bodies of law regarding families who entrust themselves to the therapists' ministrations. Their curriculum should include not only the Uniform Code of Military Justice but also grounding in a respect for the ethos, history, traditions, values, benefits, and mission of the military establishment.

SUPERVISION ACCOUNTABILITY

Supervision entails the overseeing of work or workers during execution of a task. Implicit is the fact that the supervisor carries some responsibility for the quality of the work of the supervisee and therefore is in a position of authority and power. The supervisor is accountable to the agency director, board members, community, and clientele for the type and quality of service rendered (Kaslow, 1972b). In the past 20 years, with the advent of Peer Standards Review organizations and committees (PSROs and PSPCs) and the mounting number of inquiries from third-party insurance payers, including CHAMPUS, about the nature of the therapeutic services rendered, supervisors have had to carefully monitor the practice of their supervisees. They must ensure that records accurately reflect practice and that the quality of treatment is meritorious enough to pass a review committee's standards and/ or to warrant reimbursement. Whenever a supervisor has to sign or cosign reports and insurance forms, the responsibility becomes more obvious and weightier.

In recent years, mental health professionals have become increasingly aware of their vulnerability to malpractice suits and more cognizant of liability issues. Slovenko's (1980) discussion of the legal aspects of psychotherapy supervision heightens the reader's conscious awareness of the supervisor's responsibility for the practice of his/her supervisees. He stresses that one may be held legally responsible not only for one's own faulty behavior but also for that of others. According to the doctrine of "vicarious liability" or "imputed negligence," an employer can be held liable for the tortious conduct of a supervisee committed in his or her work role by virtue of their employer/employee relationship. Modern legal theory makes a "metaphysical identification of the employer and employee as a single 'persona' jointly liable for the injury. The employer is made to carry the risk as his enterprise benefits economically . . . by the acts of employees" (Slovenko, 1980, p. 453). Since primary responsibility for overseeing a clinician's practice devolves on the supervisor, he or she has not only authority but also carries legal accountability.

Thus, the therapy supervisor bears clinical responsibility equivalent to that borne were the patient(s) under his/her care directly. Only because this is so is there sufficient ethical justification for assigning troubled individuals to the care of partially trained students, who are likely to make "errors" based on naïveté, inexperience, and lack of knowledge and clinical wisdom. Supervisors must require, for example, that trainees keep adequate records that support and document the treatment plan, maintain confidentiality, and make appropriate arrangements for coverage if they will be unavailable, that patients are told of their trainee status, and that they understand that they (and their records) can be subpoenaed by a court. If the supervisee does receive a subpoena, the supervisor is obligated to provide as much preparation assistance and backup support as necessary. Slovenko (1980) concludes ominously that litigation involving supervisors may be considered the suit of the future and that the supervisor must be a watchdog and perhaps even a bloodhound. With these admonishments in mind, perusal of this topic becomes a serious and compelling matter.

BRIEF HISTORY OF THE FIELD

Since the early 1950s the field of family therapy has burgeoned (Guerin, 1976; Kaslow, 1980). As its theory has developed, its practice has evolved in many outpatient and inpatient settings with diverse patient populations. Initially, only a handful of courageous pioneers experimented with seeing family members conjointly, and they are reputed to have practiced family therapy covertly. Referrals were made for family therapy as an intervention when all else seemed to have failed, as in the case of families with a schizophrenic member. In the past three decades family therapy has been catapulted into the therapeutic limelight as a major philosophic system of thought and treatment modality,

> an entity unto itself with a magnetic appeal for fledgling and experienced therapists alike. The awakening of the psychiatric-psychological-social work establishment to the centrality of the family system and its impact and hold on all family members has led to an increasing demand for professionals trained in family therapy who can function as an integral part of the staff of many kinds of human service agencies. In many localities, treatment-oriented agencies are considered deficient, or not fully staffed, if they do not have a family therapist. The mounting interest in and conviction of the efficiency and efficacy of family therapy has alerted professionals—practitioners and administrators, as well as educators—to the need for programs to train competent therapists. The

response has been the establishment of a vast array of educational, supervisory, and training programs to meet the demand. (Kaslow, 1977b)

SUPERVISION AND TRAINING—ACROSS TIME AND SPACE

In this section, a sample of extant training programs will be mentioned,
and several supervisory models will be described and analyzed in terms
of learning objectives, techniques, and treatment goals. A synthesis of
the literature and of observations derived from clinical experience,
teaching, training, and consultation activities will also be presented
(Kaslow, 1991).

Content and Process

Satir (1963) reported the results of a 3-year training program at the
Mental Research Institute in Palo Alto, California. It was one of the
first such programs in the family therapy field that was described in
print. She delineated three programs goals. In addition to expecting
trainees to acquire intervention skills, this project sought to

- Have them become proficient in consultation and in-service
  trainings.
- Return them to their respective institutions, where they would
  teach what they had learned.
- Provide them with the necessary tools for conducting research in
  family processes, dynamics, diagnosis, and treatment.

To Satir's list, I would add, at a minimum, that any training program should turn out professionals who possess a sound theory and
knowledge base, a familiarity with and commitment to the ethical precepts of their profession (Kaslow, 1984), and be conversant with the
larger ecosystem/context in which their patients reside and work.

A healthy, if perplexing, lack of unanimity remains as to the identity of the couples, family, sex, divorce, and remarriage therapist and
what he or she needs to know and be able to do in order to be designated as such. Some believe family therapy is a separate mental health
discipline; others posit that a family systems perspective is a way of
conceptualizing the patients' world and construction of reality (Reiss,
1981), and that it transcends intervention strategies. Others in the
helping professions do not recognize family therapy as a specialty and
go so far as to claim that no extra or special training or practicum is
needed. This is a naïve stance; treating members of families conjointly

has been shown to require knowledge of how systems operate, how to join and exit from families, how to express multilateral partiality (Boszormenyi-Nagy & Spark, 1973), how to avoid getting enmeshed in the family system, how to bring about first- and second-order change (Watzlawick, Weakland, & Fisch, 1974), and many other concepts and strategies not usually taught in graduate and professional programs that focus predominantly on individual psychotherapy.

As recently as 1974, professional rivalries and territoriality issues were exemplified in such statements as that by Malone (1974) that "there is no established clear-cut theoretical model" for training child psychiatrists in family therapy and that consequently "professional identity and professional role lack clarity, and the staff and trainees . . . experience a considerable amount of strain" (p. 454). When these comments were written, Malone was director of child psychiatry training at the Philadelphia Child Guidance Clinic, a facility already geared to family therapy practice. Yet he attributed the problems in training partially to the conflict and polarization that existed between analytically oriented child psychiatrists and family therapists. Malone recognized that, along with the myriad advantages of family therapy, there is also the risk that its overutilization can lead to a distorted view of the nature of the dysfunction and the misperception that this treatment modality is a panacea for all. Complete reliance on family therapy is as ill-advised as total reliance on individual psychotherapy. He stated that one "danger of family therapy involves the temptation for inexperienced therapists to escape the rigors, growing pains, and vicissitudes of understanding and working with intrapsychic conflict and pain," even though it makes possible "direct exploration of intrapsychic derivatives at the level of interpersonal process" (pp. 456–457). He posited that one can avoid dealing with intrapsychic problems by depending solely on environmental manipulation to achieve desired ends. The teacher-trainer who allows this does not encourage trainees to learn about "psychic development and unconscious dynamics" (p. 457).

This author finds his statements to still be cogent and accurate and believes that those advocating the teaching of family therapy to clinicians treating military personnel should bear these pitfalls in mind. Although it may be essential to use short-term, solution-oriented, systemic treatment models (de Shazer, 1985) with many military families because they can be deployed at any time on brief notice—necessitating termination of treatment—I believe an understanding of each individual's intrapsychic dynamics as well as the interpersonal transactional patterns is an important springboard for efficacious, focused interventions.

This political and ideological battle between the professions of psychiatry and family therapy was particularly lamentable, given that in the Group for the Advancement of Psychiatry (GAP; 1970) report, *The Field of Family Therapy,* released over two decades ago, the credible authors stated that "family therapy combines two bodies of knowledge: personality dynamics and multiperson system dynamics." They stressed the need for integration of these "two systems levels into a comprehensive theory" and urged that the *focus on the transactional multiperson level of functioning should be considered an addition to, not a replacement for, the individual system level of understanding and treating behavior dynamics* (pp. 565–566). Their decrying of polarization has influenced some practitioners in the various mental health disciplines, and they have incorporated couples and family systems theory and practice into their graduate and professional school curricula. Nonetheless, many psychiatrists, psychologists and social workers still complete their formal professional training without course work or clinical experience in multiperson system dynamics and intervention strategies. Similarly, some marriage and family therapy graduate programs give scant attention to psychodynamic theories of behavior, unconscious motivation, the ego and its mechanisms of defense (Freud, 1971), psychopathology, and personality disorders (Kernberg, 1975; Slavinska-Holy, 1988; Solomon, 1989).

Fortunately, during the 1980s the trend toward judicious integration of individual, couples, and family therapy concepts and the selective determination of when to use which modality and for whom accelerated. Individuals like Diane and Sam Kirschner (1986) in their comprehensive family therapy approach, Sam Slipp (1988) in his conceptualization and practice of objects relations family therapy, and Ellen and Paul Wachtel (1986) in their incisive exposition of family dynamics in individual psychotherapy have sought to incorporate the salient epistemology of both mainstreams of clinical theory and practice. This author hopes that these endeavors will receive widespread acceptance and herald the philosophic direction of training programs in the next few decades (Kaslow, 1987).

Generally, to be licensed to practice as a marital and family therapist one needs a minimum of a masters degree either in marriage and family therapy, in psychology, or social work, or an M.D. degree with a specialization in psychiatry. All need a strong course emphasis in couples and family dynamics, family life cycle, theories and techniques of couples and family therapy, professional ethics, family law, statistics and research methodology. Usually supervised practicum and internship experiences are also an essential component of one's training.

PREPARATION TO TREAT MILITARY FAMILIES

Ideally, anyone treating military families should have studied and mastered the content delineated above. It also seems imperative that they become cognizant of the numerous issues that typify military families, such as frequent and prolonged separations and relocations, and the kinds of circumstances that contribute to the occurrence of incest (Crigler, 1984), sexual abuse, substance abuse (Williams, 1984), and violence (Schwabe & Kaslow, 1984). How these behaviors are perceived and dealt with when they come to the attention of a commanding officer and their likely impact on later promotion possibilities, as well as the interface of civil law jurisdiction with military law when violations of the law occur by civilian members of a military family, must be understood. Therapists treating military families should also become familiar with the myriad other issues discussed throughout this book, like acclimating to foreign cultures, being in life-threatening situations, and the nuances of early retirement (Kaslow, 1986a).

Clearly, not all mental health trainees or professionally educated staff therapists will have the requisite background and knowledge when they are employed or assigned. Thus, for adequate treatment to be given, they must acquire it while on the job within the institutional setting of a military base or other facility.

If several members of the departments of psychiatry, psychology, or social work at a military base or hospital are skilled family therapy theorists and practitioners, they can conduct the requisite training on site. If not, the in-house teaching staff can be supplemented by having a consultant with expertise in marital and family therapy come to the base weekly for several hours to conduct training courses.

It might at times be advantageous to include in the training activities civilian therapists who treat military families at military family service centers, in community agencies, and in private practice, if it is permissible. Not only does this serve to augment their understanding of military families and of family therapy, thus adding to the resource network available to provide treatment, but it is also likely to foster better cooperation and collaboration between the military and civilian sectors of the community.

Such training should include, at a minimum, didactic coursework similar to what was mentioned earlier. A current bibliography of top books and journals on family theory and therapy should be distributed and readings assigned so that trainees quickly immerse themselves in the best literature of this field. Special emphasis should be placed on materials that describe and discuss military families.

Also essential for inclusion is the clinical component. Since training often must occur fairly rapidly in order to create a cadre of therapists competent to treat military families, the "how to" or diagnostic and intervention skills portion should be introduced early in an integrated way. For example, for the first 4 to 6 weeks, one of the instructors could see a family in a live interview. This session can be viewed by the trainees over a one-way screen or on videotape. If neither of these is available because the base is in some isolated, outlying area, or if the presence of trainees is desired as a learning approach, then arrangements can be made for trainees to sit in the treatment room and to participate, if this is acceptable to the consultant *and* the patients (Brodsky & Myers, 1986; Landau-Stanton & Stanton, 1986). Confidentiality and the limits of confidentiality should be explained to all patients and therapists involved, and requisite informed consent should be obtained in writing after a careful explanation of the training and treatment process is given and all questions are answered. Where the lead therapist is in the military and is also subject to unexpected transfers, having other team members who are familiar with the patients available to take over enhances the continuity of treatment.

Following each treatment session, sufficient time should be allocated for the trainees to give feedback on what they have observed and experienced. They can do this as individuals, and/or they can be constituted as a reflecting team to generate their own systemic hypothesis about the family's transactional system and symptomatology (Cade et al., 1986; Hoffman, 1981). The training therapist can decode his/her map of the family and elucidate the thinking that undergirded the assessment and intervention methodology. By using such an instructional format, a shared teaching/learning environment is co-created that is likely to be highly satisfying and clinically productive.

Brief therapy (de Shazer, 1985), crisis intervention strategies, and stress management approaches often constitute the treatments of choice for military families. These are the best suited to their life reality, particularly when they truly have no control over the time frame in which events occur, such as the eruption of a war and the deployment of troops, including their battalion, squadron, or submarine.

It is essential for therapists treating military families to be cognizant of the other resources available and to network with individuals within facilities that provide allied services so that referrals can be expedited. For example, young wives experience great loneliness when their husbands ship out. Participation in a wives' support group may open channels for much-needed friendship with women who are experiencing a similar dilemma and who are also expected to react courageously. Husbands with military wives who are sent overseas, as was true in the Gulf War, may need to be connected with a child care service and to an agency in which they can quickly acquire the requisite homemaking skills. If a family learns a loved one has been killed in combat, traditional therapy may need to be supplemented by attendance at a grief counseling group composed of others who are in mourning for a similar loss. Utilization of chaplaincy services can be very important as an adjunct to or in place of psychotherapy, both on the battlefront and the homefront. All of this entails an appreciation and respect for the larger military system and the services it makes available to members of the far-flung, enormous military family.

Experience gleaned in working with residents in adult psychiatry and psychology training programs in the Navy and Air Force and in conducting CE workshops on army and marine bases, as well as for military family service center staffs, has convinced me that the interspersing of didactic materials with clinical segments is imperative. If trainees and staff members can have the real families they are treating come in for a session, this is preferable. Several formats can be utilized in addition to the ones described earlier. If the presenting therapist is a novice with no or little experience in treating families, the trainer/consultant may conduct the session with the trainee and others watching. The consultant must be careful to return the case to the primary therapist and not encourage the family to think they can transfer to him or her, particularly if said consultant resides in the same community and it would be logistically possible (Nielsen & Kaslow, 1980). Following the formal session, the primary therapist(s) can be asked to comment and ask questions of the consultant, and then the discussion can be opened to the others in the audience. If family members appear able to benefit from remaining to participate in part or all of the session, they may be invited to do so, providing both consultant *and* therapist agree that this would be beneficial to them.

If the trainee or staff member is further along in their family therapy training, they can be offered the option of serving as a cotherapist with the consultant or of conducting the session alone, with the consultant observing and either giving feedback during the session through such live supervisory techniques as calling in (Kaslow, 1977b; Liddle & Schwartz, 1983), entering the room to make suggestions, or coconducting the treatment. Or the therapist can take a short break from the family to discuss what is transpiring with the consultant and perhaps other observers who have been constituting a part of a team that is helping to formulate the diagnosis or systemic hypothesis, an appropriate treatment plan that flows out of their dynamic understanding of the system's functioning and interactions, and the most efficacious interventions to expedite reaching the treatment goals (Madanes, 1981). Whenever possible, families being seen should be military families so that the trainees and/or workshop participants can become conversant with the similarities and differences between military and civilian families as two separate aggregates and the unique qualities within different military families.

The kinds of consultation/training formats elucidated above maximize the freedom of trainees to analyze and critique how others conduct therapy. They provide the possibility for selecting role models from several different mentors and give participants a chance to expand their observational sensitivity, clinical assessment, and intervention repertoire. To the consultant, it affords new challenges and can be a creative endeavor as well as a route for fulfilling one's own patriotic objectives.

As a teacher/consultant during training programs of some duration I sometimes ask trainees to bring their significant other in for at least one session. We consider such issues as how they can interpret to their partner what family therapy is about, the likely impact of this kind of training on their own family of creation, what apprehensions are present regarding what they will learn about family dynamics in their own families (Charny, 1982), and what concerns may arise in connection with an evolving close rapport with a cotherapist of the opposite sex. After the initial discomfort is overcome, these usually become productive sessions that enhance the kind and depth of communication the couples have together about their world, individually and together. With military couples, facilitating such open and honest expression of concerns and emotions can lead to their acquiring or augmenting a skill that will serve them well when they are relocated or separated by "the call of duty."

Some programs require that trainees be in marital or family therapy as an integral part of their experiential, clinical learning about self in intense, close interpersonal relationships and also what it is like to be a participant in conjoint therapy (Guldner, 1978). Others believe this is nonessential and even ill-advised. Bowen (1978) urged his trainees to do genograms and make voyages home to rework relationships in order to become more fully individuated and to gain a deeper understanding of intergenerational issues and transmissions. Many others use variations of genograms for teaching/training purposes (Guerin & Fogarty, 1972). Whatever methods are utilized to encourage trainees to reexplore and rework their heritage, their conflicts, and the ties that bind and bond in their family of origin and family of creation, I believe that getting in touch with one's personal roots, animosities, blocks, feelings of deprivation and gratitude, affection and longings is quintessential on the path to becoming a family therapist.

With trainees in military settings, the exigencies of pressing and unanticipated therapy needs due to a large-scale crisis or disaster may mean that training has to occur much more rapidly than is the case in graduate or professional school courses in the civilian sector. Such techniques as genogramming and sculpting, which can be used with multicultural military populations, may need to be taught quickly and absorbed at a fast-forward pace. Or they may not be feasible in situations where brief therapy is the only viable option.

SUPERVISION

Supervision is considered essential in family therapy training programs and is one of the core processes used to produce skilled therapists. One overall goal of supervision is the transmission of specific pertinent material, the how-to techniques for treatment of a particular family by the novice. Supervision also entails the inculcating of a deeper understanding of the principles of family dynamics, relationships, and structure and how to stimulate changes in desired directions.

At its best, the supervisory relationship is an alliance that facilitates the trainee's accessing the vast and valuable reservoir of the preceptor's experience. An essential element in the evolution of the therapist is willingness to tell about clinical progress, as well as to reveal impasses with patient families, to another, more senior therapist who has traveled similar, often rough and problematic terrain. The growth process, enhanced through supervision, should be characterized by mutuality and reciprocity, providing a vehicle for the expansion of the knowledge, competencies, and self of the supervisee and the supervisor, and the improvement of the quality of clinical services rendered (Kaslow, 1984).

Supervision is multifaceted; it extends along a continuum. At one end is the emphasis on content and technique; at the other is a concentration on the deeper process of facilitating self-awareness and personal growth (Charny, 1982). Supervision, as used here, denotes therapy of the therapy, not of the therapist. Treatment and supervision are perceived as parallel processes; in this view trainees are often seen as duplicating in their practice how they are dealt with in supervision (Abroms, 1977). Initially, trainees may benefit most from a content/technique orientation as they strive to master the material that forms the conceptual base for practice. More advanced trainees and practitioners, seeking to add to their treatment armamentarium, should become immersed in the more sophisticated and complex interpretations of family history, transactions, structures, myths, loyalties, and intergenerational legacies. They can be encouraged to read, think about, and try not only treatment of one family at a time but also such other intervention strategies as couples group therapy (Kaslow & Lieberman, 1981), multiple family therapy (Lacquer, 1972), and network therapy (Speck & Attneave, 1972). As clinicians become more proficient, supervision should be more on an "as needed" rather than mandatory weekly basis.

A supervisee with some experience and confidence may gain a great deal from supervision conducted as a process of learning and thinking geared toward achieving greater self-understanding and potency, as well as independence as a person, family member, and therapist.

Learning Objectives

Cleghorn and Levin (1973) indicated that the articulation of clear-cut learning objectives as a continuous facilitative process leads to identifying areas of need and provides both supervisor and supervisee with realistic expectations of progress. Setting goals directs the student's learning along a definitive, appropriate, and productive pathway and is conducive to periodic assessment of progress. Each category of learning objectives carries with it the idea of essential skills to be mastered and, concomitantly, the best type of supervision. They highlighted three categories of skills to be acquired and honed: *perceptual skills, conceptual skills,* and *executive abilities.* (See Cleghorn and Levin's excellent discussion for explication of these three aspects).

Executive skills bear further mention here since these are the ones least often described. They include being able to (1) revamp the therapeutic contract periodically, (2) demonstrate the relationship between transactions and the symptomatic problem, (3) be a facilitator of changes, (4) develop a style of interviewing consistent with one's own personality, (5) take control of maladaptive transactions, (6) foster adaptive behaviors and rewards for them, and (7) relinquish involvement with the family by terminating when adaptive patterns evolve and become reasonably stabilized (Kaslow, 1984).

Techniques and Methods

Much has been written about various techniques of supervision, and the interested reader is referred to several of the respected texts for an in-depth discussion of each (see, e.g., Hess, 1980b; Liddle et al., 1988;

Kaslow, 1977b, 1986b; Mead, 1990). What follows is only a brief listing highlighting the major approaches.

1. *The traditional model*—one-to-one supervision that is indirect. It consists of the supervisor meeting with the trainee before and/or after a lapse of time following the therapy session(s). The discussion revolves around the interview case report, usually a process record for beginners, and a summary for the more advanced. Usually, sessions are held weekly. Either or both may determine and control the agenda. Disadvantages may emanate from the indirect nature of the model, the selective aspects of subjective reporting, and the delay between therapy and supervision. The supervisor learns about the case secondhand and so has no way to determine if perceptions are distorted. Significant nonverbal behaviors are not observed.

2. *Cotherapy* has many advantages as a supervisory approach. The supervisor as cotherapist can demonstrate various intervention approaches in vivo, can diminish the adverse effects of countertransference, and minimize the number and extent of therapeutic errors. Many arguments have been promulgated about the efficacy of the cotherapist team (Napier & Whitaker, 1978). Just by being there and working together cooperatively or disagreeing constructively, they serve as good, live role models for the patients. They also symbolize a pair who can function as different kinds of parent surrogates, and offer needed reparenting and reeducation. When the therapists are a heterosexual cotherapy team, patients of each sex have someone they can identify with; if they are more able to relate to members of the opposite sex, this too is offered.

The preceptor who doubles as cotherapist must also reserve time to serve as supervisor. Ethically, the cotherapy team should tell patients the true nature of their relationship so that seeming power and status differentials are correctly perceived and do not exacerbate patients' concerns and projections about power and control, major themes in treating military personnel.

In cotherapy used as a supervisory tool, the supervisor is actively engaged. His/her knowledge of the trainee's diagnostic and treatment skills results from direct observation and shared experience and does not just reflect the trainee's selective reporting. That the preceptor is willing to risk demonstrating how he or she actually practices so that trainees can watch, participate, query, and comment makes supervision a livelier process and is congruent with the ethos of the field that the leaders are willing to be observed and invite feedback. Trainees often find such experiences exhilarating and highly productive (Kaslow, 1972a).

Tucker, Hart, and Liddle (1976) had cotherapists, who were all train- ees, discuss their reactions and perceptions before the supervisors and other trainees in group sessions. They were expected to describe their feelings about their patient families and each other in order to facili- tate the learning and growth experience. Supervisors helped resolve conflicts between cotherapists by seeking resolution of differences. Their rationale for this approach was that they "believed that family therapists need to be aware of and sensitive to their own and their cotherapist's emotional state to work with families in a facilitative fash- ion" (p. 270).

As to negative aspects, trainees may feel overwhelmed by and resent- ful of the supervisor's advanced competence. They may stifle their own creativity and remain silent while the supervisor conducts the major part of the therapeutic action. Ideally, the supervisor will help them express their own individuality, find their own style, trust their intu- ition, and feel free to intervene more so that eventually the team will become better balanced. The trainee must also take responsibility for initiating an active role.

Ordinarily, the advantages of supervision through cotherapy out- weigh the disadvantages. Through stimulating affective reactions in the trainee cotherapist, the supervisor can acquire greater leverage for promoting his or her learning. In processing their interaction as well as discussing the patient family, they acquire experience in listening respectfully to one another's thoughts and negotiating conflicts.

3. *Direct supervision using delayed feedback.* The proliferation of one- way mirrors, films, videotapes, and playback equipment, plus closed- circuit video monitors, have made live, direct supervision an important vehicle in training (Berger, 1970). Such equipment enables supervi- sors to observe the actual therapy session, either when it occurs or anytime thereafter. Videotaped segments can be rerun for analysis and discussion. The selective omissions or distortions that exist when written records are utilized do not occur. Therapist and/or client verbal and nonverbal contradictions become obvious. What the supervisor sees and hears is wholly authentic, which contributes to greater accuracy in interpreting dynamics and discussing treatment planning.

A trainee may feel apprehensive about having his/her work observed, but this should diminish quickly in a setting where such a format is the norm and as trainees become acclimated to such procedures (Fried- man & Kaslow, 1986). In fact, some supervisees feel neglected if such methods are not utilized.

Some limitations that accompany this method are that watching tapes or live sessions may be much more time-consuming and geo-graphically inconvenient for a busy supervisor than reading reports. The equipment is costly, and a technician may be needed to operate and repair it (a cost private practices and small institutes may not be able to afford). Some critics also consider the lack of instantaneous guidance a drawback; they view the supervisor as the immediate expert and do not believe trainees should learn through trial and error and following their own therapeutic inner drumbeat.

4. *Direct supervision with instant feedback* (see Birchler, 1975, for fuller discussion). In this approach, the best aspects of the three models described above can be combined creatively with an added dynamic dimension—instant feedback. The supervisor who observes the live treatment interviews through a one-way mirror or video monitor may interrupt and intervene directly by calling in to the therapist or actually entering the treatment room and participating. When the supervisor as expert is invited in or voluntarily enters the session, he or she may confront or interpret in a way designed to jolt the patients into realigning their family system. To administer a fast and painless "psychological shock" (Kaslow, 1984), one may prescribe the symptom, relabel the symptomatic person as the "savior" to whom they should all be grateful, or issue a paradoxical injunction (Selvini-Palazolli, Boscolo, Cecchin, & Prata, 1980). Such unexpected interventions tend to intercept repetitive patterns and unfreeze stuck ways of thinking, thereby opening pathways for the initiation of more productive ways of relating. Both patient and trainee-therapist may profit from such unanticipated supervisor behaviors.

The probability of and rationale for such external input are given in advance. The specific kind of intervention is based on the supervisor's epistemology, the goals of the therapy and the kind of two-way communication system to be utilized.

Another variation of the *instant feedback* scenario is for the therapist to leave the room and go to speak to the supervisor/observer. Although at times such a departure is disruptive to the flow of therapy and may undercut the patients' confidence in the therapist's capacity to competently conduct the therapy, in the past decade and a half having an unseen observer/team/chorus in the anteroom has become an approach used with increasing frequency (Cade et al., 1986; Papp, 1980). The team usually participates in formulating the systemic hypothesis and framing a succinct prescription (Selvini-Palazolli et al., 1980).

Critics of this approach believe it sabotages the trainee-therapist's ability to formulate his or her own diagnoses, hypotheses, and treatment plan and fosters dependence instead of independence and initiative. Other difficulties seem inherent—like battles for control and feelings of being a pawn manipulated on a chessboard. Yet devotees of this method insist that these dangers are outweighed by the benefits of avoiding therapeutic errors, because the supervisor's superior skill can be pressed into service immediately, and the trainee has solid support available on call (Kaslow, 1977a).

Ethically, patient permission to have anyone observe should be obtained and an explanation given that the viewer may periodically interrupt to call in questions or observations. The therapist's status as a trainee must be disclosed, as should be the supervisor's rank. Military personnel are especially attuned to acknowledgment of rank and hierarchy.

5. *Group supervision.* Tucker et al. (1976), in discussing group supervision, state that a basic assumption of their sequential model is that the (group) supervisory process progresses through a series of phases over the course of a semester or full year. Each session moves "through an observable, definable, and systematic sequence" (p. 269). Their supervision consisted of 1- to 1½-hour meetings of 10 students with three supervisors, after group observations of two family sessions. Each student participated both as observer and therapist. Cotherapy teams were composed of trainee-trainee, supervisor-supervisor, or trainee-supervisor.

The aims of their supervisory sequence include (1) having participants deal with the cotherapists' reactions to each other and to the session by discussing their responses in front of the group in order to minimize distortions and biases; (2) assessing observed family interactions and generating hypotheses about the family as a system; (3) conceptualizing about families and family therapy; and (4) planning for future sessions and exploring various intervention strategies that might be utilized.

The second and third phases of this model (Tucker et al., 1976) focus on the same genre of perceptual and conceptual learning objectives formulated by Cleghorn and Levin (1973); their Phase 4 goals are similar to the latter authors' executive skills objectives.

During the last phase of this model, discussion centers on feelings evoked in prior supervisory sessions. The supervisor acts as group facilitator. Supervision is aimed at both guiding the students' therapeutic activity and encouraging them to let their individual styles evolve.

In group supervision there is a chance for dialogue about conceptual notions and the opportunity for trainees to build a sense of cohesiveness and trust in working with colleagues. Trainees often sense relief when they realize that others also feel overwhelmed or ignored by their patients (Abels, 1970). This process may contribute to reducing apprehensiveness about self-disclosure while providing a here-and-now experience in a small group that partially replicates a family and may serve to reactivate feelings of sibling rivalry and bonding, repressed resentment toward adult authority figures (the supervisors, cast in parental roles), and longing to have one's dependency needs met. In creating a context in which these emotions can be expressed and dealt with, it is probable that unfinished issues from the past will well up into consciousness, ripe for resolution within the group or in family of origin work. This will help insulate against their becoming blockages to treating families.

The presence of a guest or the addition of a new member after a supervision group has coalesced heightens the trainees' awareness of their sense of group identity. They often react to the newcomer as if he or she is a resented intruder. Experiencing this bonding increases their awareness of why it is difficult for a therapist to enter a family that perceives them as a potentially disruptive intruder and therefore someone they collude to extrude (Kaslow, 1972a).

Group supervision expands the repertoire of action techniques supervisees can acquire. For example, it affords opportunities for members to participate in various role plays, to experiment when enacting the therapist with myriad interventions conducive to different outcomes. Also, with sufficient supervisees present, the supervisor may demonstrate family sculpting (Duhl, Kantor & Duhl, 1973; Satir, 1972), a *nonverbal technique* useful for both diagnosis and treatment. In brief, any member of the family can be asked to sculpt (i.e., to mold the family members in a living collage, each in a position the sculptor believes is characteristic, revealing, and typical of their interactional pattern. The first sculptor can be requested to rearrange the family as he/she would like them to be, thus offering an opportunity for them to convey their needs and desires and to make some input into the family's thrust toward change through restorying and fashioning a new direction. Or another member may be asked to rearrange the family physically, depicting how they would like it to be. Thus, varying perceptions of the family's alliances and emotions can be choreographed (Papp, 1976) in an intriguing manner. Another variation is to ask trainees to sculpt their own families, utilizing each other as substitute family members. This affords both a chance to experiment with the technique before trying it with patients and a chance to place themselves in their simulated family while emotionally and physically reexperiencing the actual family ties and cutoffs.

Since group supervision has received scant attention in the literature, this summation has tried to provide some depth and breadth of description and analysis. It is posited here that small-group supervision is a valuable approach because it encourages trainees to selectively choose from the large array of extant concepts and techniques from numerous schools of therapy and to be creative within the parameters mandated by the family and its context (Kaslow, 1981). A skilled leader/ supervisor can model commitment to flexibility and responsiveness in order to illuminate hidden conflicts and trainee responsibility for his/her contribution to the family's process in treatment with analogous parallel supervisor responsibility for the training group's development.

6. *Additional supervisory objectives and techniques for their realization.* It is important that the supervisor of new trainees, such as interns and residents (Friedman & N. Kaslow, 1986), *promote trainee self-awareness and a sense of their own personal history and intrapsychic and interpersonal dynamics in relation to their family of origin and, if married, family of creation.* One can urge (or require) trainees to make *voyages home,* a la Bowen (1978), to work toward resolving unfinished relationship conflicts from the past; to repair cutoffs from parents, siblings, and other relatives; to become aware of invisible and not so invisible loyalties (Boszormenyi-Nagy & Spark, 1973); and to gain knowledge about their own heritage. Having students work on their own family genograms of at least three generations is a productive way of fulfilling their quest to comprehend their complex roots and ultimately to tap into these as a reservoir of energy and illumination.

Supervisees, like patients, can be requested to bring in and tell stories about family photographs (Kaslow & Friedman, 1977), using these projectively to elicit memories and repressed feelings. As the supervisees explore who they are and how they came to be that way within their family constellation, they acquire mastery of intervention strategies that can be utilized to help patients for whom brief therapy focused on the here and now is insufficient, reconstruct their life stories, and heal old narcissistic injuries and family schisms.

Since numerous individuals—and today couples, too—join the military to escape from dealing with family-of-origin conflicts, and/or because of long periods of time away from family members, photographs may be one of the few reminders that spur memories of significant others and are usually readily accessible. Before furloughs, family-of-origin and family-of-creation issues often resurface, causing apprehension mingled with the hope that somehow, miraculously, something might be different and better. Military and civilian therapists who have had the good fortune to be coached in doing their own family of origin reconstruction can in turn coach their service personnel patients in how to make home visits more productive and beneficial whenever such an approach may constitute the treatment of choice.

7. The idea of requiring *therapy for therapist trainees* has become controversial. Certainly one profound way of learning about the experience of therapy is to be in treatment and experience it from a patient's vantage point. Seeking and accepting help may be quite ego-dystonic. In the patient position one learns personally how painful it can be to open up repressed conflict areas and how hard it is to accept interpretations and confrontations. This process of seeing oneself more clearly and accepting responsibility for what happens rather than projecting blame onto others becomes even more troublesome and compelling in the presence of one's spouse and children. Because experiencing this as a recipient rather than as a provider of therapy can be both devastating and enriching, I believe that whenever feasible it is important for marriage and family therapists to have at least a few treatment sessions (Kaslow, 1977a) with their close relatives participating. (This cannot be made mandatory because the training/educational program has no authority over those outside of its student population.)

In the event that a supervisee's own marriage is fraught with severe strife, the resultant stress and turmoil may have a negative impact on his/her therapeutic objectivity. Thus, trainees should be expected to become aware of and control their resistances and defenses and resolve any difficulties that are likely to impede their effectiveness in the therapist role. Marital therapy is certainly one route through which this is accomplished.

In working with mental health personnel in the military, a supervisor must be cognizant of the need to accord respect based on rank and title, to adhere to requirements inherent in the hierarchical structure of the armed services, and to convey the importance of this to all supervisees.

SUPERVISOR–SUPERVISEE MATCH

Supervision, in its most ideal form, is an existential process that enhances the being and becoming of all participants. To the extent possible, the process and expectations should be adapted to the trainee's personal and professional developmental level (Friedman & N. Kaslow,

1986). For example, a 28-year-old graduate school psychology intern or psychiatric resident at Wilford Hall, Lackland Air Force Base, San Antonio, Texas, usually will be at a much earlier level of professional development than a 40-year-old psychiatrist at the rank of major who is taking on new responsibilities for treating families in Wiesbaden, Germany. Each will need supervision that takes into account their prior personal and professional history, as well as their level of intelligence and motivation and various personality factors. Variables such as age, race (Royster, 1972), religion, ethnicity (Kutzik, 1972), and gender (Brodsky, 1977, 1980) may also play a part in determining which supervisor–supervisee match is likely to be most efficacious. A good blend of similarities and differences is apt to maximize learning. When in some situations only one supervisor is available, the pair just must resolve difficulties and work together; there are no other choices. Thus, it is incumbent upon those in charge of supervision/training endeavors to make every effort to ensure that supervisory assignments and subsequent interventions are appropriately attuned to the supervisee's personal background, substantive knowledge, clinical experience, and level of skill; and in the armed services, rank also might be an important consideration. Training efforts should flow from a synthesized theory of how learning occurs and how this may vary depending on whether one is a neophyte or an advanced therapist. Sometimes personality incompatibilities are so severe that they are difficult to resolve and impede learning and, ultimately, therapeutic outcome. When totally different value systems or life views become evident and are deemed to be irreconcilable, they may need to be circumvented. For example, a soft-spoken and somewhat docile Philippine-born and -bred female psychiatrist could have many problems overseeing the practice of a rigid, authoritarian German male resident who is also several years her senior in age.

U.S., Israeli, Norwegian, and other governments in recent decades have made great strides in integrating their armed forces in terms of race and sex. Thus, in dealing with military personnel, it is essential that clinicians understand what it means to experience covert or overt prejudice, exclusion, or being bypassed for promotion because one is black, Chicano, Asian, or female. These are issues that the supervisor may need to handle with a clinician whose background and thinking is provincial and/or ethnocentric. Because supervision and therapy have been posited here to be parallel processes, if supervisor and supervisee are of different racial, ethnic, or socioeconomic status, the way any conflicts emanating from these differences are handled is likely to be duplicated between therapist and patients when similar difficulties arise.

Sexualizing the supervisory relationship is as unethical and unprofessional as sexualizing the treatment relationship (Brodsky, 1977; Kaslow, 1986b). Power and control needs may become intertwined with gender issues if the authority exercised by the supervisor exceeds that inherent in the supervisory role. To illustrate: Bob R, PhD, who was supervising Sue K, a female doctoral intern in a VA hospital, was quite domineering and did not perceive her as a serious young professional. He acted as if she had no right to be in the training program, and he did all he could to push her to drop out. Sue persevered by staying task-focused and tried to change his stereotypical role image of women, but Dr. Bob was unrelenting. Unless issues like these are confronted and resolved in supervision, they may hamper the trainee's ability to handle analogous issues raised by patients.

When a supervisee is experienced and competent and requests supervision to fulfill personal, agency, or licensure requirements, a good "match" remains an important aspect of the teaching/learning process. Such a supervisee has a better base of comparison and may be more demanding, critical, and appreciative if the quality is excellent. In numerous workshops on advanced supervision that I have conducted, the following profile for an "ideal supervisor" has emerged from the participants. The person should:

1. possess and be able to impart a vast store of knowledge and stimulate the supervisee to read and pursue new learning;
2. have a clear theoretical position, be able to utilize a variety of approaches, and be flexible about accepting and respecting that the supervisee may have a different orientation;
3. have a good sense of humor and awareness of life's absurdities;
4. be challenging and provocative;
5. be courageous;
6. be alive and energetic—not too busy or "burned out";
7. be honest and authentic;
8. be task-oriented and make optimal use of time;
9. assume appropriate responsibility and accountability;
10. be confident of his or her own skills and position so that he or she is not threatened by the supervisee's knowledge and accomplishments;
11. be up to date and at the cutting edge of developments in key areas of his/her practice;
12. be nonauthoritarian yet able to model high standards of practice;

13. be reasonably healthy emotionally; and

14. not attempt to become supervisee's therapist.

Under the tutelage of such a supervisor, training is an exciting adventure.

Where prejudice, insensitivity, or narrow-mindedness exist in the intense dyadic relationship called supervision, these decrease the quality of learning and often cause negative fallout within the larger institutional context. For this reason and others, directors of training should not only require and read supervisor's *evaluations* of supervisees but also trainees' assessments of their supervisors. If similar complaints are voiced repeatedly about the same supervisor, whoever is in charge must cope with the problem to eliminate it; or if this is not possible, change the person's assignment. The evaluation process should be relatively standardized.

The issue of match is less salient in group supervision because the group process can help defuse strong negative interactions. The leader rarely can attack one trainee without others coming to the rescue, or joining together to seek recourse from a higher authority (Abels, 1970; Kaslow, 1972a). In addition to being knowledgeable about the subject matter and skills they are to impart, group supervisors should be adept in leading role playing and simulations and in critiquing case records and videotapes. Merely being an adequate facilitator of group process is not sufficient.

SUMMARY AND CONCLUSIONS

Supervision can be conceptualized as a didactic learning experience that supplements classroom training and personal reading. It involves the communication of information and provides the necessary foundation for the mastery of theory and therapeutic skills. It should pay ample attention to the ethical precepts and value assumptions that undergird clinical interventions. Information on the legal context and the laws that regulate clinical practice should be incorporated into the training. When the supervisees are treating military families, it is essential that the family therapy being taught take cognizance of the body of both military and civilian law relevant to family affairs.

During the training phase and beyond, clinicians should be encouraged to explore their own assumptions, hunches, and theoretical positions, and to engage in therapy as both a scientific and creative process. Supervisors should be deeply committed to humanistic values and able to stimulate learning by leading supervisees along challenging intellectual and emotional pathways and engaging in illuminating brainstorming and problem solving with them. Such process, content, people, and outcome-oriented supervising perceives the student as a total person rather than as a recipient of indoctrination.

The supervisee should be motivated to examine, critique, reformulate, and validate his/her own framework for meaning and value, as this is the springboard from which therapeutic intervention evolves. No clinician should assume that his/her beliefs and attitudes are the most desirable ones nor superimpose them on patients, yet the therapist should be fully aware of his/her value base and be able to articulate it when necessary. Only then can one determine which kinds of problems one probably will be ineffective in treating and refer those presenting such problems to a therapist less likely to be "turned off" by the specific behavior constellation. For instance, a therapist who thinks homosexuality or divorce is intrinsically sinful should not endeavor to treat gay people or divorcees.

Verbal and written evaluations should be done at periodic intervals to ascertain if the treatment outcomes sought are being delivered and to determine if the learning objectives are being met. The evaluation should be shared with the trainee, who can append a response before it is filed for future reference. Each evaluation should be considered in setting learning objectives for the next training period.

Therapists treating military families should endeavor to achieve mastery of the basic recommended curriculum *plus* all of the additional material one needs to know about this population as a "special" group and about the military law that influences their lives. Given that some members of each family are apt to be civilians, when co-trainers are used, a team of a military and a civilian leader is recommended.

To supplement the training the military can provide directly, graduate and medical school courses as well as family institute offerings can be utilized. If adequate skilled supervision/consultation is not accessible within the service's own departments or agencies, these too can be purchased from competent individuals in the civilian sector.

Marital and family therapy is a stimulating, challenging and rewarding field. It lends itself to ingenuity and innovation and requires as well solid thinking and clear mapping of family dynamics, structure, and treatment plans and goals. For these reasons, it appeals to the more creative individuals in the therapist community. Therefore, some defining and standardization to maintain quality without squelching experimentation or fostering rigidity is essential.

The family remains the most basic institution in all societies. Therapists are among those who can help revitalize and enrich family life and connectedness so that it becomes more satisfying for the members as a group and for each person individually. For our country to continue to flourish, military families, like their civilian counterparts, need to have the best services we can offer them. And in an era when an increasing number of servicemen and women are married and have children, attention must be paid to family dilemmas and concerns.

REFERENCES

Abels, P. (1970). On the nature of supervision: The medium is the group. *Child Welfare, 49*(6), 305–307.

Abroms, G. M. (1977). Supervision as metatherapy. In F. W. Kaslow (Ed.), *Supervision, consultation and staff training in the helping professions*. San Francisco: Jossey-Bass.

Austin, L. (1950). Supervision of the experienced caseworker. In C. Kasius (Ed.), *Principles and techniques in social casework*. New York: Family Service Association of America.

Austin, L. (1952). Basic principles of supervision. *Social Casework, 33*(10), 411–419.

Austin, L. (1956). An evaluation of supervision. *Social Casework, 37*(8), 375–382.

Austin, L. (1960). Supervision in social work. In R. H. Kurtz (Ed.), (vol. 14), *Social Work Yearbook*. New York: National Association of Social Workers.

Austin, L. (1963). The changing role of the supervisor. In H. J. Parad & R. R. Miller (Eds.), *Ego oriented casework*. New York: Family Service Association of America.

Berger, M. M. (Ed.) (1970). *Videotape techniques in psychiatric training and treatment*. New York: Brunner/Mazel.

Birchler, G. R. (1975). Live supervision and instant feedback in marriage and family therapy. *Journal of Marriage and Family Counseling, 1*(4), 331–342.

Boszormenyi-Nagy, I., & Spark, G. (1973). *Invisible loyalties*. New York: Harper & Row. (Reprinted, 1984, New York: Brunner/Mazel).

Bowen, M. (1978). *Family therapy in clinical practice*. New York: Aronson.

Brodsky, A. M. (1977). Countertransference issues and the woman therapist. *Clinical Psychologist, 30*, 12–14.

Brodsky, A. M. (1980). Sex role issues in the supervision of therapy. In A. K. Hess (Ed.), *Psychotherapy supervision: Theory, research and practice.* (pp. 509–524). New York: Wiley.

Brodsky, S., & Myers, H. H. (1986). In vivo rotation: An alternative model for psychotherapy supervision. In F. W. Kaslow (Ed.), *Supervision and training: Models, dilemmas and challenges* (pp. 95–104). New York: Haworth.

Cade, B. W., Speed, B., & Seligman, P. (1986). Working in teams: The pros and cons. In F. W. Kaslow (Ed.), *Supervision and training: Models, dilemmas and challenges* (pp. 105–118). New York: Haworth.

Charny, I. W. (1982). The personal and family mental health of family therapists. In F. W. Kaslow (Ed.), *The international book of family therapy* (pp. 41–55). New York: Brunner/Mazel.

Cleghorn, J. M., & Levin, S. (1973). Training family therapists by setting learning objectives. *American Journal of Orthopsychiatry, 43*(3), 429–446.

Crigler, P. W. (1984). Incest in the military family. In F. W. Kaslow & R. I. Ridenour (Eds.), *The military family: Dynamics and treatment* (pp. 98–124). New York: Guilford,

de Shazer, S. (1985). *Keys to solutions in brief therapy.* New York: Norton.

Duhl, F., Kantor, D., & Duhl, B. (1973). Learning, space and action in family therapy: A primer of sculpture. In D. Block (Ed.), *Techniques of family therapy.* New York: Grune & Stratton.

Freud, A. (1971). *The ego and the mechanisms of defense* (rev. ed.). New York: International Universities Press. (Original work published 1936)

Friedman, D., & Kaslow, N. J. (1986). The development of professional identity in psychotherapists: Six stages in the supervision process. In F. W. Kaslow (Ed.), *Supervision and training: Models, dilemmas and challenges* (pp. 29–50). New York: Haworth.

Group for the Advancement of Psychiatry (1970). *The field of family therapy* (Report 78). New York: Author.

Guerin, P. J. (1976). Family therapy: The first twenty-five years. In P. J. Guerin (Ed.), *Family therapy and practice* (pp. 2–22). New York: Gardner Press.

Guerin, P., & Fogarty, T. (1972). Study your own family. In A. Ferber, M. Mendelsohn, & A. Napier (Eds.), *The book of family therapy* (pp. 445–467). New York: Science House.

Guldner, C. A. (1978). Family therapy for the trainee in family therapy. *Journal of Marriage and Family Counseling, 4*(1), 127–132.

Hess, A. K. (Ed.). (1980a). *Psychotherapy supervision: Theory, research and practice.* New York: Wiley.

Hess, A. K. (1980b). Training models and the nature of psychotherapy for supervision. In A. K. Hess (Ed.), *Psychotherapy supervision: Theory, research and practice* (pp. 15–28). New York: Wiley.

Hoffman, L. (1981). *Foundations of family therapy.* New York: Basic Books.

Kaslow, F. W. (1972a). Group supervision. In F. W. Kaslow (Ed.), *Issues in human services: A sourcebook for supervision and staff development.* San Francisco: Jossey-Bass.

Kaslow, F. W. (Ed.). (1972b). *Issues in human services: A sourcebook for supervision and staff development.* San Francisco: Jossey-Bass.

Kaslow, F. W. (Ed.). (1977a). *Supervision, consultation and staff training in the helping professions.* San Francisco: Jossey-Bass.

Kaslow, F. W. (1977b). Training of marital and family therapists. In F. W. Kaslow (Ed.), *Supervision, consultation and staff training in the helping professions.* San Francisco: Jossey-Bass.

Kaslow, F. W. (1980). History of family therapy: A kaleidoscopic overview. *Marriage and Family Review, 3*(1,2), 77–111.

Kaslow, F. W. (1981). A diaclectic approach to family therapy and practice: Selectivity and synthesis. *Journal of Marital and Family Therapy*, 7(3), 345–351.

Kaslow, F. W. (1984). Training and supervision of mental health professionals to understand and treat military families. In F. W. Kaslow & R. I. Ridenour (Eds.), *The military family: Dynamics and treatment* (pp. 269–305). New York: Guilford Press.

Kaslow, F. W. (1986a). Consultation with the military: A complex role. In L. C. Wynne, T. T. Weber, & S. H. McDaniel (Eds.), *Systems consultation* (pp. 383–397). New York: Guilford Press.

Kaslow, F. W. (Ed.). (1986b). *Supervision and training: Models, dilemmas, and challenges*. New York: Haworth.

Kaslow, F. W. (1987). Marital and family therapy. In M. B. Sussman & S. Steinmetz (Eds.), *Handbook of marriage and the family*. New York: Plenum.

Kaslow, F. W. (1991). Marital therapy supervision and consultation. *American Journal of Family Therapy*, 19(2), 129–146.

Kaslow, F. W., & Friedman, J. (1977). Utilization of family photos and movies in family therapy. *Journal of Marital and Family Therapy*, 3(1), 19–25.

Kaslow, F. W., & Lieberman, E. J. (1981). Couples group therapy: Rationale, dynamics and process. In G. P. Sholevar (Ed.), *The handbook of marriage and marital therapy* (pp. 347–362). New York: SP Medical and Scientific Books.

Kernberg, O. (1975). *Borderline conditions and pathological narcissism*. New York: Jason Aronson.

Kirschner, D. A., & Kirschner, S. (1986). *Comprehensive family therapy*. New York: Brunner/Mazel.

Kutzik, A. J. (1972). Class and ethnic factors. In F. W. Kaslow (Ed.), *Issues in human services: A sourcebook for supervision and staff development* (pp. 85–114). San Francisco: Jossey-Bass.

Lacquer, M. P. (1972). Multiple family therapy. In A. Ferber, M. Mendelsohn, & A. Napier (Eds.), *The book of family therapy* (pp. 618–636). New York: Science House.

Landau-Stanton, J., & Stanton, D. M. (1986). Family therapy and systems supervision with the "Pick-a-Dali Circus" model. In F. W. Kaslow (Ed.), *Supervision and training: Models, dilemmas and challenges* (pp. 169–182). New York: Haworth.

Liddle, H. A., Breunlin, D. C., & Schwartz, R. C. (Eds.). (1988). *Handbook of family therapy training and supervision*. New York: Guilford.

Liddle, H. A., & Schwartz, R. (1983). Live supervision/consultation: Pragmatic and conceptual guidelines for family therapy trainees. *Family Process*, 22, 477–490.

Madanes, C. (1981). *Strategic family therapy*. San Francisco: Jossey-Bass.

Malone, C. A. (1974). Observations on the role of family therapy in child psychiatry training. *Journal of American Academy of Child Psychiatry*, 3(3), 437–458.

Mead, D. E. (1990). *Effective supervision: A task-oriented model for the health professions*. New York: Brunner/Mazel.

Napier, A. Y., & Whitaker, C. A. (1978). *The family crucible*. New York: Harper and Row.

Nielsen, E., & Kaslow, F. (1980). Consultation in family therapy. *American Journal of Family Therapy*, 8(4), 35–42.

Papp, P. (1976). Family choreography. In P. Guerin (Ed.), *Family therapy: Theory and practice*. New York: Gardner Press.

Papp, P. (1980). The Greek chorus and other techniques of paradoxical therapy. *Family Process*, *19*, 45–57.

Piercy, F. P. (Ed.). (1986). *Family therapy: Education and supervision*. New York: Haworth.

Reiss, D. (1981). *The family's construction of reality*. Cambridge, MA: Harvard University Press.

Richan, W. C. (1972). Indigenous paraprofessional staff. In F. W. Kaslow (Ed.), *Issues in human services: A sourcebook for supervision and staff development* (pp. 51–71). San Francisco: Jossey-Bass.

Richan, W. C. (1977). Training of lay helpers. In F. W. Kaslow (Ed.), *Supervision, consultation and staff training in the helping professions* (pp. 115–132). San Francisco: Jossey-Bass.

Roth, S. A. (1986). Peer supervision in the community mental health center: An analysis and critique. In F. W. Kaslow (Ed.), *Supervision and training: Models, dilemmas and challenges* (pp. 159–168). New York: Haworth.

Royster, E. C. (1972). Black supervisors: Problems of race and role. In F. W. Kaslow (Ed.), *Issues in human services: A sourcebook for supervision and staff development* (pp. 72–84). San Francisco: Jossey-Bass.

Satir, V. (1963). The quest for survival: A training program for family diagnosis and treatment. *Acta Psychotherapeutica et Psychosomatica*, *11*, 33–38.

Satir, V. (1972). *Peoplemaking*. Palo Alto, CA: Science & Behavior Books.

Schwabe, M., & Kaslow, F. W. (1984). Violence in the military family. In F. W. Kaslow & R. I. Ridenour (Eds.), *The military family: Dynamics and treatment* (pp. 125–146). New York: Guilford Press.

Selvini-Palazzoli, M., Boscolo, L., Cecchin, G., & Prata, G. (1978). *Paradox and counterparadox*. New York: Jason Aronson.

Selvini-Palazzoli, M., Boscolo, L., Cecchin, G., & Prata, G. (1980). Hypothesizing, circularity, neutrality: The guidelines for the conductor of the session. *Family Process*, *19*(1), 3–12.

Slipp, S. (1988). *The technique and practice of object relations family therapy*. New York: Aronson.

Slovenko, R. (1980). Legal issues in psychotherapy supervision. In A. K. Hess (Ed.), *Psychotherapy supervision: Theory, research and practice* (pp. 453–473). New York: Wiley.

Slavinska-Holy, N. (1988). *Borderline and narcissistic patients in therapy*. Madison, WI: International Universities Press.

Solomon, M. F. (1989) *Narcissism and intimacy*. New York: Norton.

Speck, R., & Attneave, C. (1972). Social network intervention. In C. Sager & H. S. Kaplan (Eds.), *Progress in group and family therapy* (pp. 416–439). New York: Brunner/Mazel.

Tucker, B. Z., Hart, G., & Liddle, H. A. (1976). Supervision in family therapy: A developmental perspective. *Journal of Marriage and Family Counseling, 2*(3), 260–276.

Wachtel, E. F., & Wachtel, P. L. (1986). *Family dynamics in individual psychotherapy.* New York: Guilford.

Watzlawick, P., Weakland, J., & Fisch, R. (1974). *Change: Principles of problem formation and problem resolution.* New York: Norton.

Williams, T. G. (1984). Substance misuse and alcoholism in the military family. In F. W. Kaslow & R. I. Ridenour (Eds.), *The military family: Dynamics and treatment* (pp. 73–97). New York: Guilford.

PART II

Broader Social Issues: Policies, Programs, and Services Geared to Military Families

Military Family Service Centers: Their Preventive and Interventive Functions

Richard J. Brown III, PhD

For over 10 years, all branches of the armed services have been operating community- or installation-level family centers to provide a broad range of services to military personnel and their families. In late 1992, there were over 360 family centers in the Department of Defense (DoD), down from 375 in 1991. That number will continue to drop as congressionally mandated base closures are carried out. However, even with fewer active installations across the DoD, the number of family centers should be above 300 for some time into the future. This chapter chronicles the growth of military family service centers and highlights their mission.

BRIEF HISTORY
Changing Family Demography

Much has been said about the former culture of the military as a bastion of male singleness (Brown, Carr, & Orthner, 1983). The military has not been isolated from the major shifts in family demography occurring in the United States over the past 30-plus years. The dominant demographic characteristic of singleness began changing long before the cultural attitudes began to recognize that change.

Among most senior leadership in all services, there was a strong resistance to acceptance of these demographic shifts and even more resistance to recognizing the policy implications of the changes. However, in the mid-1970s these attitudes began to adjust.

Today, well over 50% of all military service members are married. Among officers, the percentage approaches 70% (Orthner, Giddings, & Quinn, 1986). This is a far different service composition than was the case when the military was largely composed of single males. As military family demography changed along with the rest of society, it became increasingly clear to military leadership that the connection between family members' attitudes and the military member's commitment to the military and ability to perform the mission were strongly intertwined.

This position was increasingly supported by a growing body of research from the late 1970s to the early 1980s. By the mid-1980s, the common conclusions of an increasingly large body of military family research reflected strong links between family support and mission support (Orthner et al., 1987). These findings became well known to the senior leadership in all branches of the armed forces, and gradually leadership support for family centers in the military became firm and constant.

A Catalytic Moment in California

In the late 1970s, a few forward-thinking military leaders happened to be in the right place at the right time. The time was September 1977; the place was San Diego, California. Under the leadership of Edna J. Hunter and D. Stephen Nice, the Family Studies Branch of the Naval Health Research Center in San Diego and the Naval Postgraduate School in Monterey sponsored the Conference on Current Trends and Directions in Military Family Research (Hunter & Nice, 1978). That 3-day conference, which had been projected to draw about 50 participants, topped an audience of 500. The timing and makeup of participants could not have been more catalytic, and the little research conference turned into the pivotal moment for launching an action plan. Among those in attendance were two very senior leaders from the Navy and the Air Force, Vice Admiral James D. Watkins, later to become chief of naval operations, and Chaplain Brigadier General Richard Carr, who became Air Force chief of chaplains. Within a year, important things began to happen.

Navy Family Awareness Conference

In the fall of 1978, the Navy convened the first navy-wide Conference on the Family in Norfolk. A 1980 study of retention revealed that spousal attitudes were the single most important determinant in decisions regarding staying in the service among Navy personnel (Smith, 1982). These data and the impetus of the 1978 Navy conference laid the groundwork for the establishment of the first Navy Family Service Center at the Norfolk Naval Base in 1980. This beginning in the Navy was soon followed by a second Family Service Center in San Diego. Over the next few years, the Department of the Navy expanded their family center program to be on site at all Naval and Marine Corps installations (Smith, 1982).

In November 1988, the Department of the Navy conducted a second family conference, titled the Navy and Marine Corps Family Support Conference. Held in Norfolk, Virginia, this conference cast the shape of the Navy and Marine Corps family center program for the foreseeable future.

The Air Force Started with Research

In 1979, the Air Force embarked on a service-wide study of military family life, published in January 1980 as *Families in Blue*. Following the publication of *Families in Blue* (Orthner, 1980), Air Force Chief of Staff General Lew Allan established the Air Force Office of Family Matters (AFFAM) in the spring of 1980. AFFAM sponsored the first Air Force Conference on Families in September 1980, in San Antonio, Texas. This conference recommended that base-level family centers be established as soon as possible. The Air Force Family Support Center program was launched in July 1981 with the establishment of four prototype centers, which were fully funded by HQ USAF, and three additional centers locally funded by their bases.

THE ARMY TOOK THE LEAD

At the time these beginnings were taking place in the Navy and the Air Force, the Army had already been operating its Army Community Service Centers (ACSCs) for 15 years. Although not specifically identified as family centers, the ACSCs were focused on many of the issues that came to be known as "family issues," and many of their services were identical to those later developed in the family centers of the other branches of the military. Initially staffed primarily by volunteers, ACSC staffing was gradually shifted to a core of full-time employed professional staff and an adjunct staff of volunteers. Also, in the mid-1970s, the Army Chaplain Service was the primary sponsor of several Family Enrichment Centers that were established on major Army installations in the United States. These Family Enrichment Centers were staffed by qualified Army chaplains who had advanced training in pastoral counseling and marriage and family enrichment programs. Often, the Family Enrichment Centers were additionally staffed by qualified social workers. Thus, the Army was already in the installation-level family support business when the other services began their initiatives in the late 1970s and early 1980s.

THE FAMILY CENTER PROGRAM IN THE DoD

As of January 1992, there were 159 Army family centers, 80 Navy centers, 116 Air Force centers, and 18 Marine Corps centers, for a total of 373. Family center staff allocations by branch of service were as follows: Army, 1026; Navy, 987; Air Force, 1005; and Marine Corps, 197. Although these centers are service-specific in terms of programs offered as well as the organizational models employed, there are certain core programs and services that are offered by all DoD family centers. Also, the organizational rationale of service support for family programs and the expected organizational benefits are common across the military.

The commonality of organizational rationale and service models across the branches of the military cannot be attributed to any formal central organizational influence on the services since the DoD Office of Family Policy, Support and Services was not organized until the mid-1980s, several years after the start of the family centers in the separate branches of service.

In the early 1980s the Armed Services YMCA established the Military Family Resource Center. Over the next few years, this resource center became a major source of resource support for the growing military family center field. In 1986, the DoD Family Policy Office was established in the Pentagon under the Office of the Assistant Secretary of Defense, and the resource center became a part of this new DoD office. In 1988 this office became the DoD Office of Family Policy, Support and Services and was expanded to include family policy, family advocacy, and the military family resource center.

NAVY FAMILY SERVICE CENTERS

Navy family service centers (FSCs) generally have between 10 and 50 staff members, depending upon the size, location, and support characteristics of the installation. The director is a Navy line officer of the rank of lieutenant commander through captain. The Navy made this decision at the beginning based on the belief that a line officer would be better able to influence senior base leadership. The deputy director in Navy centers is always a human services professional, usually either a psychologist or a social worker. The remainder of the FSC staff is usually a combination of civilian employees, contract personnel, and military members. Most of these have degrees in some area of human services. The Navy has always placed strong emphasis upon appropriate professional training for FSC staff members. All staff members delivering direct counseling services must be appropriately credentialed.

The overall mission of Navy FSCs is to be a focal point for family and people concerns on base. They are there to serve whole families, family members, and single military members through a comprehensive information and referral service, marriage and family counseling services, education in effective money management, a transition assistance program for military members leaving the service, a family relocation program to assist during moves, and support for family members before, during, and after duty separations. While seeking to not be too crisis-oriented, the FSC is, by virtue of its mission, a primary point of crisis intervention on base. Since the Navy does not have an extensive mental health service within the medical services on base, the emergency mental health needs are more likely to fall to the FSC. Navy FSCs also manage child and spouse abuse programs.

Above all, the Navy sees the FSC as a primary resource for the command structure to improve the quality of life at the installation. This last part of the mission of a Navy FSC is in sync with all other military FSCs. An organizationally sponsored FSC is there to help the decision makers or power structure of the organization meet the needs of the people who serve the needs of the organization.

For 10 years, the Navy FSCs have addressed the following areas: volunteer development and management, child and spouse abuse (family advocacy), family life education, financial education and counseling, family separation and deployment assistance, cultural adjustment support, general counseling, spouse or family member employment assistance, personal and family crisis assistance, and relocation assistance. The general emphasis in services and programs has been on the former, descending to the latter items listed.

With the enormous changes occurring in the Department of Defense in the early 1990s, the program/service balance in military family centers has been shifting. The growing emphasis in Navy FSCs, as in the family centers of all other branches of service, is on transition and relocation assistance. Both of these programs are congressionally mandated and have a great deal of visibility. Other programs receiving emphasis are family advocacy, personal financial management, exceptional family member program, and crisis assistance. Following the experiences of the Gulf War, there is also increased emphasis on providing assistance to reserve members and their families.

MARINE CORPS FSCS

FSCs in the Marine Corps were established in 1980 as a result of the White Paper on Marine Families issued by the commandant of the Marine Corps. There is a strong focus upon supporting the commander in meeting the needs of the Marine members and their families. The primary mechanism for providing this support is that of positioning the FSC as the base focal point of family issues. Several of the specific services offered by the FSC assist with this positioning. The first is information, referral, and follow-up, and the second is counseling assistance. Both of these are direct services and put the FSC in the position of being one of the first places marines and their family members turn for help. All counseling services seek to follow a nonmedical model and are to be provided only by qualified and credentialed staff members.

Other services offered by Marine Corps FSCs are almost identical to those offered by Navy FSCs. They are as follows: financial counseling, relocation assistance, family separation and deployment support, spouse and child abuse services through the family advocacy program, employment resource center, and special needs families. As is true of all other military family centers at this time, special emphasis is being placed on member and family transition assistance and family relocation assistance.

AIR FORCE FSCS

FSCs in the Air Force have gone through two distinct stages in the evolution of their services and programs. The first was from their beginning in July 1981 through 1988. The exact range and nature of the services and programs the service wanted the FSCs to deliver was not always clear, and as a result the centers developed a wide range of programs and services. Most often these addressed needs and concerns of the local base. In the fall of 1988, the air force convened a Family Support Review Panel to determine the most appropriate role and structure for the FSCs. The results of this review were published in January 1990 with endorsement by the Air Force chief of staff, and from that time the Air Force FSCs have been guided by a much clearer statement of mission, organization, and service delivery.

The dual-focus mission of Air Force FSCs is to help the service understand and respond to the needs of Air Force families while also helping them to understand the needs of the organization and to adjust to the life-style required by the organization. There are four functional areas identified to serve as a structure from which to fulfill the dual-focus mission:

- *Information, referral, and follow-up counseling* to help family members access existing resources on base and in the civilian community.

- *Leadership consultation* to provide assistance to unit commanders and supervisors in their task of responding to family issues in the most positive ways possible.

- *Policy, planning, and coordination* to help commanders develop family supportive policies and practices, and to facilitate better coordination of programs and services which seek to enhance family well-being.

- *Direct services* to provide family life education and skill development in support of family adaptation to the military life style.

The direct service area within Air Force FSCs is comparable to that in all other military family centers, with the exception of child and spouse abuse services through the family advocacy program. Unlike the other military services, the Air Force operates the family advocacy program from the medical services arena. It is an extension of the mental health center located within the medical services of each base. The Air Force has a career field for military members who are trained and credentialed social workers. The family advocacy program is operated primarily by those in this career field.

Other areas of direct service correspond almost exactly with the other military family centers. As is the case across all DoD family centers during the early to mid-1990s, two programs receiving a great deal of attention and use are the transition program and the relocation assistance program. Other direct service programs are financial management counseling and education, family member job and career assistance, and family separation and mobility support.

Staff size is generally from 5 to 15; the director is a civilian human services professional and the deputy director a senior enlisted military member. The Air Force chose to use a senior enlisted person as the military staff member who would seek to enhance the center's acceptance and voice with the military leadership on base. In a few cases, the FSC director has been a uniformed social worker borrowed from the mental health career field for one assignment. This practice has been utilized for the most part in locations adverse to civilian placement.

ARMY COMMUNITY SERVICE CENTERS

As noted earlier, the Army community service (ACs) center program began in 1965. Staffed in the early days mostly by volunteers, today, the ACS program has grown into a professional social service network offering a broad range of programs and services very similar to the family centers in the other military services. Information, referral and follow-up is a core component of ACS services. Relocation assistance and transition assistance are two major services available during the downsizing of the military. As in the Navy and Marine FSCs, the Army ACS operates the family advocacy program to address the problems of child abuse and neglect, spouse abuse, and foster care needs. Other staple programs cover consumer affairs and financial assistance, family member employment assistance, and exceptional family members— a program that assists family members with special social, medical, or personal needs.

KEY ISSUES RELEVANT TO ALL FSCs IN THE MILITARY

Credentialing of Counselors. All of the service branches except the Air Force provide ongoing counseling services in their centers. These services require that staff members providing counseling must be properly trained and appropriately certified or licensed. The Air Force centers do not provide ongoing counseling services of any type and therefore do not require any form of counseling training or certification for staff members.

Confidentiality. There is no form of privileged information between counselors or other staff members and any person using services in any of the military family centers; that is, reports can be, and occasionally are, requested by a commanding officer. Family center staff members must take care to let all clients or program users know of this limitation and that they have the choice of using a civilian provider who can maintain greater confidentiality. Disclosures later shared with commanding officers can impede upward career mobility and/or lead to dismissal from service.

Liability Risks for FSC Staff Members. Staff members who are a part of civil service are insured by the federal government as long as they are operating within the normal scope of their job requirements. However, contract staff members who are not a part of civil service or on active military duty are not insured by the government and are subject to malpractice suits.

Prevention versus Intervention. Most programs and services offered by military family centers are preventive in nature. That is certainly the intent of most of these efforts. Those programs that are primarily interventive are family advocacy and individual, marital, and family counseling. The family advocacy programs are both interventive and preventive, since they each have a rather large effort geared toward education and prevention.

IMPACT OF OPERATION DESERT STORM

The overall impact of the Persian Gulf operations was to give military family programs intense visibility. The services of all family centers were utilized to the maximum. More than at any time in the past, the families of reserve military members were affected. As a result, all military family centers are strengthening their outreach to the family members of reservists, and each of the services has initiated special programs for their reserve components.

MILITARY FAMILY CENTERS AND THE FUTURE

The mid-1990s will continue to see dramatic changes in the military services of the United States. During this period of downsizing and reorganization, support of families through strong family centers will be essential. At the present time, leadership support for family programs is strong. To maintain this support, family center programs must be well developed, effectively delivered, and complimentary to existing services. The centers must maintain competent, high-quality staff and constantly improve efforts to coordinate with existing services. Additional efforts must be made to overcome the perceptions that military family centers are primarily there to provide services to families with serious problems and to respond to crises. This perception has plagued the centers from their beginnings (O'Keefe, Eyre, & Smith, 1984).

The DoD Office of Family Policy, Support and Services is presently developing initiatives to address many of the issues facing military family centers, especially those related to standards for operating centers and credentialing of center staff. This commitment to professional development within the respective FSC was clearly seen in the first DoD conference for directors of military family centers held in conjunction with the Annual Conference of the National Council on Family Relations in November 1982 in Orlando, Florida. This 2-day conference stressed professional development and preparing military family center staff for the challenges of the remainder of this decade and beyond the year 2000.

REFERENCES

Brown, R. J., Carr, R., & Orthner, D. K. (1983). Family life patterns in the Air Force. In F. D. Margiotta, J. Brown, & M. J. Collins (Eds.), *Changing U.S. military manpower realities* (pp. 207–220). Boulder, CO: Westview Press.

Hunter, E. J., & Nice, D. S. (Eds.). (1978). *Military families: Adaptation to change.* New York: Praeger.

O'Keefe, R. A., Eyre, M. C., & Smith, D. L. (1984). Military family service centers. In F. W. Kaslow & R. I. Ridenour (Eds.), *The military family: Dynamics and treatment* (pp. 254–268). New York: Guilford Press.

Orthner, D. K. (1980). *Families in blue: A study of married and single parent families in the U.S. Air Force* (USAF Contract No. F33600-79-C-0423). Washington, DC: Office of the Chief of Chaplains, USAF.

Orthner, D. K., Early-Adams, P., Devall, E., Giddings, M., Morley, R., & Stawarski, C. (1987). *The Army family research program: Community satisfaction and support programs* (U.S. Army Contract No. MDA 903-87-C-0540). Athens: University of Georgia.

Orthner, D. K., Giddings, M. M., & Quinn, W. H. (1986). *Youth in transition: A study of adolescents from Air Force and civilian families.* Athens: University of Georgia.

Smith, D. L. *Military family programs and policy: U.S. Navy family efforts.* Paper presented at the National Council on Family Relations, Pre-Conference Workshop on Family Life in the Military, Washington, DC.

CHAPTER NINE

Weathering the Storm at Home: War-Related Family Stress and Coping

Charles R. Figley, PhD

THE ABRUPT END OF THE GULF WAR, FOLLOWING ONLY 100 HOURS OF GROUND conflict, surprised most Americans. Few were fully prepared for the postwar period. The general public expected few postwar problems to persist among the troops who had served in the war and the families who waited and worried at home. In this chapter, seven basic points are discussed. These points emerged from the few available professional sources of information about Gulf War veterans and their families and the cumulative literature on military and veteran family studies compiled over the past 50 years (Department of Veterans Affairs, 1991; Figley, 1978; Hill, 1949) and are as follows:

1. The psychosocial impact of the war on *families as well as on the troops* has already been quite profound—in spite of the duration and intensity of the war—because *duration and intensity are only two of many factors* that cause posttraumatic stress.

2. By the time troopers are reunited with their families, many of the families *may have endured more profound stress than the troopers had.*

3. Home coming—for both the troops and the families—may be more stressful than the departure was.

4. To effectively help these servicepeople and their families recover quickly from war we must understand the sources of stress, methods of coping, and potential mental health consequences.

5. The characteristics of all helping—no matter if the help comes from professionals or volunteers or from the military or civilian sector—must include four fundamental elements: respect, information, support, and empowerment.

6. Military family specialists can play a vital role in promoting postwar recovery.

One program that evolved during the Gulf War is described in some detail here. *It is hoped that, if similar crises occur in the United States or other countries in the future, the premises delineated and the interventions cited here can provide a model for services to be developed rapidly.*

BACKGROUND

Our involvement with Gulf War families at Florida State University (FSU) began shortly after American troops were mobilized at the start of Operation Desert Shield. I direct an interdisciplinary PhD program, a fully functioning Marriage and Family Therapy Center/Clinic, and the Psychosocial Stress Research Program at FSU. The disadvantages of administration are well known to research professors; the advantages, however, enabled us to mobilize considerable resources to apply to understanding and reacting to the growing crisis in the Middle East.

September 6 Conference on the Gulf Crisis

Recognizing the enormous strain on family systems, with members suddenly being deployed, and/or on the professionals responsible for their care, we acted quickly to help. We organized a conference at FSU, which was held on September 6, 1990, at the Florida State Conference Center in Tallahassee.

The purpose of the meeting was to bring together those responsible for identifying and meeting the needs of American families most affected by the Middle East crisis: those with members who were either being held hostage by Iraq or members being deployed in military service. The goals of the conference were threefold: (1) to identify the major needs of these military families, (2) to summarize the various programs being utilized or that needed to be utilized to assist these families, and (3) to determine how additional resources could be organized to minimize the negative consequences of the mobilization on these families and on those who serve them.

The sessions were videotaped (available through the FSU Marriage and Family Therapy Center), and major conclusions were transcribed into brief proceedings (Figley, 1990). Among the many recommendations emerging from this conference was one to convene a national conference to focus attention on the families affected by the Middle East conflict, especially the children, and to mobilize the private sector to assist in effective ways.

National Conference on the Gulf Crisis

A national conference was convened in Washington, DC, on October 4, 1990, at the Washington Hilton, in conjunction with the annual meeting of the American Association for Marriage and Family Therapy (AAMFT). As with the Tallahassee conference, this one focused on *both* military and hostage families. Presenters included top professionals within the Departments of Defense, State, and Health and Human Services who were responsible for either military or hostage families. Also presenting were professionals from the private sector, representing the Red Cross, the USO, Family Service Association of America, National Organization for Victim Assistance, USA-Give, and others. In addition to alerting each other about everyone's mission and efforts in this crisis, together they forged a national agenda for action. An audiotape collection of these sessions was produced (AAMFT, 1990). Later an edited proceedings emerged (Figley, 1991c) that focused on military families.

Gulf War Family Support Project

In response to growing tension within Gulf War families living in Tallahassee, our center established the Gulf War Family Support Project in early December 1990. The project still continues today, thanks in part to a generous contribution by the Vietnam Veterans Aid Foundation. The project maintains a 24-hour hotline for consultation and referral for a wide variety of services, ranging from child care to legal consultation and tax preparation. Most of the assistance, however, focuses on marriage and family counseling and consultation. The center has received over 500 phone calls and has made contact with hundreds of family members, including several dozen who sought counseling. Many of the calls and contacts involve concern about the welfare of children exhibiting symptoms of stress and anxiety associated with war. The project also maintains a resource clearinghouse of relevant materials for both family members and the professionals who serve them (Figley, 1991d).

March 1 Conference on the Homecoming and Postwar Adjustment

Shortly after the ceasefire was declared we sponsored another conference for family professionals working with Gulf War families. The conference was again held at the Florida State Conference Center on the campus of FSU in Tallahassee, on March 1, 1991. The primary focus was preparing for the homecoming and the postwar readjustment. A videotape was produced and is also available through the FSU Marriage and Family Therapy Center (Figley, 1991e).

Workshop for Volunteer Coordinators

On March 2–3, the center cosponsored and provided the plenary speakers for a training workshop for Florida Army Reserve and National Guard volunteer coordinators working at family support centers. The focus was also on the homecoming and postwar readjustment, with special attention to children, parent-child relationships, and the marital relationship. A videotape of the major sessions is available through the center; the training manual is available through the 81st Army Command in Atlanta, Georgia.

Need for a National Policy for Military Families

Since early 1991 the center staff has consulted with many individuals and institutions. These included other family-centered institutions, military service assistance programs, national mental health associations, and other professional organizations. Most wanted to help military families. It was obvious throughout this period that no plan of action existed on either a national or regional level. Few communities (Cleveland is a major exception) reacted to this emergency in a unified manner. As a result, agencies were groping for direction in coordinating their efforts with others in their area.

There is a critical need for national policies that focus on helping military families, especially in times of war. We need an emergency plan to identify and attend to the needs of our military families, especially our children, during periods of crisis. Currently, we will be starting a regional research project that will study the postwar readjustment stressors and methods of coping of military and reservist families in the Army, Air Force, and Navy (Figley, 1991e).

In the next part of this chapter some of the major sources of stress experienced by American families with loved ones affected directly by the war (either in the military or living in or near a war zone) are discussed. Then several research questions that must be answered before an effective intervention program can be drafted to prevent and treat children and families affected by war and other traumatizing events are proposed.

THEORETICAL ORIENTATION

Today traumatologists view individuals who are exposed to traumatic events as members of traumatized systems (Figley, 1978, 1989b). People, as family members, can both traumatize and be traumatized by other family members. Each time an *individual traumatized person* is considered, one must simultaneously suspect a *traumatized family* within which this person seeks social support. Theoretically, the family system and its members can be exposed to or "infected" with external traumatic information in numerous ways. Among others, family members are traumatized by imagining what may be happening to a relative (e.g., one held as a hostage or engaged in a war). They can be profoundly affected by direct exposure to the member's descriptions of or actions caused by her or his traumatizing experiences. Prevention and amelioration of systemic traumatization require effective cognitive appraisal management. That is why information is so critical to traumatized families and individuals.

Thus, it is important in our effort to help such devastated families to be sensitive to their special circumstances. Among other things, we need to know (1) the perceived sources of stress, (2) the methods families employed in coping with stressors, (3) the methods that resulted in reducing stress and those that had the opposite effect, and (4) the patterns that emerged within the family that were functional in managing the traumatic crisis but which may not be functional following the crisis. Such a family traumatic stress assessment is useful in both studying and treating traumatized families.

IMMEDIATE SOURCES OF STRESS

Troopers

Although the focus of this chapter is mainly on the Gulf War families, a brief review of several major sources of stress for the troopers—

regardless of their roles in the war—seems pertinent. Based on the cumulative knowledge of the impact of war, there will most definitely be postwar stress among those who have served in any war zone. A number of troops will continue to experience posttraumatic stress disorder (PTSD) long after the specific war is over. This has even been the case following the Gulf War, despite its short duration and low intensity. This position was expressed in a recent report to Congress by the Department of Veterans Affairs (DVA, 1991). The report was the result of several months of investigation and interviews among both DVA and Department of Defense (DoD) installations with the most contact with Gulf War veterans. The existence of postwar stress was due, in part, to the nature of the war and the homecoming.

During the War

The Gulf War was like no other in American history. It differed from previous wars in many ways: (1) many troops—and the rest of the world—were kept up to the minute on the various developments via satellite television (including live broadcasts of Allied bombing raids before the start of the war was officially declared); (2) there was a greater and constant threat of biochemical and nuclear warfare to the troops; (3) never before were so many troops massed so quickly to do battle with a single country; (4) never before was America threatened with terrorist attack associated with a war; and (5) there was extraordinary support of the American people for the war effort, especially for the troops and their families. Other features of this war, though not unique, were no less stressful for those who had to serve and fight in the war zone: (1) changes in climate, routine, danger level; (2) the long period of anticipation of the war and one's role in it; (3) the constant stress of being under attack from SCUD missiles; (4) being away from home and family and all of the associated comforts; (5) the dangerous preparation for war, including maneuvers and war simulations; (6) the war itself and the actual confrontation with the enemy—both alive and dead, and (7) the horrific and pathetic scenes during the mopping-up phase (DVA, 1991; Figley, 1991a, Hobfoll et al., 1991).

Following the War

Conventional wisdom suggests that the stress and anxiety disappear once the war is over. Research on the immediate and long-term psychosocial consequences of war, however, clearly indicate that the immediate postwar period is as stressful for both the troops and their families as is the prewar period (Figley, 1978; Kulka et al., 1990; Milgram, 1985). And for Gulf War troops, the preliminary findings indicate that this trend continues (cf. Brigham, 1991; Wolfe, 1991). Among the many stressors for the Gulf War troops were: (1) frustrations of not leaving for home fast enough; (2) the culture shock resulting from the short duration between the war theater and home, once troops finally left (i.e., "fox hole to front porch" period); (3) the conflicted emotions associated with the reunion (happy to be home but confused about the events in the war and their various meanings); (4) pressures of meeting the immediate needs of others versus one's own; (5) pressures of returning to work versus enjoying life back home; and (6) the extraordinary contrast between being in the middle of an intense and huge war effort and dealing with the routine of life at home (Figley, 1991c; Hobfoll et al., 1991).

Families

Though they are far from the war zone, families experience an entire plethora of war-related stressors. Unfortunately, these families and their struggles go largely unnoticed by military and military veteran mental health specialists (Figley, 1978; Figley & Southerly, 1980). The postwar stressors affecting the family system vary greatly among families. This review supports the second major point of this paper: by the time troopers are reunited with their families, many *families have endured more stress than the troopers had*. Based on research on previous American wars (e.g., World War II [Hill, 1949], Vietnam [cf. Figley, 1978]) and other types of traumatizing events—especially those involving separation (e.g., Iranian hostage crisis [Figley, 1980])—it is likely that some family members will experience postwar stress and in some cases PTSD, regardless of the outcome of the war.

During the War

The Gulf War, which was unique in many respects, created specific stressors for the families of the troops. Perhaps the most profound impact resulted from the use of the media. Conventional and satellite-transmitted television, commercial radio, computer modem, fax machine, and shortwave radio provided up-to-the-minute information about the war. As a result, many family members and friends felt compelled to monitor these sources of new information as much as possible. By doing so, they were exposed to rumors and misinformation and had to forgo other activities in order to maintain this vigil.

Among the numerous sources of stress for families during the war were the following: (1) disruption of life patterns and routines; (2) assumption of roles, tasks, and obligations vacated by the trooper; (3) assumption of new roles associated with helping family members and friends cope with the crisis; (4) decreased source of income (especially among reservist nuclear families); (5) decrease in the quality of health care for dependents for families away from military medical facilities and the Civilian Health and Medical Program of the Uniformed Services (CHAMPUS); (6) constant uncertainty about their trooper's welfare; (7) inability to plan because of the uncertainty of the trooper's tour of duty; (8) children's welfare (psychological, developmental, and medical) as a result of being deprived of a parent for so long and with the parent in danger; (9) confusion and frustration with military bureaucracy, policies, procedures, and expectations, especially for reservist families; (10) media reports associated with the length, outcome, and appropriateness of the war; (11) worry about the trooper's criticism or other comments associated with how things are being handled at home; and (12) anxiety about the long-term effects of the war on the trooper.

During the Homecoming

Most assume that the homecoming is a time of pure joy and satisfaction. Yet for many families, this period is extremely stressful. They and the returning trooper not only share the relief of the separation finally ending, but they soon face a large number of challenges that quickly intrude on the joy of reunion. These challenges are associated with the strains of reviewing what has happened to them during the separation and attempting to reorganize their lives as quickly as possible. There is often conflict over what is to be reorganized, by whom, and in what way.

It is often a period that holds considerable ambivalence, the mixture of great relief and exhilaration. Among the many challenges faced by reunited veteran families during this period have been the following: (1) family conflict over what was done at home, how, and by whom; (2) evaluation of the frequency and quality of letters, calls, and other communications from the trooper during her or his absence; (3) family rearrangement (reorganization of family roles, routine, and rules due to the trooper's absence); (4) shifts in the friendship support network (e.g., the trooper may discourage continuing contact with the family system); (5) marital conflict over potential or real extramarital affairs; and (6) conflict over each person's homecoming fantasies (competition among the trooper and family members about activities to do when, where, and with whom).

Thus, the third point of this chapter is that *the homecoming—for both the troops and the families—may be more stressful than the departure*. In contrast to the homecoming, there was often little time to prepare for the departure, with almost complete attention to the preparation and little to the implications of the separation.

Long-Term Postwar Stressors

After the parades, the delayed second honeymoons and vacations, and the parties to welcome the troops home, the family must settle down to face many concerns. These include issues unresolved at the time of deployment that may have become exacerbated, such as major purchases or repairs, marital conflicts, and career decisions.

Additional sources of stress may have emerged as a result of the physical separation and the hardships each experienced associated with the war. Among these are (1) struggling to return to the prewar/ separation lifestyle and interaction, which may require more time than expected; (2) making decisions about careers and the household quickly, due to the delays imposed by the war; (3) confronting the long-term resentments of family members who felt forced to assume new roles and responsibilities at home with little support from others; and (4) reestablishing personal relationships with family members that were affected by the war—especially the marital relationship and trooper-child relationships (Figley, 1991, 1991b, 1991c).

STRESS REACTIONS

Stressors manifested themselves in a variety of reactions during and following the war, including, but not limited to, the following list. Mental health professionals, especially military family service providers, would be wise to ask family members about the presence of these reactions prior to any intervention.

- shame over some failure
- depression or letdown that follows high levels of energy and activity
- poor reaction to changes, including those associated with the war
- excessive talking about stressors, especially those experienced during the war
- crying and extreme emotionality associated with the stressors

- difficulty sleeping
- minor illnesses
- low energy
- overeating
- rumination about minor issues
- inability to concentrate
- overdependency on others or on activities that appear to relieve the stress
- guilt about actions or lack of actions
- abusive actions against family members

METHODS OF COPING

Family members are faced with coping with an extraordinary accumulation of stressors. Most are able to endure and draw upon their strengths and resources. Some appear to become hardier, even more resilient and functional. Yet other families and family members, as a result of the war-related stressors and/or because of their own personality factors, employ coping strategies that do more harm than good and become additional sources of stress.

Positive Coping Methods

Elsewhere (Figley, 1989a) I have identified 11 characteristics that are applicable in differentiating between functional and dysfunctional family coping. These include (1) clear acceptance of the stressor, (2) family-centered locus of the problem, (3) solution-oriented problem solving, (4) high tolerance of other family members, (5) clear and direct expressions of commitment and affections, (6) open and effective communication utilization, (7) high family cohesion, (8) flexible family roles, (9) efficient resource utilization, (10) absence of violence, and (11) infrequency of substance use.

With regard to contemporary military families who struggle with the stressors of war mobilization, engagement, and reunion, there are several additional methods of coping that appear to be important, at least based on our knowledge of Gulf War military families. These include (1) talking to others about everyday matters and, if necessary, starting a support group; (2) increasing the network of people willing and able to help; (3) channeling energy into doing something to help others and the troops (e.g., organizing the community to display yellow ribbons, volunteering as a Red Cross worker, starting a newsletter for families with members in the armed services, particularly the war zone; (4) writing letters to the trooper and others to express feelings and emotions; (5) becoming educated about the war and the region within which it is being fought; (6) engaging in appropriate physical exercise; and (7) becoming preoccupied with hobbies and other activities.

Negative Coping Methods

Conversely, faced with a crisis situation and the cascade of stressors, families may engage in coping methods that are not useful and that may become additional sources of stress. Elsewhere I (Figley, 1989) have noted 11 characteristics of negative coping that are the obverse of positive coping. These are (1) denial or misperception of the stressor, (2) individual-centered locus of the problem, (3) blame-oriented problem solving, (4) low tolerance for other family members, (5) indirect or missing expressions of commitment and affections, (6) closed or ineffective communication utilization, (7) low or poor family cohesion, (8) rigid family roles, (9) inefficient resource utilization, (10) utilization of violence, and (11) abuse or frequent use of habit-forming substances to control stress.

With regard to contemporary military families who struggle with the stressors of war mobilization, engagement, and reunion, there are several additional methods of coping that tend to *increase stress* rather than abate it, or so it appears, based on our knowledge of Gulf War military families. These include (1) blaming oneself for all or most of the negative life circumstances, (2) avoiding all responsibility for negative life circumstances while unfairly blaming the military or "the government," (3) being overly cynical about life circumstances, (4) lack of motivation for engaging in necessary daily tasks and responsibilities, (5) taking frustrations out on others—particularly loved ones, (6) excessively seeking information to clarify one's current situation (e.g., "CNN syndrome"), and (7) exercising excessively to control the stress or to avoid thinking about the stressors.

WAR-RELATED STRESS DISORDERS

A relatively small percentage of those war veterans and family members who are unable to cope effectively will develop one or more associated mental disorders. Mental health professionals need to be alert to this possibility and utilize standardized protocols to effectively diagnose the presenting problems. This relates to my fourth point: *To effectively help these troopers and families recover quickly from the war we must understand their sources of stress, methods of coping, and potential mental health consequences.*

Disorders Affecting Individuals

Those diagnoses affecting individual family members and veterans are as follows:

1. *War-related PTSD.* Nearly all of the field of traumatology, particularly literature on PTSD, focuses on individual pathology. However, it is important to recognize that family members of the traumatized are also vulnerable to this disorder, which can be experienced vicariously. This might involve, for example, imagining the death and pain of the trooper in the war zone, or it might involve being traumatized in the process of helping the trooper overcome her or his memories of war experiences.

2. *War-related clinical depression.* This disorder is a result of the dramatic shift from the extraordinary war-related stress to the relatively calm and routine postwar period.

3. *Substance abuse.* This problem is expected to be greater for family members than for veterans. Family members may have turned to alcohol or other substances as a means of self-medication to control the stress during the war. Spouses left back home without the companionship of the trooper were especially vulnerable. In contrast, all substance use in the Gulf War theater was restricted. Troopers may have experienced for the first time in their adult life what it felt like to be free of alcohol, for example.

4. *Phobic disorders.* War-related phobic disorders are normally associated with danger, information about danger, and interpersonal contact. However, such disorders are highly treatable and often disappear spontaneously.

Disorders Affecting Relationships and Family Systems

The study and classification of trauma-related systemic disorders is in the very early stages of development (Figley, 1985, 1989a). Therefore, a simple listing of various possible systemic or family/interpersonal relationship disorders connected with the war is not possible. However, mental health professionals should be especially observant in systems in which at least one family member is diagnosed with a stress disorder. If left untreated, the family system tends to reorganize around the disorder and remains dysfunctional even after the individual family member is successfully treated.

Elsewhere (Figley, 1989a) I have defined traumatized families as those who have been exposed to stressors that resulted in disruptions of their life routine. As a result, their beliefs, points of view, perceptions, frames of reference, or cognitive appraisals of family members—both separately and collectively—have been altered. This unsatisfactory situation causes considerable tension within the family and among its members.

Among the warning signs that a family may not be coping well during the postwar recovery period are the presence of the following characteristics: (1) A "parentified child," or a child who has been given adult responsibilities as a result of a missing or dysfunctional parent or parents (Whitaker & Keith, 1981); (2) excessively permeable boundaries of the marital and parent-child subsystems by extended family members and friends as a result of a missing or dysfunctional parent or parents (Figley, 1989b); (3) overidentification or idealization of a family member with either the veteran or with the another family member as a result of the war (Figley, 1990b); (4) excessive blaming of other family members for the current tension within the family; (5) intolerance among family members (Figley & McCubbin, 1983); (6) inflexible family roles and routines (Watzlawick, Beavin, & Jackson, 1967); and (7) evidence and tolerance of family abuse toward one another (Figley, 1983).

ROLE OF HELPERS AND PROFESSIONALS

Before treating those families who wish help in dealing with war trauma–related problems, mental health professionals should consult the growing body of literature on this topic (e.g., Figley, 1989b). There are specific, theory-based steps to take to assess and treat traumatized families and children. However, many families will not present themselves for formal therapy but still need some form of assistance. Given the likelihood of war-related problems among family members and close friends, practitioners should attempt to screen and educate all family members. Only a minority will require intensive, long-term psychotherapy. Most require attention of a different sort. Gulf and other war families deserve and require kindness, attentiveness, and the appreciation deserved by all who have sacrificed so much for their country during war time.

Based on my nearly two decades of work with people in crisis or those who have been traumatized, it is apparent that four fundamental elements are required to prevent or reduce the predictable stress experienced by warrior family members and friends. These elements, or principles, which have emerged from five decades of research focusing on individuals and family systems caught in crisis situations, are associated with effective functioning during the crisis and the speed of recovery following it. This is related to the fifth and final point: *The characteristics of all helping—no matter if the help comes from professionals or volunteers or from the military or civilian sector—must include four fundamental elements: respect, information, support, and empowerment* (*RISE*). This RISE model of intervention is briefly discussed below.

Respect

In this context, families and other close supporters of war veterans merit the kind of respect that could be defined as "someone deserving high or special regard, esteem; the expression of respect or deference; to have concern for." Thus, those who worry about loved ones endangered during a war should be treated with *respect*. They require respect for their privacy, for their sacrifices, and for their stressful life circumstances.

Information

It was noted earlier that one of the distinguishing features of the Gulf War was the profound impact of the electronic media. Information, often in a raw and unreliable form, was available almost instantaneously. And Gulf War families had to cope with the consequences. They felt compelled to monitor those sources of new information as much as possible, despite knowing that much of the information might be unreliable. Clinicians need to help families fill this vacuum with immediate, accurate, and reliable information about whatever is of concern to them. Most often the concern will be associated with the reason the family sought professional assistance in the first place.

If the problems involve the immediate and long-term psychosocial consequences of war—for both veterans and their families—mental health professionals can serve a vital role by providing psychoeducational information in a variety of forms. In contrast to the dearth of information available during earlier wars, today books, newspaper and magazine articles, and videotapes of documentaries and lectures are available on the topic of PTSD and other consequences of war-related experiences.

Practitioners need to be sensitive to the specific needs of individual family members (Figley, 1989a). Many family members would rather hear a brief summary, while others can not bear to listen and would rather get the information more gradually and in "doses" they can handle under their own control. Therefore, even though most family members require information regarding the stressors on their family, they may differ on *how* this information should be imparted.

Support

In contrast to other recent American wars, the Gulf War, its troops, and their families have enjoyed unprecedented *public support*. This support has been helpful to the troops and their families, who need to know that their sacrifices were useful and appreciated. Yet, this widespread, public support decreased steadily in the months following the war. The various welcoming receptions and parades were appreciated by these families, but were viewed by the general public as the final payment of gratitude. This rather abrupt shift in sentiment may be perceived by these veterans and families as a form of abandonment and neglect, especially if the war-related problems continue long afterward.

An equally important source of support for these veterans and their families comes from services established specifically for them (e g., military or DVA). These services must be accessible, reliable, effective, and delivered with professionalism. Otherwise, these clients will feel abandoned and unappreciated.

Another source of support for veterans and their families is from *other veterans and their families*. The family support groups that functioned so well during the war are also vital for those adversely affected in the aftermath of the war. Practitioners should enable veterans and families to seek out and find support among those who share common experiences.

Empowerment

The final element in the RISE model, empowerment, is a component of a general model of intervention. We attempt to *empower the family to make peace with the past* and take charge of their lives (Figley, 1989a). Making peace with the past requires confronting the most disturbing, confusing, or threatening memories and finding understanding and acceptance. An even better peace would be transforming a traumatizing memory into one that inspires and educates. This involves helping a 6-year-old son, for example, to understand why his father was gone during his birthday and to come to appreciate that a delayed celebration was worth it, that his father is a "hero" now, in part because of the son's sacrifices.

The empowerment element is prevention-oriented. It attempts to mitigate the presenting stress and enable the family to avoid unwanted future stress.

Empowering families, in contrast to simply "treating" them involves (1) accurately assessing their current sources of stress, (2) identifying functional and dysfunctional coping styles, (3) educating them about traumatic stress and recovery, (4) building supportiveness among family members toward one another, and (5) developing family relationship skills that strengthen and mobilize the family to solve their own problems. These skills might include strategies for "reframing," or viewing their challenges in alternative or more positive ways; effective methods of stress management; improved interpersonal communication and empathy; improved problem solving and conflict management; and other behaviorally based skills.

Empowering families means working with generally functional families and enabling them to apply their strengths to the current crisis. Moreover, it involves facilitating the family in such a way that they take credit for facing the challenges associated with war separation and mastering them. As a result of their struggles, they will feel more confident and prepared for future challenges as a family.

SUMMARY AND CONCLUSION

This chapter is concerned primarily with military families most affected by the recent Gulf War. Even as late as August 1991, some military families still were separated due to this war as the final troops were returning to their original military installations, were being deactivated, or were leaving the service entirely. Yet the lessons learned from this war and from all those that preceded it suggest that we know a great deal about how military families cope with the stress of war.

The kinds of information that would assist mental health practitioners to work more effectively with military and war veteran families has been delineated herein. In the process we have tried to make six fundamental points. These are (1) the psychosocial impact of the war *on families as well as on the troops* has already been quite profound—in spite of the duration and intensity of the war—because *duration and intensity are only two of many factors* that cause posttraumatic stress; (2) by the time troopers are reunited with their families we will find that the *families may have endured more profound stress than the troopers have*, (3) homecoming—for both the troops and the families—may be more stressful than the departure; (4) to effectively help these servicepeople and their families recover quickly from the war we must understand the sources of stress, methods of coping, and potential mental health consequences; (5) the characteristics of all helping—no matter if the help comes from professionals or volunteers or from the military or civilian sector—must include four fundamental elements: respect, information, support, and empowerment; and (6) military family specialists can play a vital role in promoting postwar recovery.

The importance of the family to troops, especially those who have chosen the military as a career, became quite evident during the Gulf War. In a recent study conducted by the Army's comptroller office, it was found that troops interviewed during the war were most concerned about the welfare of their families; they tended to perform more effectively if they believed their families were being well taken care of back home; and plan to make the service a career if they had a family. Interestingly, however, military medicine in general and mental health services in particular are oriented to individuals, especially the serviceperson. Perhaps it is time to consider shifting resources in these areas toward a more family-centered approach, one that includes family practice medicine and family therapy mental health services.

REFERENCES

Brigham, D. (1991). Veterans benefits outreach to active duty military members. In Department of Veterans Affairs (VA Persian Gulf Returnees Working Group) (Eds.), *War zone stress among returning Persian Gulf troops: A preliminary report* (pp. B1–B6). West Haven, CT: National Center for PTSD.

Department of Veterans Affairs (VA Persian Gulf Returnees Working Group). (1991). *War zone stress among returning Persian Gulf troops: A preliminary report.* West Haven, CT: National Center for PTSD.

Figley, C. R. (1978). *Stress disorders among Vietnam veterans: Theory, research. and treatment.* New York: Brunner/ Mazel.

Figley, C. R. (1983). Catastrophe and the family. In C. R. Figley (Ed.), *Stress and the family: Vol. 2. Coping with catastrophe.* New York: Brunner/Mazel.

Figley, C. R. (Ed.). (1980). *Mobilization I: The Iran Crises, Final Report of the Task Force on Families of Catastrophe.* West Lafayette, IN: Purdue Research Institute.

Figley, C. R. (1989a). *Helping traumatized families.* San Francisco: Jossey-Bass.

Figley, C. R. (Ed.) (1989b). *Treating stress in families.* New York: Brunner/ Mazel.

Figley, C. R. (Ed.). (1990). *Families in crisis: The Gulf War challenges and consequences.* Tallahassee, FL: FSU Center for Professional Development.

Figley, C. R. (1991a). Critical services for the veterans of the Gulf War. In Department of Veterans Affairs (VA Persian Gulf Returnees Working Group) (Eds.), *War zone stress among returning Persian Gulf troops: A preliminary report* (pp. D3–D14). West Haven, CT: National Center for PTSD, D3-D14.

Figley, C. R. (1991b). *Investigation of war-related stress among families of Gulf War military service personnel.* Unpublished research proposal, Tallahassee, FL: FSU Marriage and Family Therapy Center.

Figley, C. R. (1991c). *Strengthening military families: Mobilizing national resources.* Tallahassee, FL: FSU Marriage and Family Therapy Center.

Figley, C. R. (1991d). *Prisoners in paradise: Recognizing and strengthening Gulf War families.* Columbus, GA: Bradley Center Hospitals and Outpatient Clinics.

Figley, C. R. (1991e). *War and separation of the family.* Keynote presentation. Tallahassee, FL: FSU Marriage and Family Therapy Center, T. Whidden US Army Reserve Center.

Figley, C. R., & McCubbin, H. I. (Eds.). (1983). *Stress and the Family: Vol. 2. Coping with catastrophe.* New York: Brunner/Mazel.

Figley, C., & Southerly, W. T. (1980). Psychosocial adjustment of recently returned veterans. In C. R. Figley and S. Leventman (Eds.), *Strangers at home.* New York: Brunner/Mazel.

Hill, R. (1949). *Families under stress.* New York: Harper & Row.

Hobfoll, S. E., Spielberger, C. D., Breznitz, S., Figley, C., Folkman, S., Lepper-Green, B., Meichenbaum, D., Milgram, N. A., Sandler, I., Sarason, I., & van der Kolk, B. (1991). War-related stress: Addressing the stress of war and other traumatic events. *American Psychologist, 46*(8), 848-855.

Kulka, R. A., Schlenger, W. E., Fairbank, J. A., Hough, R. L., Jordan, B. K., Marmar, C. R., Weiss, D. S., with Gradey, D. A. (1990). *Trauma and the Vietnam War generation: Report of findings from the National Vietnam Veterans Readjustment Study.* New York: Brunner/Mazel.

Milgram, N. A. (Ed.). (1986). *Stress and coping in time of war: Generalizations from the Israeli experience.* New York: Brunner/Mazel.

Watzlawick, P., Beavin, J., & Jackson, D. D. (1967). *Pragmatics of human communication.* New York: Norton.

Whitaker, C. A., & Keith, D. V. (1981). Symbolic-experiential family therapy. In A. S. Gurman & D. P. Kniskern (Eds.), *Handbook of family therapy.* New York: Brunner/Mazel.

Wolfe, J. (1991). Preliminary report of a reunion survey on desert storm returnees. In Department of Veterans Affairs (VA Persian Gulf Returnees Working Group) (Eds.), *War zone stress among returning Persian Gulf troops: A preliminary report* (pp. C1–C14). West Haven, CT: National Center for PTSD.

CHAPTER TEN

The Military Family and the Health Care System

D. Stephen Nice, PhD

"IN PRIMITIVE SOCIETY THE BODY OF MAN IS THE PARADIGM FOR THE DERIVATION of the parts and meanings of other significant objects; in modern society, man has adopted the language of the machine to describe his body" (Manning & Fabrega, 1973).

Within the military, the importance of medical benefits to service members and their families has long been recognized (Stumpf, 1978); however, the importance of the reciprocal influence of the military family on the health care system has not been fully appreciated. As perhaps the most important context within which illness occurs and is resolved, the family serves as a basic unit in health and medical care (Litman, 1974). Familial factors affect the adoption and maintenance of health behaviors, the definition of illness and validation of the sick role, the decision to practice lay care or utilize professional health care services, and the recovery or rehabilitation process. Litman (1974) points out that the family has variously been treated not only as an independent, dependent, and intervening variable but as a precipitating, predisposing, and contributory factor in the etiology, care, and treatment of both physical and mental illness and as a basic unit of interaction and transaction in health care as well.

191

Over the past two decades, much of the work of medical and social scientists has focused on familial influences on the utilization of health services. While rising sales cause joy in most industries, increasing outlays for health care are causing distress not only among those who must pay the bills but among health care providers themselves (Aaron & Schwartz, 1990). Official forecasts project that the United States will be devoting 15% of total gross national product to health care by the year 2000 (Aaron & Schwartz, 1990). In fiscal year (FY) 1989, the Department of Defense (DoD) medical appropriations totaled nearly $13.2 billion (McDavid, 1990).

The military family is often challenged by living a dual existence between the military and its adjacent civilian community (Rodriguez, 1984). The point of greatest intersection between the family and the military is the health care system. Health care for military beneficiaries, primarily active-duty and retired personnel and their respective dependents, is provided through a dual system. In this system, the Army, Navy, and Air Force operate 137 hospitals and numerous clinics in the United States, and this "direct care" system is augmented by the Civilian Health and Medical Program of the Uniformed Services (CHAMPUS) (Hosek et al., 1990). The CHAMPUS program is a traditional health insurance program that reimburses for care primarily provided to military beneficiaries below the age of 65. Most direct care services are free, while CHAMPUS generally charges a small deductible plus copayments of 20% to 25% (Hosek et al., 1990). In FY90 there were approximately 852,000 hospitalizations and 48 million outpatient visits to Army, Navy, and Air Force medical facilities (Naval Medical Data Services Center; Special Studies Branch, U.S. Army Patient Administration Systems and Biostatistics Division; Headquarters, Air Force Office of Medical Systems/SGSI; personal communication, April 12, 1991). Dependents of active and retired military personnel accounted for about half of all inpatient admissions (436,000) and outpatient visits (21.7 million).

In FY89, dependents of active and retired personnel (excluding California and Hawaii) accounted for an additional 235,000 hospital admissions and 6.8 million outpatient visits to CHAMPUS programs. The average CHAMPUS cost is approximately $5,000 per hospital admission and $75 per outpatient visit. CHAMPUS costs for FY89 were about $2.6 billion, or 20.5% of the total DoD medical appropriations.

Although it is clear that military families have a direct impact on the demand for health care services, it is important to remember that utilization is only one of many subtle and complex health and medical care processes that are multidetermined but strongly influenced by familial factors. While a visit to the doctor represents the most tangible intersection of the military family and the health care systems, this event is linked to a larger continuum of processes that operate within the family. The purpose of this chapter is to consider the influence of the military family on health and medical care and suggest a broader consideration of the military family across a range of health-related efforts.

A PERSPECTIVE ON MILITARY FAMILIES

The majority of military personnel today are married, as opposed to earlier times when most personnel were single (see Chapter 8, this volume). However, despite the change in composition, the military has not considered family concerns a policy priority (Hunter, 1982; Kohen, 1984). The provision of medical care for military dependents has been largely reactive. Between 1884 and the end of World War II, dependent medical care at Army expense or at Army facilities was offered only on an emergency basis and at the discretion of the facility commanding officer (Potter, 1990). During the World War II mobilization that began in 1940, however, events overwhelmed the system as commanders of Army bases faced large numbers of young, pregnant wives who had followed their husbands (Potter, 1990). Unlike the two previous mobilizations (in 1898 and 1917) the World War II mobilization coincided with large-scale dislocations of the Great Depression and changing work norms which prompted wives of military inductees to seek work close to where their husbands were stationed (Potter, 1990). As a preliminary solution to the ensuing health care crisis, the Emergency Maternity and Infant Care section of the Social Security Act of 1935 was used as a statutory vehicle through which to provide medical care for those individuals in the four lowest pay grades (Potter, 1990).

In 1956 Congress enacted the Dependents' Medical Care Act, which established the lawful right to medical care for military dependents (Potter, 1990). It was not until 1973, however, that benefits were firmly established for male dependents of female active-duty members. Lieutenant Frontiero, an Air Force officer, and her civilian husband were denied housing assistance and medical benefits because of her inability to demonstrate that she was the sole source of more than one-half of her husband's living expenses—a condition not required under the same statute for male service members. Although the statute was upheld in a federal district court, it was reversed by the Supreme Court, which found that sex-based classifications should be deemed inherently suspect and that the government could sustain them only by proving that a compelling government interest existed in the different treatment (Beans, 1975).

HEALTH PROMOTION

The case for primary prevention of disease and injury through the adoption of healthful life-style behaviors has been well established (Kalmar, 1979), and the family represents the most powerful context in which such behaviors can be acquired. It is generally recognized that the pattern of life-style behaviors is more similar within families than between families (Glueck, Laskarszewski, Rao, & Morrison, 1986). Although Turk and Kerns (1985) conclude that each type of health behavior may have its own unique determinants and reinforcers, certain families are more likely to engage in a broad variety of health-related behaviors (Pratt, 1976; Turk & Kerns, 1985).

In her analysis of dual-parent middle-class families, Pratt (1976) found a positive association between positive health-related behaviors and family characteristics such as egalitarian family decision making, joint parental involvement in raising the children, emphasis on individual autonomy, active problem solving as a coping strategy, and extensive contacts and involvement with community institutions. Conversely, both the lack of availability and perceived adequacy of family support among women after surgery for breast cancer has been linked to greater reliance on accommodation of emotion-focused coping such as more smoking, eating, and drinking (Bloom, 1982).

Smoking

Despite the fact that cigarette smoking has long been identified as the single most important source of both preventable and premature mortality in the United States and that the public's awareness of the relationship between cancer and cigarettes has increased (USDHHS, 1989), smoking rates among U.S. military personnel remain higher than among civilians, with the highest levels occurring in the Navy (44%) and the Army (42%) (Bray et al., 1988). Although there are no reliable estimates of the impact of smoking on the military, in 1983 smoking was estimated to cause more than 350,000 deaths and generate $5 billion to $8 billion in excess health care costs in the nation (Johnson & Eakin, 1983). Compared to individuals who never smoked, heavy smokers at age 25 can expect a 25% shorter life (Rogers & Powell-Griner, 1991). Although much of the excess mortality was originally concentrated among men, changes in women's smoking behavior have prompted Jacobson (1981) to conclude that in their patterns of smoking-related mortality, women are achieving "an equality in death that most have never achieved in life."

Studies of smoking behavior have demonstrated concordance for smoking status between spouses (Barrett-Connor, Suarez, & Criqui, 1982; Venters, Jacobs, Luepker, Maiman, & Gillum, 1984) and familial influences of smoking on children (Graham, 1987). In a study of family influences on smoking, Nolte, Smith, and O'Rourke (1983) found that children were twice as likely not to smoke if neither parent smoked and almost twice as likely to smoke if both parents smoked. Three out of four children are aware of cigarettes before they reach their fifth birthday, and if parents smoke or are permissive in their attitude toward smoking, children are more likely to become smokers (Baric, 1979; Charlton, 1986; Graham, 1987). A number of studies also suggest a sex linking in the generational patterns of smoking attitudes and behavior, with a stronger association between mothers and their daughters than between fathers and their sons (Rawbone, Keeling, Jenkins, & Guz, 1979).

In addition to attitudinal and behavioral influences, smoking within the family also subjects family members to the hazards of passive smoke. The most researched passive smoker is the unborn (Graham, 1987). Large cohort studies have linked maternal smoking and lower birthweight, an increase in perinatal mortality, and long-term child development problems (Butler & Alberman, 1969; Fogelman, 1980; Peters et al., 1983). In a well-controlled study of 5-year-old children, a range of health and behavioral problems were found to be more common among those whose mothers were smokers (Butler & Golding, 1986). These problems included stomachache, ear discharge, squint, wheezing, bronchitis, pneumonia, and mouth breathing.

Efforts to change smoking behavior are particularly difficult when attempted in isolation, without the social supports that sustain a person's daily activities (Stunkard, Felix, & Cohen, 1985). Research has shown that social support is an aid in smoking cessation and the maintenance of nonsmoking behavior (Lichtenstein, Glasgow, & Abrams, 1986; Venters, 1989). Moreover, married smokers are more likely to quit than are separated, divorced, or widowed smokers, as well as to maintain a nonsmoking status (Venters et al., 1986). Given the concordance of smoking between spouses and the importance of social support in smoking behavior, military smoking cessation programs should consider reaching spouses as well as active-duty members. This could be done through the encouragement of cessation programs for couples in conjunction with media and environmental efforts focused in areas such as exchanges, commissaries, and health care clinics where spouses may be present. Although a recent study showed that smoking cessation interventions that were integrated into primary care practice were not very effective, the authors speculated that more intensive interventions on multiple occasions based on relapse prevention strategies hold promise for success (Thompson et al., 1988).

Other Life-Style Behaviors

As Turk and Kerns (1985) point out, family influences are important determinants of a number of important life-style behaviors, including eating habits and food preferences (Bryan & Lowenberg, 1958), weight and overweight (Garn & Clark, 1976; Garn, Cole, & Bailey, 1976), use of alcohol (Tennant & Detels, 1976), and exercise (Perrier, 1979). Epidemiologists, in fact, have expressed concern that continually eating high-fat convenience foods, smoking cigarettes, maintaining sedentary physical behavior, and living a time-pressured life-style are patterns into which certain segments of the population are socialized at a very early age (Blackburn & Gillum, 1980; Venters, 1989).

Heavy alcohol consumption, perhaps more than any other behavior, impels a family synergism of enormous destructive potential. Despite recent declines in the overall volume of alcohol consumption among military personnel, in 1988 over 80% of all U.S. military personnel were drinkers, and 9% were heavy drinkers (Bray et al., 1988). Adverse alcohol-related health outcomes from fetal alcohol syndrome (Streissguth & Little, 1985) and through chronic disease and death (Kolb & Gunderson, 1985; Popham, Schmidt, & Israelstam, 1985) are well documented. Alcohol has also been considered a contributor to approximately one half of this nation's motor vehicle fatalities (about 27,000 to 28,000 yearly) (Hingson, Scotch, Sorenson, & Swazey, 1981).

Within the military community, family influences on alcohol use have received attention. In a study of drinking patterns of military wives in overseas base communities, Garrett and colleagues (Garrett, Parker, Day, Van Meter, & Cosby, 1978) concluded that the alcohol consumption among these military wives was higher than that of their civilian counterparts. They identified a number of environmental, occupational, and social factors associated with heavier drinking among military wives overseas (Garrett et al., 1978). In a later analysis of substance misuse and alcoholism in military families, Williams (1984) also developed associations between certain military environmental pressures, such as family separation, and alcohol use. Given the enormous health and social costs of heavy alcohol use, it is important to recognize and facilitate the role of the family in prevention, treatment, and rehabilitation efforts (Moos, 1985).

In 1986, the DoD established a formal, coordinated, and integrated health promotion policy (DoD Directive No. 1010.10), which was designed to improve and maintain military readiness and the quality of life of DoD personnel and beneficiaries. Health promotion was defined as those activities designed to support and influence individuals in managing their own health through life-style decisions and self-care. The health promotion directive identified six broad program areas: smoking prevention and cessation, physical fitness, nutrition, stress management, alcohol and drug abuse prevention, and prevention of hypertension (Bray et al., 1988).

As part of a national movement to change unhealthy life-styles, health promotion efforts have included a combination of approaches to enhance awareness, change behavior, and create environments that support healthy practices or discourage unhealthy ones. Helping people make changes in their lives, however, has proved remarkably difficult (Foreyt, Goodrick, & Gotto, 1981; Nice & Woodruff, 1990). Although behavior change often has been obtained during the course of an intervention project, the behavior often reverts to baseline levels after discontinuation of the intervention. Baranowski and Nader (1985) believe that families may be key components in preventing this backslide, and they support family involvement in health behavior change programs. This involvement, it is argued, has the potential for training and motivating all family members, attempting to minimize barriers posed by family members, and training family members to support the behavior change process. Given the importance of the family in the establishment, maintenance, and potential modification of important life-style behaviors, DoD health promotion efforts, including media, environmental, and individual interventions, should be broadened to address the entire family.

ILLNESS AND HEALTH CARE

As Litman (1974) observed, the role of the family as a hereditary, causal agent or source of communication in the disease process has been the subject of numerous socioepidemiological investigations. These investigations have noted both the association in the occurrence of chronic illness in both spouses (Downes, 1947) and the concentration or clustering of illness episodes within families (Fox & Hall, 1972). In addition to genetic factors, the common infectious diseases afford the clearest evidence of the important part the family may play as a source of illness (Haggerty & Alpert, 1963; Litman, 1974). The direct spread of infectious agents may occur more easily within the family than in any other social context, and stress-related influences on immunosuppression may be most directly established within the family context.

Stress and Social Support

A military career is not based on taking a job but on joining a total institution for a contracted portion of one's life (Kohen, 1984). Given this commitment, organizational imperatives such as geographic mobility, family separation, cultural isolation, and the potential of international conflict are stressors for the entire family. Reviews of the literature on military family stress are available and will not be addressed in detail (cf., Hunter & Nice, 1978a, 1978b; Jensen, Lewis, & Xenakis, 1986; Kaslow & Ridenour, 1984; Kohen, 1984). These stresses, and the individual and family adaptations to them, have important health-related implications for the military.

The physiological basis for a relation between illness and the events and conditions of the social environment was first provided in the work of Hans Selye (1976) in the 1950s. The import of this early work on stress was not the identification of any special characteristic of the social or physical environment as inherently stressful but the establishment of a relationship between stressors and a pattern of bodily responses clearly recognized as a disease state (Levin & Idler, 1981). Since this early work, the relationship between stress and illness has been supported through an immense amount of epidemiological research.

Within the family context, maladaptive situations and stresses have been implicated in the etiology and course of a variety of both acute and chronic diseases (Meyer & Haggerty, 1962; Minuchin, 1974; Turk & Kerns, 1985). The key role of the family in the development and maintenance of health, as well as in the expression of and response to somatic illness, has long been known intuitively by health care providers and has contributed to the emergence of family medicine as a subspecialty. Turk and Kerns (1985) point out that the distinguishing feature of family medicine is the insistence upon the need to enlarge the conceptual field within which a physician attempts to understand the pathology of the considered individual. This enlargement of perspective includes the patient not only holistically but also as a biological and social member of an intimate social group—the family (Carmichael, 1976).

In considering the unique stresses of military life and the relationship between stress and illness, it must be remembered that the family is a powerful determinant of behavior and can foster adaptive as well as maladaptive activities (Turk & Kerns, 1985). The family system, confronted with continuous internal and external demands for change, may be able to respond with growth, flexibility, and structural evolution (Shapiro, 1983). Within the military family literature, the coping and adaptational processes that are perhaps best documented are those used by the families of the prisoners of war and those missing in action during the Vietnam War (Hunter, 1984; McCubbin, Dahl, Lester, Benson, & Robertson, 1975; McCubbin, Hunter, & Metres, 1974).

In a study of the families of Naval aviators who were held as prisoners of war in Vietnam, Nice and colleagues (1981) found that five years after repatriation there were no significant differences in the marital adjustment or family environment of these families and their matched controls (Nice, McDonald, & McMillian, 1981). However, the availability of normative data on the Family Environment Scale (Moos, 1974) suggested an interesting comparison between these Naval aviator families and the broader constituency of civilian families sampled in the development of the scale norms. A standard score profile of the military families (POWs and Controls) generally resembled the structure-oriented families discussed by Moos and Moos (1976). These families exhibited relatively high standard scores on cohesion, moral-religious emphasis, and organization, and relatively low standard scores on conflict.

Moos and Moos (1976) found that structure-oriented families typically show a strong emphasis on structuring family activities and on explicitness and clarity with regard to family rules and responsibilities. In addition, family members are strongly committed to the family and consider themselves, in general, to be mutually helpful and supportive (Moos & Moos, 1976). We speculated that such emphasis on structured activities, role clarity, and intrafamily support within these military families may represent an adaptation of the family system in order to stabilize the effects of disruptions, such as family separation and geographic mobility, which are inherent in Navy life (Nice et al., 1981). This interpretation was believed consistent with McCubbin's hypothesis that families manage their internal affairs to maximize the flow of energy into the utilization of coping behaviors effective in diverting, reducing, or possibly removing the sources of stress (McCubbin, 1979).

In a recent study, Eastman, Archer, and Ball (1990) used the Family Environment Scale to assess 785 Navy enlisted families and reported that Navy sailors and wives placed substantial value on family cohesiveness, expressiveness, and organization and deemphasized conflict in relation to their civilian counterparts. This replication of our previous work with the families of Naval aviators (Nice, Mcdonald, & McMillian, 1981) suggests the potential of an ongoing adaptational process whereby families can more effectively manage the stresses of military life.

The adaptational and coping capacity of families is important in the context of health and illness because it is the family that is most likely to act as a buffer to absorb the strains and stresses its members experience. The import of social support in avoiding or minimizing the disease process has been well documented (Berkman & Syme, 1979; Cassel, 1974, 1976; Cobb, 1979; DiMatteo & Hays, 1981; Gore, 1978). One of the first studies that directly assessed the potential of social support as a buffer between stress and illness was conducted in North Carolina with 170 military enlisted families who were having their first baby (Nuckolls, Cassel, & Kaplan, 1972). Results of this study showed that women who experienced the largest number of life changes before and during pregnancy had one-third fewer complications when their psychosocial asset scores were high rather than when they were low. In a subsequent large-scale follow-up of an epidemiological study conducted in Alameda County, California, Berkman and Syme (1979) assessed the impact of social ties and networks on mortality from all causes. One of their most dramatic findings was that for each age and sex group in the population studied, mortality rates for the married were lower than for the nonmarried, whether single, separated, divorced, or widowed, and these differences were particularly pronounced for men. Sarason (1988) identifies both theoretical and clinical reasons for believing that the support provided by social relationships contributes to positive adjustment and personal development and also provides a buffer against the deleterious effects of stress.

Weiss (1974) suggested that there are six major provisions of social relationships: attachment, social integration, opportunities for nurturance, reassurance of personal worth, a sense of reliable alliance, and the availability of guidance. Although the relative contributions of the expressive and instrumental aspects of social support as mediating structures in the relationship between stress and disease have not been determined, there is compelling epidemiological evidence that social support is a critical factor. Therefore, those military policies that strengthen and support the family may have direct implications for the health and readiness of the active-duty force.

Health Care Utilization

Physicians are well aware that neither illness nor seeking medical attention is a random event; both are influenced by many factors, including those related to family characteristics (Schor, Starfield, Stidley, & Hankin, 1987). Over the past three decades, the Health Belief Model has provided a major organizing framework for understanding and predicting a number of health behaviors, including health care utilization. As reviewed by Janz and Becker (1984), the Health Belief Model consists of four dimensions.

- *Perceived susceptibility* refers to one's subjective perception of the risk of contracting a condition.
- *Perceived severity* refers to feelings concerning the seriousness of contracting an illness and includes evaluations of both medical/clinical consequences and possible social consequences.
- *Perceived benefits* refers to an appraisal of the effectiveness of the various actions available in reducing the disease threat.
- *Perceived barriers* refers to the potential negative aspects of a particular health action.

A kind of cost-benefit analysis is thought to occur wherein the individual weighs the action's effectiveness against perceptions that it may be expensive, dangerous, unpleasant, inconvenient, or time-consuming (Janz & Becker, 1984). As Rosenstock (1974) points out, "The combined levels of susceptibility and severity provided the energy or force to act and the perception of benefits (less barriers) provided a preferred path of action." Each of these decision processes is believed to be strongly influenced by demographic, social, psychological, and family factors.

The majority of symptoms and conditions of ill health reported by the general public are not treated by a medical practitioner or any other health professional but are addressed through self-care or family care (Dean, 1986; Roghmann & Haggerty, 1972; Wilkinson, Darby, & Mant, 1987). The decision as to whether a member's illness should be treated at home or with the assistance of a professional caregiver tends to be negotiated within the family (Litman, 1974). Within this context, the decision to seek some form of professional assistance for an ill family member generally resides with the wife/mother (Litman, 1974).

In a historical analysis of the development of the medical profession, Levin and Idler (1981) point out that health care for family members has always been a function of families. As currently practiced, family care is a self-contained system of symptom recognition, interpretation and assessment, treatment, and evaluation of effectiveness. Although there are no data on family care in U.S. military families, the high level of self-care practiced in the context of a nationalized health service in Great Britian (Fry, 1973; cited in Levin & Idler, 1981) suggests that it may be high among military families as well.

Although there is evidence to suggest that self-care actions for minor symptoms or complaints are usually appropriate (Wilkinson et al., 1987), concern has been expressed regarding the extensive use of nonprescriptive medications, a market estimated to be $9 billion in the United States in 1980 (Maiman, Becker, & Katlic, 1986). Information from the United States and Britain reveals that adult consumers ignore the label warnings on nonprescriptive medications, exceed the correct dosage, and overextend recommended periods for administration without seeing a physician (Maiman et al., 1986). These adults also frequently diagnose and initiate treatment, including nonprescriptive medications, for ailments in their children. In a study of parents' responses to the management of hypothetical episodes of fever or nasal congestion in their children, Maiman and colleagues (Maiman, Becker, Cummings, Drachman, & O'Connor, 1982) found that 79% of parents would medicate their children for fever without first consulting a health professional (the rate for nasal congestion was 54%). In addition to utilizing over-the-counter medications, patients self-medicate by manipulating the medical profession, primarily through obtaining repeat prescriptions for psychoactive drugs (Dean, 1986; Graham-Smith, 1975).

While much of the self-care or lay care occurs within the family context, the family also plays a decisive role in the decision to seek professional health care. In a study of the effects of family membership on health care utilization, Schor and colleagues (1987) found that a small proportion of families account for a disproportionately large share of health care utilization. Parental influence on children's utilization was particularly significant, with mothers generally being two to three times more powerful in this regard. In this study of more than 80,000 ambulatory visits made by 693 families enrolled in a prepaid group medical practice over a period of at least 6 consecutive years, the authors found that intrafamilial patterns of morbidity were apparent for several major groupings of diagnoses, most notably for acute health problems, and that these patterns remained stable over time. In addition to factors such as genetic influences and exposure patterns, intrafamilial consistencies in health care utilization may be largely determined by similarities in the social and psychological influences within the family system (Picken & Ireland, 1969). Intrafamilial stress, for example, is associated with increased use of health services (Roghmann

& Haggerty, 1972). In a study conducted in a solo family practice, 4% of the families accounted for more than 10% of the visits and 32% of the physician's time (Collyer, 1979). These family members presented with recurrent somatic complaints, and at least one member of the family was ultimately diagnosed as depressed.

Psychosocial problems and symptoms of emotional distress play a prominent role in patients reporting to primary care settings (Barsky, Wyshak, & Klerman, 1986; Berkanovic, Hurwicz, & Landsverk, 1988; Klerman et al., 1987) and psychologically distressed patients use a disproportionate share of ambulatory services and hospitalizations. It is estimated that approximately 60% of the outpatient visits in a prepaid health maintenance organization (HMO) are made by patients who demonstrate an emotional, rather than an organic, etiology for their symptoms (Cummings & Follette, 1976; Garfield et al., 1976).

A study of 1,743 outpatient visits to two Navy hospitals revealed that approximately one-fourth of the visits were precipitated or aggravated by social or emotional factors (Nice, 1982). The most frequent diagnoses were depression, anxiety, obesity, irritable bowel syndrome, and fatigue. Because the ambulatory visit rates of civilian beneficiaries of the military health care system closely approximate those of a large HMO (Thorner, 1978), the actual social or emotional contribution to visits may be quite high. Sears (1977) has written of the profound implications of the nonmedical use of Navy medical facilities.

Within the military, periods of separation from a spouse or parent represent a frequent and significant stress to the family (Abbe, Naylor, Gavin, & Shannon, 1986; Beckman, Marsella, & Finney, 1979; Isay, 1968; Nice, 1983; Peck, 1976). It is estimated that 245,000 children living in the United States have a parent serving in the military overseas; at least 50% of these are Navy dependents whose sponsors are on duty afloat (Strabstein, 1983). In a retrospective study of the wives of fleet ballistic missile submarine personnel, Snyder (1978) reported that wives recalled being far more ill and seeking more medical attention when their husbands were at sea than when they were at home. In a subsequent controlled study of Navy family separation and physician utilization, Nice (1980) found that during a 7-month deployment, separated and control wives did not differ on the number of symptoms, but separated wives visited the physician significantly more frequently. In a more recent cohort-controlled study of Navy family separation, Abbe and colleagues (Abbe, Naylor, Gavin, & Shannon, 1986) found that the total number of medical visits of separated wives was significantly increased only after their husbands' return. When only stress-related visits were considered, however, separated wives were seen more often both during the spouses' absence and after his return. Given the importance of continuity of care during stressful periods, such as family separation, and the high levels of Navy patient satisfaction with family practice physicians, priority admittance to family practice programs should be considered for families anticipating deployment separation (Nice, 1983).

Rehabilitation and Recovery

The importance of the family is particularly great in the rehabilitation and recovery of patients. As Levin and Idler (1981) point out, the most obvious contributions occur in the management of chronic diseases. They cite the efficacy of self-administered diabetes care as the classic example and also conclude that many other chronic conditions have been found to be not only amenable to self- or family care but significantly benefit by the involvement of the patient and family. In a retrospective study of patients who had a diagnosed cardiovascular accident with partial paralysis, Anderson and her colleagues concluded that, in the majority of cases, the education of the patient and his/her family was as important for maintaining the patient's rehabilitative status as was the use of public health nursing and community resources (Anderson, Anderson, & Kotke, 1977). Given that nearly 50% of our civilian population has one or more chronic diseases and a substantial proportion of the bedfast elderly live at home, support of the chronically ill has been identified as a normative family function (Levin & Idler, 1981; Pratt, 1976). In 1971, less than 5% of adults with chronic diseases were institutionalized (American Hospital Association, 1971). Although the dominant theories of family health behavior view the family as increasingly incompetent to cope effectively with illness of long duration without serious consequences of discordance, disaffectation, general deterioration of its integrity, and ultimate negative impact on the welfare of the chronically ill family member (Levin & Idler, 1981), this view has not received empirical support in the literature and remains an open question (Brown, Rawlinson, & Hardin, 1982).

Within the generally youthful active-duty military population, the rehabilitative and recovery role of the family may be more oriented toward injury- or combat-related disabilities. The psychological and physical residuals of war inexorably challenge the family's recuperative power and may exact a toll on the family's emotional reserve (Brende & Parson, 1985). Between 1965 and 1972, U.S. military forces suffered 303,598 injuries from enemy action in Vietnam (Johnson,

1980). Over half of these casualties required hospital care. The physical and psychological injuries incurred in this and other wars generally have been treated or tended to during the recovery or rehabilitation process within the family. This context provides continuity of care, a commitment that allows the individual to count on this support in interpreting the implications of the injury or disability, and the reassurance necessary to focus and sustain the patient's motivation for adaptation or recovery (Levin & Idler, 1981). Although this rehabilitation process, as well as the reintegration of combat veterans, may strain the family system, there appear to be no long-term adverse effects on marital functioning or dissolution (Call & Teachman, 1991; Card, 1983).

CONCLUSIONS

The military family has dramatic implications for military medicine. As military medicine approaches the challenges of the coming decade, the strategic plans and programs of the health care community are expected to become increasingly oriented toward a broader, more holistic perspective. Continuing demand in a scarce resource environment has placed enormous pressure on military medicine over the past decade. As demands for medical efficiency increase, there are potentially correlative increases in staff burnout and consumer dissatisfaction. Paradoxically, the pressures on the military health care system may be ultimately reduced by expanding its role to involve and influence the social structures mediating health behaviors and outcomes.

In areas of health promotion, self-care, and utilization decision processes, aggressive programs to involve, educate, and empower family members appear warranted. In recent years, the military has demonstrated great leadership in promoting health and physical readiness among its active-duty members. The expansion of these efforts to all beneficiary populations could generate a number of positive medical and personnel-related outcomes. As Williams (1973) noted, everybody knows that health begins at home, yet health care authorities, both national and international are slow to recognize this.

In the area of self-care, Levin and Idler (1981) note that since 1975 we have seen a wide range of diagnostic, monitoring, and treatment technology added to the traditional household standbys of thermometer, hot water bottle, and elastic bandage. In the diagnostic category, for example, new technology includes home throat cultures, diabetic self-monitoring, bowel cancer screening, detection of urinary tract infections, blood pressure monitoring, and pregnancy testing. A need exists to simplify medical technology further for home use and to educate consumers in its proper application.

The processes involved in the decision to seek medical care in the military are not well understood. However, interventions to modify the demand for medical services have been viewed as successful in HMOs by some in the private sector (Follett & Cummings, 1967; Goldberg, Krantz, & Locke, 1970; Jones & Vischi, 1979; Klerman et al., 1987; Rosen & Wiens, 1979) and may be appropriate for the fee-free military health care system. Given the multicultural, heterogeneous nature of medical beneficiaries in the military, initiatives to modify demand should be preceeded by a program of research to identify appropriate strategies. Approaches to contain costs through sensitizing consumers to health care costs have not always had the intended effect. In a study of cost sharing, competition-based cost containment strategies, Hibbard and Weeks (1987) reported:

> For those who are less able to determine when medical care is neces-
> sary, who do not pursue alternative sources of information on providers,
> diagnosis, and treatment, who do not know how to negotiate in the health
> care encounter, and who are not knowledgeable about the health care
> delivery system, the only choice may be to forego care or pay higher out-
> of-pocket costs. (p. 1020)

Thus, cost sharing may have serious adverse consequences for vulnerable sectors of the population (Lohr et al., 1986). Given the complexity of the determinants of utilization and the special characteristics of the military health care system and its beneficiaries, intervention strategies should be developed on a sound empirical basis.

Levin and Idler (1981) have identified networking as an effective method of integrating mediating structures such as the family into the health care process. They define networking as "putting community resources in touch with each other as a way of promoting their synergistic benefit to the community as a whole" (p. 254). Within the military context, networking should extend both vertically and horizontally. Many family issues can be best addressed through coordinated efforts of the medical and personnel communities, and many lessons can be shared between service branches.

When the organizational perspective on the active-duty service member is broadened to consider the individual realistically, within his/her fundamental social context, initiatives toward the involvement of families and family priorities in health care planning and other strategic processes appear well advised. The challenge for military medicine is to enjoin these family resources in the development of a fundamental paradigm shift toward wellness.

REFERENCES

Aaron, H. A., & Schwartz, W. B. (1990). Rationing health care: The choice before us. *Science, 247*(4941), 418–422.

Abbe, J. S., Naylor, G. S., Gavin, M., & Shannon, K. M. (1986). Temporary paternal absence and health care utilization: A cohort-controlled study. *Military Medicine, 151*(9), 469–472.

American Hospital Association. (1971). *Report of a conference on care of chronically ill adults.* Chicago: Author.

Anderson, E., Anderson, T. P., & Kotke, F. J. (1977). Stroke rehabilitation: Maintenance of achieved gains. *Archives of Physical Medicine and Rehabilitation, 58*, 353.

Baranowski, T., & Nader, P. R. (1985). Family involvement in health behavior change programs. In D. C. Turk & R. D. Kerns (Eds.), *Health, illness, and families: A life-span perspective* (pp. 81–107). New York: John Wiley & Sons.

Baric, L. (1979). Acquisition of the smoking habit. *Health Education Journal, 38*, 71–76.

Barrett-Connor, E., Suarez, L., & Criqui, M. H. (1982). A spouse concordance of plasma cholesterol and triglyceride. *Journal of Chronic Diseases, 35*, 333–340.

Barsky, A. J., Wyshak, G., & Klerman, G. L. (1986). Medical and psychiatric determinants of outpatient medical utilization. *Medical Care, 24*(6), 548–560.

Beans, H. C. (1975). Sex discrimination in the military. *Military Law Review, 67*, 19–83.

Beckman, K., Marsella, A. J., & Finney, R. (1979). Depression in the wives of nuclear submarine personnel. *American Journal of Psychiatry, 136*, 524–526.

Berkanovic, E., Hurwicz, M., & Landsverk, J. (1988). Psychological distress and the decision to seek medical care. *Social Science and Medicine, 27*(11), 1215–1221.

Berkman, L. F., & Syme, S. L. (1979). Social networks, host resistance and mortality: A nine-year follow-up study of Alameda County residents. *American Journal of Epidemiology, 109*, 186–204.

Blackburn, H., & Gillum, R. (1980). Heart disease. In J. M. Last (Ed.), *Maxcy-Rosenau Public Health and Preventive Medicine* (p. 1168). New York: Appleton-Century-Crofts.

Bloom, J. (1982). Social support, accommodation to stress, and adjustment to breast cancer. *Social Science and Medicine, 16A*, 1329–1338.

Bray, R. M., Marsden, M. E., Guess, L. L., Wheeless, S. C., Iannacchione, V. G., & Keesling, S. R. (1988). *1988 worldwide survey of substance abuse and health behaviors among military personnel* (Contract No. MDA903-87-C-0854). Research Triangle Park, NC: Research Triangle Institute.

Brende, J. O., & Parson, E. R. (1985). *Vietnam veterans: The road to recovery.* New York: Plenum Press.

Brown, J. S., Rawlinson, M. E., & Hardin, D. M. (1982). Family functioning and health status. *Journal of Family Issues, 3*(1), 91–110.

Bryan, M. S., & Lowenberg, M. E. (1958). The fathers' influence on young children's food preferences. *Journal of the American Dietetic Association, 34,* 30–35.

Butler, N., & Alberman, E. (Eds.) (1969). *Perinatal problems: Second report of the 1958 British perinatal mortality survey.* Edinburgh: Churchill Livingstone.

Butler, N., & Golding, J. (1986). *From birth to five.* Oxford: Pergamon Press.

Call, V. R. A., & Teachman, J. D. (1991). Military service and stability in the family life course. *Military Psychology, 3*(4), 233–250.

Card, J. (1983). *Lives after Vietnam: The personal impact of military service.* Lexington, MA: D. C. Heath.

Carmichael, L. P. (1976). The family in medicine: Process or entity? *Journal of Family Practice, 3,* 562–571.

Cassel, J. (1974). An epidemiological perspective of psychosocial factors in disease etiology. *American Journal of Public Health, 64,* 1040–1043.

Cassel, J. (1976). The contribution of the social environment to host resistance. *American Journal of Epidemiology, 104,* 107–123.

Charlton, A. (1986). Children who smoke. *Health School, 1,* 125–127.

Cobb, S. (1979). Social support and health through the life course. In M. W. Riley (Ed.), *Aging from birth to death: Interdisciplinary perspectives.* Washington, DC: American Association for the Advancement of Science.

Collyer, J. A. (1979). Psychosomatic illness in a solo family practice. *Psychosomatics, 20,* 762.

Cummings, N. A., & Follette, W. T. (1976). Brief psychotherapy and medical utilization. In H. Darken (Ed.), *The professional psychologist today: New developments in law, health insurance, and health practice.* San Francisco: Jossey-Bass.

Dean, K. (1986). Lay care in illness. *Social Science and Medicine, 22*(2), 275–284.

DiMatteo, M. R., & Hays, R. (1981). Social support and serious illness. In B. H. Gottlieb (Ed.), *Social networks and social support.* Beverly Hills, CA: Sage.

Department of Defense. (1986). *Health promotion* (DoD Directive No. 1010.10). Washington, DC: Author.

Downes, J. (1947). Chronic illness among spouses. *Milbank Memorial Fund Quarterly Bulletin, 25,* 334.

Eastman, E., Archer, R. P., Ball, J. D. (1990). Psychosocial and life stress characteristics of Navy families: Family environment scale and life experiences scale findings. *Military Psychology, 2*(2), 113–127.

Fogelman, K. (1980). Smoking in pregnancy and subsequent development of the child. *Child Care Health Developmental, 6,* 233–249.

Follett, W., & Cummings, N. A. (1967). Psychiatric services and medical utilization in a prepaid health plan setting. *Medical Care, 5,* 25–35.

Foreyt, J. P., Goodrick, G. K., & Gotto, A. M. (1981). Limitation of behavioral treatment of obesity: Review and analysis. *Behavioral Medicine, 4,* 159–174.

Fox, J. P., & Hall, L. E. (1972). Continuing surveillance of families for studying the epidemiology of viral infection. *International Journal of Epidemiology, 17*(1), 31.

Garfield, S. R., Collen, M. F., Feldman, R., Soghikian, K., Richart, R. H., & Duncan, J. H. (1976). Evaluation of an ambulatory medical care delivery system. *New England Journal of Medicine, 294,* 426.

Garn, S. M., & Clark, D. C. (1976). Trends in fatness and the origins of obesity. *Pediatrics, 57,* 443.

Garn, S. M., Cole, P. E., & Bailey, S. M. (1976). Effect of parental fatness levels on the fatness of biological and adoptive children. *Ecology of Food and Nutrition, 6,* 1–3.

Garrett, G. R., Parker, B., Day, S., Van Meter, J. J., & Cosby, W. (1978). Drinking and the military wife: A study of married women in overseas base communities. In E. J. Hunter & D. S. Nice (Eds.), *Military families: Adaptation to change* (pp. 222–237). New York: Praeger.

Glueck, C. J., Laskarszewski, P. M., Rao, D. C., & Morrison, J. A. (1986). Familial aggregation of coronary risk factors. In W. Connor & D. Bristow (Eds.), *Complications in coronary heart disease.* Philadelphia: Lippincott.

Goldberg, J. D., Krantz, G., & Locke, B. Z. (1970). Effect of a short-term outpatient psychiatric therapy benefit on the utilization of medical services in a prepaid group practice medical program. *Medical Care, 8,* 419–428.

Gore, S. (1978). The effect of social support in moderating the health consequences of unemployment. *Journal of Health and Social Behavior, 19,* 157–165.

Graham, H. (1987). Women's smoking and family health. *Social Science and Medicine, 25*(1), 47–56.

Graham-Smith, D. (1975). Self-medication with mood-changing drugs. *Journal of Medical Ethics, 1,* 132.

Haggerty, R. J., & Alpert, J. J. (1963). The child, his family and illness. *Postgraduate Medicine, 34,* 228.

Hibbard, J. H., & Weeks, E. C. (1987). Consumerism in health care: Prevalence and predictors. *Medical Care, 25*(11), 1019–1032.

Hingson, R., Scotch, N. A., Sorenson, J., & Swazey, J. P. (1981). *In sickness and in health: Social dimensions of medical care.* St. Louis: C. V. Mosby.

Hosek, S., Anderson, M., Dixon, L., Thomas, N., Zwanziger, J., Blake, D., Polich, S., Rahman, A., & Bamezai, A. (1990). *Preliminary results from an evaluation of the CHAMPUS reform initiative* (Contract No. MDA903-85-C-0030). Santa Monica, CA: The Rand Corporation.

Hunter, E. (1982). *Families under the flag: A review of military family literature.* New York: Praeger.

Hunter, E. J. (1984). Treating the military captive's family. In F. W. Kaslow & R. I. Ridenour (Eds.), *The military family: Dynamics and treatment* (pp. 167–196). New York: Guilford Press.

Hunter, E. J., & Nice, D. S. (Eds.). (1978a). *Children of military families: A part and yet apart.* Washington, DC: U.S. Government Printing Office.

Hunter, E. J., & Nice, D. S. (Eds.). (1978b). *Military families: Adaptation to change.* New York: Praeger.

Isay, R. A. (1968). The submariners' wives syndrome. *Psychiatric Quarterly, 42,* 647–652.

Jacobson, B. (1981). *The ladykillers: Why smoking is a feminist issue.* London: Pluto Press.

Janz, N. K., & Becker, M. H. (1984). The health belief model: A decade later. *Health Education Quarterly, 11*(1), 1–47.

Jensen, P. S., Lewis, R. L., & Xenakis, S. N. (1986). The military family in review: Context, risk, and prevention. *Journal of the American Academy of Child Psychiatry, 25,* 225–234.

Johnson, L. (1980). Scars of war: Alienation and estrangement among wounded Vietnam veterans. In C. R. Figley & S. Leventman (Eds.), *Strangers at home: Vietnam veterans since the war* (pp. 213–227). New York: Praeger.

Johnson, T. A., Jr., & Eakin, K. M. (1983). Health maintenance and screening. In R. B. Taylor (Ed.), *Fundamentals of family medicine* (pp. 295–319). New York: Springer-Verlag.

Jones, K. R., & Vischi, T. R. (1979). Impact of alcohol, drug abuse and mental health treatment on medical care utilization. *Medical Care, 17*(12), 1–81.

Kalmar, V. (1979). An integrative summary. In D. A. Hamburg (Ed.), *Healthy people: The surgeon general's report on health promotion and disease prevention background papers, 1979.* Washington, DC: U.S. Government Printing Office.

Kaslow, F. W., & Ridenour, R. I. (Eds.). (1984). *The military family: Dynamics and treatment.* New York: Guilford Press.

Klerman, G. L., Budman, S., Berwick, D., Weissman, M. M., Damico-White, J., Demby, A., & Feldstein, M. (1987). Efficacy of a brief psychosocial intervention for symptoms of stress and distress among patients in primary care. *Medical Care, 25*(11), 1078–1088.

Kohen, J. A. (1984). The military career is a family affair. *Journal of Family Issues, 5*(3), 401–418.

Kolb, D., & Gunderson, E. K. E. (1985). Research on alcohol abuse and rehabilitation in the U.S. Navy. In M. A. Schuckit (Ed.), *Alcohol patterns and problems* (pp. 157–177). New Brunswick, NJ: Rutgers University Press.

Levin, L. S., & Idler, E. L. (1981). *The hidden health care system: Mediating structures and medicine.* Cambridge, MA: Ballinger.

Lichtenstein, E., Glasgow, R. E., & Abrams, D. B. (1986). Social support in smoking cessation: In search of effective interventions. *Behavior Therapy, 17,* 607–619.

Litman, T. J. (1974). The family as a basic unit in health and medical care: A social-behavioral overview. *Social Science and Medicine, 8,* 495–519.

Lohr, K. N., Brook, R. H., Kamberg, C. J., Goldberg, G. A., Leibowitz, A., Keesey, J., Reboussin, D., & Newhouse, J. P. (1986). Use of medical care in the Rand health insurance experiment: Diagnosis and service specific analyses in a randomized controlled trial. *Medical Care, 24,* 75.

Maiman, L. A., Becker, M. H., Cummings, K. M., Drachman, R. H., & O'Connor,

P. A. (1982). Effects of sociodemographic and attitudinal factors on mother-initiated medication behavior for children. *Public Health Reports, 97*, 140–149.

Maiman, L. A., Becker, M. H., & Katlic, A. W. (1986). Correlates of mothers' use of medications for their children. *Social Science and Medicine, 22*(1), 41–51.

Manning, P. K., & Fabrega, H. (1973). The experience of self and body: Health and illness in the Chiapas Highlands. In G. Psathas (Ed.), *Phenomenological sociology* (p. 283). New York: John Wiley and Sons.

McCubbin, H. I. (1979). Integrating coping behavior in family stress theory. *Journal of Marriage and the Family, 41*, 237–243.

McCubbin, H. I., Dahl, B., Lester, G., Benson, D., & Robertson, M. L. (1975). *Coping repertoires of families adapting to prolonged war-induced separations* (Report No. 75-56). San Diego, CA: Naval Health Research Center.

McCubbin, H. I., Hunter, E. J., & Metres, P. J., Jr. (1974). Children in limbo. In H. McCubbin, B. Dahl, P. Metres, Jr., E. Hunter, & J. Plag (Eds.), *Family separation and reunion: Families of prisoners of war and servicemen missing in action.* Washington, DC: U.S. Government Printing Office.

McDavid, P. T. (1990). *CHAMPUS chartbook of statistics* (5400.2-CB). Aurora, CO: Information Systems Division, Statistics Branch.

Meyer, R. J., & Haggerty, R. J. (1962). Streptococcal infections in families: Factors altering individual susceptibility. *Pediatrics, 29*, 539.

Minuchin, S. (1974). *Families and family therapy.* Cambridge, MA: Harvard University Press.

Moos, R. H. (1985). Creating healthy human contexts: Environmental and individual strategies. In J. C. Rosen & L. J. Solomon (Eds.), *Prevention in health psychology* (pp. 366–389). Hanover, NH: University Press of New England.

Nice, D. S. (1980). *Navy family separation and physician utilization* (Report No. 80-34). San Diego, CA: Naval Health Research Center.

Nice, D. S. (1982). *The contribution of social and emotional factors to the utilization of navy outpatient medical facilities* (Report No. 82-4). San Diego, CA: Naval Health Research Center.

Nice, D. S. (1983). The course of depressive affect in navy wives during family separation. *Military Medicine, 148*(4), 341–343.

Nice, D. S., McDonald, B., & McMillian, T. (1981). The families of Vietnam POWs five years after reunion. *Journal of Marriage and the Family, 43*(2), 432–437.

Nice, D. S., & Woodruff, S. (1990). Self-selection in responding to a health risk appraisal: Are we preaching to the choir? *American Journal of Health Promotion, 4*(5), 367–372.

Nolte, A. E., Smith, B. J., & O'Rourke, T. (1983). The relative importance of parental attitudes and behavior upon youth smoking behavior. *Journal of School Health, 53*, 264–271.

Nuckolls, K. B., Cassel, J., & Kaplan, B. H. (1972). Psychosocial assets, life crisis, and the prognosis of pregnancy. *American Journal of Epidemiology, 95*, 431–441.

Peck, B. B. (1976). Psychotherapy with the father-absent military family. *Journal of Marriage and Family Counseling, 2*, 23–31.

Perrier Corp. (1979). *Fitness in America. The Perrier study.* Great Waters, NY: Author.

Peters, T., Golding, J., Butler, N., Fryer, J., Lawrence, C., & Chamberlain, G. (1983). Plus ca change: Predictors of birthweight in two national studies. *British Journal of Obstetrics and Gynecology, 90,* 1040–1045.

Picken, I. B., & Ireland, G. (1969). Family patterns of medical care utilization. *Journal of Chronic Diseases, 22,* 181–191.

Popham, R. E., Schmidt, W., & Israelstam, S. (1985). Heavy alcohol consumption and physical health problems: A review of the epidemiologic evidence. In M. A. Schuckit (Ed.), *Alcohol patterns and problems* (pp. 203–245). New Brunswick, NJ: Rutgers University Press.

Potter, M. (1990). Military dependent medical care during World War II. *Military Medicine, 155*(2), 45–47.

Pratt, L. (1976). *Family structure and effective health behavior: The energized family.* Boston: Houghton-Mifflin.

Rawbone, R., Keeling, C., Jenkins, A., & Guz, A. (1979). Cigarette smoking among secondary school children in 1975: Its prevalence and some of the factors that promote smoking. *Health Education Journal, 39,* 92–99.

Rodriguez, A. R. (1984). Special treatment needs of children of military families. In F. W. Kaslow & R. I. Ridenour (Eds.), *The military family: Dynamics and treatment* (pp. 46–72). New York: Guilford Press.

Rogers, R. G., & Powell-Griner, E. (1991). Life expectancies of cigarette smokers and nonsmokers in the United States. *Social Science and Medicine, 32*(10), 1151–1159.

Roghmann, K. J., & Haggerty, R. J. (1972). Family stress and the use of health services. *International Journal of Epidemiology, 1*(3), 279–286.

Rosen, J. C., & Wiens, A. N. (1979). Changes in medical problems and use of medical services following psychological intervention. *American Psychologist, 34*(5), 420–431.

Rosenstock, I. M. (1974). Historical origins of the health belief model. *Health Education Monographs, 2,* 332.

Sarason, I. G. (1988). Social support, personality, and health. In M. P. Janisse (Ed.), *Individual differences, stress, and health psychology* (pp. 109–128). New York: Springer-Verlag.

Schor, E., Starfield, B., Stidley, C., & Hankin, J. (1987). Family health: Utilization and effects of family membership. *Medical Care, 25*(7), 616–626.

Sears, H. J. (1977). Radical approach to health care delivery. *U.S. Navy Medicine, 68,* 15–16.

Selye, H. (1976). *The stress of life* (rev. ed.). New York: McGraw-Hill.

Shapiro, J. (1983). Family reactions and coping strategies in response to the physically ill or handicapped child: A review. *Social Science and Medicine, 17,* 913–931.

Snyder, A. I. (1978). Periodic marital separation and physical illness. *American Journal of Orthopsychiatry, 48,* 637–643.

Strabstein, J. (1983). Geographic distribution of military dependent children: Mental health sources needed. *Military Medicine, 148,* 127–132.

Streissguth, A. P., & Little, R. E. (1985). Alcohol-related morbidity and mortality in offspring of drinking women: Methodologic issues and a review of pertinent studies. In M. A. Schuckit (Ed.), *Alcohol patterns and problems* (pp. 113–155). New Brunswick, NJ: Rutgers University Press.

Stumpf, S. S. (1978). Military family attitudes toward housing, benefits, and the quality of military life. In E. J. Hunter & D. S. Nice (Eds.), *Military families: Adaptation to change* (pp. 3–16). New York: Praeger.

Stunkard, A. J., Felix, M. R. J., & Cohen, R. Y. (1985). Mobilizing a community to promote health: The Pennsylvania County Health Improvement Program (CHIP). In J. C. Rosen & L. J. Solomon (Eds.), *Prevention in health psychology* (pp. 143–190). Hanover, NH: University Press of New England.

Tennant, F. S., & Detels, R. (1976). Relationship of alcohol, cigarette and drug abuse in adulthood with alcohol, cigarette and coffee consumption in childhood. *Preventive Medicine, 5,* 70–71.

Thompson, R. S., Michnich, M. E., Friedlander, L., Gilson, B., Grothaus, L. C., & Storer, B. (1988). Effectiveness of smoking cessation interventions integrated into primary care practice. *Medical Care, 26*(1), 62–76.

Thorner, R. M. (1978). The use of health services by civilian beneficiaries of the military health care system: A comparative study. *Medical Care, 16*(4), 267–288.

Turk, D. C., & Kerns, R. D. (Eds.). (1985). *Health, illness, and families: A lifespan perspective.* New York: John Wiley & Sons.

U.S. Department of Health and Human Services. (1989). *Reducing the health consequences of smoking: 25 years of progress. A report of the surgeon general* (DHSS Publication No. CDC 89-8411). Rockville, MD: Author.

Venters, M. H. (1989). Family-oriented prevention of cardiovascular disease: A social epidemiological approach. *Social Science and Medicine, 28*(4), 309–314.

Venters, M. H., Jacobs, D. R., Luepker, R. V., Maiman, L. A., & Gillum, R. F. (1984). Spouse concordance of smoking patterns: The Minnesota heart survey. *American Journal of Epidemiology, 120,* 608.

Venters, M., Jacobs, D., Pirie, P., Luepker, R., Folsom, A., & Gillum, R. (1986). Marital status and cardiovascular risk: The Minnesota heart survey and the Minnesota heart health program. *Preventive Medicine, 15,* 591.

Weiss, R. S. (1974). The provisions of social relationships. In Z. Rubin (Ed.), *Doing unto others* (pp. 17–26). Englewood Cliffs, NJ: Prentice-Hall.

Wilkinson, I. F., Darby, D. N., & Mant, A. (1987). Self-care and self-medication: An evaluation of individuals' health care decisions. *Medical Care, 25*(10), 965–978.

Williams, C. D. (1973). Health begins at home: Reflections on the theme of W.H.O. Day. *Journal of Tropical Medicine, 76*(7), 210.

Williams, T. G. (1984). Substance misuse and alcoholism in the military family. In F. W. Kaslow & R. I. Ridenour (Eds.), *The military family* (pp. 73–97). New York: Guilford Press.

CHAPTER ELEVEN

Military Retirement in the Post-Cold War Era

Rex A. Frank, PhD

A COLLEAGUE RECENTLY TOLD ME ABOUT THE RETIREMENT PARTY FOR AN AIR Force colonel. At the peak of his career, this 51-year-old officer had managed a budget in the hundreds of millions and held authority over thousands of men and women. He had flown numerous combat missions in sophisticated, multimillion-dollar jets. As his car exited the gate of the base he had commanded, his head hung and a wistful sadness was in his eyes. He and his wife were returning to the Midwest, where they still owned a home they had briefly lived in years before. Now he had no job. He seemed to have been waiting for someone to come to *him,* but no one had come. What job could possibly compete for his interest with the position he was leaving behind? At some level he was aware that no corporate giant was looking for a CEO with no business experience at age 51. But he had been unable to lower himself actually to apply or *look* for a position for which he might qualify. He couldn't envision himself selling insurance or preparing tax returns. To all the world he appeared as a man who had lost his dearest friend.

In this chapter I hope to provide a glimpse into the world of the military retiree and the career factors that can enhance or detract from the approach to a new, civilian life. Some of these elements are the product of changes in world politics during the 1990s. Others are peculiar to the environment in which the soldier and family live and work during an active career. Finally, there are suggestions for professionals who assist military members and families to prepare for or deal with the consequences of retirement.

THE 1980s AND 1990s

From the close of the Vietnam era to the onset of Operation Desert Shield, professional military men and women have enjoyed the appearance of security generated by a peacetime military. Brief surges like Operation Just Cause reminded us that we were to be ready to move at a moment's notice. But we took comfort in the fact that the budget wouldn't permit moves for the sake of moving. Desert Storm taught us that some of the all-volunteer force enlisted to enhance education, to gain steady employment, or to achieve security, never remotely believing that we would again go to war. The political and economic forces that made military service attractive to the new volunteer in the 1970s and 1980s also impacted on the decision of the post-Vietnam veteran to remain on active duty until eligible for retirement. Jensen, Lewis, and Xenakis (1986), who report that "military families do not experience unemployment," seem to give credence to the idea of peacetime security. The retiree of the 1990s is likely to have seen little warfare. He, and evermore frequently she, will have been a midlevel manager of people, systems, equipment, supplies, or money.

Contrary to the observation of Jensen et al. (1986), the *threat* of unemployment has always existed for military men and women. Timing of retirement may be a function of factors beyond the control of the service member. Involuntary separation *before* retirement can result from a formal reduction in force (RIF) or for administrative reasons. In 1992 there was a groundswell of change focused on reductions throughout the Department of Defense (DoD). Reverberations from the end of the cold war and decomposition of the Soviet Union are being felt by members of the military services. Some 229,000 personnel with between 15 and 20 years of service are expected to be forced out of the Air Force with current reduction programs (West, 1992a). Military personnel are no longer protected from economic recession.

Similar cuts occurred following the end of the Vietnam War. However, many career personnel felt at ease with those cuts because they were based on performance. Those with good records were unconcerned. The cold war was still on; there was little risk of combat after Vietnam; careers could continue unimpeded. In late 1991 all of that changed. Within the Air Force, for example, the demise of the Strategic Air Command eliminated a host of jobs filled by quality personnel. With little notice, colonels were advised that a Selective Early Retirement Board (SERB) would be convened in January 1992 to impose early retirement on as many as 25% of them. The *criteria* for selection *were not* announced, but the writing was on the wall. Performance *was not* going to be the only criterion. Those without firm job positions at the time SERB convened would likely be retired within as little as 210 days of selection. In fact, 610 of the 2,086 colonels considered were selected for early retirement—more than 29%; 369, or 30%, of the lieutenant colonels considered were selected by this board (West, 1992b). One of my family members, caught in the draw-down, expected to complete 30 years of service but in 1991 *volunteered* for early retirement with less than 25 years rather than risk being snagged by the SERB.

Elimination or consolidation of units created wholesale early release of enlisted personnel, too. By March 1992, almost 12,000 applications for early separation with severance pay had been approved by the Air Force (West, 1992a). April headlines in military newspapers threatened a RIF. Sufficient numbers of officers had not volunteered to separate before retirement and large numbers were projected to be involuntarily separated. The *Air Force Times* (Maze, 1992a) also reported DoD's rejection of a 15-year retirement program designed to temporarily speed the process of what had euphemistically been labeled as *right sizing* the military services. This term, *right sizing,* naturally led to the tongue-in-cheek question of whether we had been previously *wrong sized.* A popular joke of this time held that Under Chief of Staff General Merrill A. McPeak's command, the Air Force crest had been modified to include two golden arches and the motto "Over one million SERB'd." At least one proposal (Maze, 1992b) has supported an additional cut 200,000 military members beyond the presently expected 500,000 by 1997. For the thousands being *involuntarily* retired there has been little planning, anticipation, or preparation.

Some studies (McBride, 1976; Palmore, Fillenbaum, & George, 1984; Wan, 1982) have suggested that retirement, as an event is not significantly stressful. However, a broad range of reports (Berkey & Stoebner, 1968; Biderman, 1964; Druss, 1965; Greenberg, 1965; Hamrick, 1989; McNeil & Giffen, 1965, 1967; Milowe, 1964) have held that military retirement differs substantially from civilian retirement. Geopolitical shock, high-tech warfare, DoD budget cutbacks, economic uncertainties, and social change all impact on the professional soldier's preparation for retirement.

WHO AND WHERE ARE MILITARY RETIREES?

Military retirees are often invisible to those around them. Nothing distinguishes them from others, except as they are willing to relate their past histories. Over 1.5 million military retirees are distributed throughout the U.S. and overseas (DoD Statistical Report on the Military Retirement System, 1991). Perhaps because of some benefits of retirement, certain states have greater concentrations of retired military personnel. Figure 11.1, shows the numbers of military retirees living in the 10 states with the greatest concentrations.

San Antonio, Texas, where there are five military installations and two major military medical centers, has the single highest concentration of retired military personnel in the country, more than 28,000. The combined annual retired pay of the San Antonio group totals more than $464 million.

DIFFERENCES BETWEEN MILITARY AND CIVILIAN RETIREMENT

Existing models of retirement, such as that of Nowak and Brice (1984), are inadequate to describe the military retiree's situation. Though some aspects of Nowak's model, such as the concept of retirement adapta-

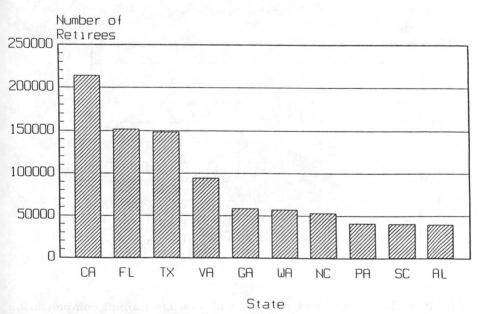

Figure 11.1. Top ten military retirement states.

tion as a complex and dynamic process, do apply to the military, civilian models do not address the almost universal necessity for a second career for the retired soldier. The term *retirement* may be misleading when applied to military personnel. Those who provide care for career service personnel can benefit from understanding the soldier's world as he or she approaches the completion of a career.

Age at Retirement

Job security aside, those who reach retirement from military service do so 15 to 25 years earlier than civilians. As shown in Figure 11.2, more than half of retired enlisted personnel are younger than 65.

For most soldiers, retirement occurs during their years of greatest productivity. Often the retiree's children are in late adolescence at the time of this family transition. Shaw (1987), in reflecting on the retiree's age and that of the children, pointed out that "just as the adolescent is struggling to resolve his own identity conflicts, he may also encounter a father who is experiencing uncertainty in his own social, economic, and occupational identity" (p. 544). Figure 11.3 shows that a higher percentage of officers retire when slightly older. Figure 11.4 reflects the actual age of the service members at retirement.

Thurnher (1976) found that in nonmilitary families middle-aged women gave less positive evaluations of marriage than did newlyweds

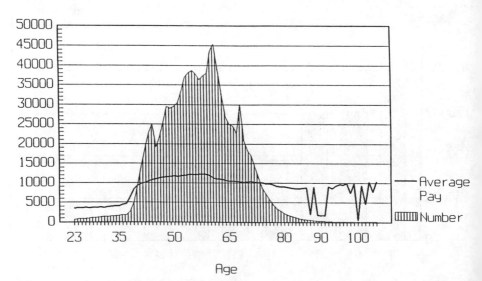

Figure 11.2. Numbers of retirees and average annual compensation (enlisted only, FY 1990).

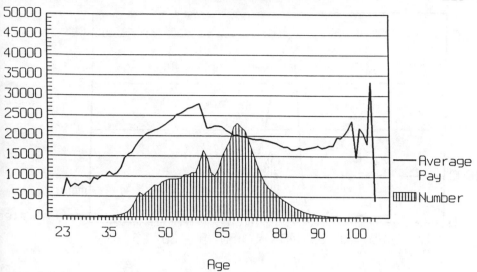

Figure 11.3. Numbers of retirees and average annual compensation (officers only, FY 1990).

or those approaching retirement age. Spouse's low satisfaction, identity conflicts of children, and financial crises are likely to place the military man's family at higher risk. Larkin's (1983) work, showing a higher frequency of medical visits for military families approaching retirement, appears to bear this out.

Officer and Enlisted Retirees

As shown in Figure 11.4, peak retirement ages differed for officers and enlisted personnel in fiscal year (FY) 1990, reflecting the later age of service entry for officers. Average retired pay for enlisted personnel (Figure 11.2) hovers at about $12,000 per year. Retired officers have a higher retirement income, but officers' pay is not as balanced across age groups as that of enlisted personnel. The average officer's peak pay is reached at about age 58 and approaches roughly $28,000.

Fuller and Redfering (1976) reported that enlisted personnel are more likely than officers to find their choice of a second career commensurate with their military duties because officers rarely move into high civilian managerial positions. Conversely, the adjustments made by one enlisted friend of mine who recently retired, illustrate the drastic shifts many retirees face. Initially trained as an administrative specialist, during his career he cross-trained to become a mental health technician. Like many military mental health technicians, he devel-

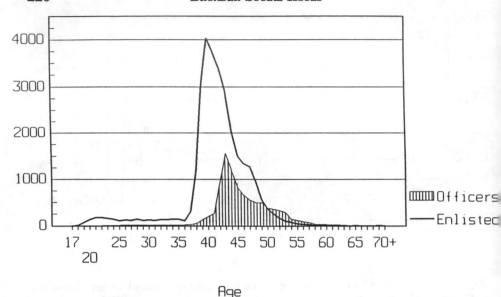

Figure 11.4. Age of personnel retired in FY 1990: all retirees, including disability, excluding reserves.

oped skills in psychological testing, office and personnel management, budgeting, and supervision and training of subordinates. Nonetheless, upon retirement he returned to the family tradition of farming, where few of his military skills were transferable.

Though Fuller and Redfering found no relationship between rank and adjustment to retirement, Berkey and Stoebner (1968) pointed out elements of the *retirement syndrome,* which they found peculiar to officers. The foremost of these was rank. They state:

> Reaching the rank of full colonel or higher is generally accepted as having achieved success in a military career. To the officers seen, retirement as a lieutenant colonel (or lower rank) was tantamount to being a vice president but not the president; the understudy but not the star. Being not as good as the next man; having some inner defect: these were the feelings conveyed by officers who had failed to attain a higher rank. Ballooning of such feelings occurs near the time of retirement as one reexamines one's past and present and looks toward the future. (p. 7)

The retirement syndrome was initially labeled by McNeil and Giffen (1967) in a study that did not differentiate officers from enlisted retirees. The reports of Bellino (1969), Biderman (1964), Druss (1965), Greenberg (1965), and Milowe (1964) all focused on problems associated with the retirement of enlisted personnel, including somatic complaints, loss of security, decreased self-worth, foreboding of loss, and a confrontation with one's own aging process (Berkey & Stoebner, 1968). This suggests that the syndrome exists for both officers and enlisted retirees.

Years with the Company

Until recently the military environment has been one in which the professional expected to remain with the *company* for 20 or more years. Company switching, golden parachutes, and the like have never been part of the military. Twenty years of success within the military system develops some coping strengths that are useful in the civilian world and others that are likely to conflict with it.

Early retirement for a civilian is often the product of a decision by the worker. For civil service employees, Schmitt and McCune (1981) found job attitude and financial variables significantly related to the decision to retire early, before the age of 70 years. Adequacy of retirement income played a major role in these early retirement decisions. Those less satisfied with work retired earlier if their income permitted. Berkey and Stoebner (1968) similarly reported "annihilation of the driving spirit to remain on active duty" and "embitterment and hurt" in retiring officers who had not been promoted to the rank of colonel.

Enforced early retirement in the military also can result from ill health or failure to be promoted. Early retirement negatively impacts on the adjustment to the retired role as a function of both its involuntary nature and poor health or lower than expected income (Beck, 1982; Kimmel, Price, & Walker, 1978; Portnoi, 1983; Sweet, Stoler, Kelter, & Thurrell, 1989). Similarly, Knippa (1979) found involuntary military retirees were less satisfied with life than were those who retired voluntarily. This might give the false impression that military retirees adapt poorly. The work of Houghton (1987) showed that retired officers were more highly educated than the average American, had a higher income than their age-equivalent peers, and average life satisfaction scores were higher than a national sample matched for age, socioeconomic status, and ethnicity. Houghton also found retired officers mean body age was 6.4 years younger than their birth age. Men who worked more years after retirement from the military had younger body ages than those who worked fewer years until full retirement.

Selection of Retirement Location

Though moving is commonplace for the civilian worker, the *decision* to move is often an active choice for him or her. Moving is rarely an active choice for the soldier, sailor, or marine. The location in which the retiring service member finds him or herself may be based entirely on personnel policy and timing. Last year one colleague found his retirement orders canceled less than a month before they were to take effect. He replanned his retirement from Saudi Arabia during Operation Desert Storm. My own retirement process also illustrates this point. In 1986 my scheduled return to the United States from Germany was delayed by 3 months because of DoD budget cuts. I had identified 13 possible locations to which I preferred assignment before retirement. Texas was not among them, though that is where I was eventually sent. Further DoD cuts led to longer assignments, and I remained in Texas until 1992. Because I am licensed in Florida, I had anticipated returning there for my second career. Recession and job uncertainties, combined with the expected income reduction from retirement, gave me pause to seriously consider the risk of a new beginning without a firm position. Job hunting cross-country was complicated, and the prospects for selling my home in a buyer's market were poor. My reluctant decision to remain in Texas required relicensing and rethinking my retirement goals. Years before I had carefully considered what quality of life I wanted in retirement and where this could be achieved and had planned for the specific date of retirement with Florida firmly in mind. My terminal assignment, however, was the principal determinant of my decision to retire in Texas. Many military families face considerable stress at retirement because they are located far from where they wish to reside.

The services provide the retiree a benefit our civilian counterparts often do not enjoy: movement to the designated place of retirement. What the service does not provide is the ability to sell one's home or the opportunity to readily scour the job market in another state. The benefit offers the fantasy that one can indeed go where one would like. The fantasy may run up hard against reality, unless the family has established a "beachhead" in this spot. A retiree needs family, friends, or a firm job in place if the move is to become reality. In dual-profession couples the number of complications in retiring to a distant location escalates dramatically.

Compensation and a Second Career

Military retirement compensation is rarely perceived by the recipient as a sufficient amount on which to live. Dunning and Biderman (1973) report that the relation of military retirement income to civilian needs often makes the choice of a subsequent civilian career a necessity.

There are three distinct retirement compensation formulas within the present military retirement system. Those who joined before September 8, 1980, are entitled to pay equal to terminal basic pay times a multiplier equal to 2.5% times the number of years of service, limited to a maximum of 75%. For those entering after September 7, 1980, the *average* of the highest 36 months of basic pay is used instead of terminal basic pay. Members entering on or after August 1, 1986, are subject to a penalty if they retire with less than 30 years. At age 62, their retired pay will be recomputed without the penalty. Until the year 2000, retirees who complete 20 to 30 years service receive between 50% and 75% of their final base pay as their deferred compensation.

The FY 1991 DoD *Statistical Report on the Military Retirement System* reflects that the highest-paid military retirees (four-star rank) receive gross annual pay of approximately $70,000, while the lowest-paid retiree receives about $4200. Garber (1971) summarized findings of a study that illustrate the need for additional employment. In the sample of 2,878 personnel who retired in May 1964, 93% were employed 1 year after retirement, 4% were still seeking employment, 1% were about to begin, and only 1% to 2% had given up looking for work.

Continued Benefits

One of the enticements for a military career has been the continuation of many benefits following retirement. Recreation services provide swimming pools, golf courses, entertainment tickets, rental equipment, and so on, at low prices. Retirees are also eligible for space-available travel on military aircraft.

Commissary and exchange benefits follow the career soldier into retirement. The exchange functions as a post or base department store, offering everything from stereo equipment to hardware free of tax and often at lower prices than in the local community. The commissary is a grocery store and typically offers better value than does the exchange. For example, at the time of this writing a carton of cigarettes in a grocery store costs approximately $22. In the commissary, a carton of generic, untaxed cigarettes may cost as little as $3.50. Such savings can be translated into cash or a much more luxurious menu, raising the standard of living. On the day of my own retirement I joked with colleagues that I knew I had joined the ranks of the retirees because I was on my way to the commissary to stand in line on a weekday morning.

Freely available medical care during the active-duty career forms an umbrella that shields the military family from escalating medical costs.

Later, the retiree and eligible family members retain access to medical benefits on a space-available basis. The space-available caveat, however, makes access to medical care questionable. Recently, in the medical center in which I practiced, I bumped into a retired chaplain I had not seen in a decade. He seemed much older than I remembered him, and explained that he had developed cancer some years before. He was irritated because his physician had told him to return in 2 weeks, but he had been told on the appointment line that the next available appointment was 6 months in the future.

When care is available and accessible, it is potentially the most valuable advantage of a military career. Military personnel and organizations that represent retired military men and women have been concerned for decades about the erosion of benefits at retirement. Paramount among these, in light of the dizzying heights of medical care and insurance costs, is the medical benefit. The fact that medical care is provided on a space-available basis does not diminish the often-held feeling that medical care is an *earned right* in retirement. Umbrella care during active-service years may also generate distrust of civilian medical care or discomfort in navigating that system. In my own military practice I often listened to a retiree or family member explain that they didn't want civilian care, though they could afford it, because "all they're interested in is money" or "I've always gotten better care from the military."

Some aspects of military health care, like emergency room services, are easier to access than others. The hospital pharmacy is available, even if a physician may not be. The retiree can have a prescription filled, though written by a civilian physician. With rising drug expenses, the pharmacy can provide substantial savings. However, because smaller military hospitals do not stock more esoteric or costly medications, if one does not live near a major medical center, pharmacy benefits may be of little value.

Availability of services has spawned retirement communities around large installations where the benefits are to be found. Base closings initiated in 1991 will likely cause psychological and social impact on these retiree communities as they find their programs evaporate.

Health Insurance and Survivor Benefits

Military retirees and eligible family members automatically receive free health insurance through the Civilian Health and Medical Program of the Uniform Services (CHAMPUS). However, copayments escalate to higher percentages than those for dependents of active-duty personnel, and coverage terminates at age 65, when the insured becomes eligible for Medicare.

The military services also offer a Survivor Benefit Program (SBP), which provides a surviving spouse with up to 55% of the service member's retired pay to age 62. At that point SBP is cut to 35% unless the service member has elected supplemental coverage at additional cost. With supplemental coverage, military retirees pay 16.88% of their retirement income for coverage. Some representatives of retirees complain that comparable benefit programs for federal employees cost only 10% of retired income. Despite the relatively high cost, 75% of officers and 46% of enlisted members enroll in the SBP at retirement (Willis, 1992).

Community of Retirees

Concentrations of retired personnel create political power in terms of sheer numbers as well as the cash they inject into the community. They also place a strain on installations that support active forces and retirees. During Operation Desert Storm, about a third of Air Force health care providers in San Antonio were shipped overseas. Military medical facilities geared up to receive massive numbers of casualties. Had those casualties materialized, health care might well have ceased for the retired population.

Frequent moves, long absences of the military member from the home, living in foreign countries, and the continuing need to adapt to new situations are among the shared stresses in the military community. However, Shaw (1987), in considering children in the military, observed that "in those instances where the parents have identified with the military way of life and assimilated the shared network of values and loyalties, many of these stresses can be significantly mitigated if not offset by the other psychosocial advantages of this community" (p. 544). Some of these advantages can be preserved in retirement.

The women's movement, two-career families, and other changes in the demographics of the military service have led to a decrease in the sense of community over the course of the past 20 years. This is reflected in the decline of military clubs, spouses' clubs, and the cherished traditions that accompanied them. Nevertheless, retirees of the 1950s and 1960s, and perhaps even the 1970s exited their careers when the military community was indeed close-knit. Combat and adversity bind former military men and women. In a military city like San

Antonio I frequently see a bumper sticker that proclaims "Retired Air Force and Damn Proud of It." I have not seen a similar sticker for a commercial enterprise.

Little (1981) pointed out the significance of the sense of community to the military member and suggested that the "loneliness of the retired status" is a cost of the intensity of friendships during active service, the dominance and pervasiveness of the military community, and the lack of segregation of occupational roles and friendship relations. Biderman (1964) found that some military retirees manage adaptation to the civilian community by essentially propagating the "old" system. Popular wisdom in San Antonio, for example, holds that the United Services Automobile Association (a major U.S. insurance and banking institution) is staffed almost entirely by retired officers and is "more military than the military." The USAA office building is known as second in size only to the Pentagon.

Other distinctions no doubt exist between military retirement and retirement from a civilian career or employment. However, the second career, sense of community, continued benefits, youthful age at retirement, and compensation programs form a unique constellation which differentiates the world of the military retiree and family from their civilian counterparts. They may feel estranged and isolated when leaving the service. Potential disaffection can be modulated if the retiree and family make thoughtful preparations for retirement.

RETIREMENT PLANNING

The career uncertainty of the 1990s jolted thousands of career-minded soldiers into immediate consideration of their prospects in civilian life. Knippa (1979) reported that positive adaptation to military retirement is associated with higher educational level, effective preparation for retirement, and a voluntary decision to retire. However, Dunning and Biderman (1973) observed that many military retirees do not prepare for the change until a few months in advance. Fuller and Redfering (1976) found that preretirement planning was the prime determinant of the military member's adjustment to retirement. If the "peace dividend" of the 1990s leads to the projected wholesale early retirements, many retirees will be deprived of both preparation and a voluntary decision.

Literature on civilian retirement focuses on the importance of planning for eventual satisfaction with retirement (Dorfman, 1989; Giordano & Giordano, 1983; Morrow, 1982; Rowen & Wilks, 1987; Shouksmith, 1983; Singleton, 1985). Kamouri and Cavanaugh (1986) found that preretirement education programs influenced retirement attitudes and behaviors as well as satisfaction. Abel and Hayslip (1987) reported that retirement preparation programs maintained both the desirability and expectancy of internal control and positive retirement attitudes. Rowen and Wilks (1987) argued for a preventive planning model to control stress factors such as loss of identity, marital problems, alcoholism, and loneliness. They suggest that a preretirement planning program might include educational content on finances, legal considerations, housing, consumerism, health planning, sociopsychological aspects, and the impact of retirement on the family. Kragie, Gerstein, and Lichtman (1989) reported that better-educated individuals plan more for retirement relative to finance and income but ignore the other areas. They found that people with a high external locus of control did not report *any* health planning. Subjects with an external locus of control and higher education were more likely to attend preretirement programs. Quick (1990) suggested that the process of retirement may be made a beneficially stressful experience, based on sources of stress that include life-style and location, spousal concerns, finances, and health. Odenwald (1986) focused on the importance of financial planning. Kaminskida Rosa (1985) presented a life-style model that deals with emotional issues surrounding retirement. This type of program covers the realities and stereotypes about retirement, leisure time, housing and relocation, relationship with spouse, and stress management. Liptak (1990) noted that life and career planning often neglect planning for leisure, while resources that do address leisure usually fail to describe the planning process.

Siegel and Rees (1992) report that planning programs for public employees, compared with private organizations, lag in participation and innovation. They found that most programs treat retirement as a point in time and fail to recognize it as a complex process. Formal and informal military retirement planning programs are typically brief, focus on administrative procedures, and rarely integrate the process of retirement. Programs that involve military family members in planning are the exception. Though military programs lag far behind their corporate counterparts, it is not *necessary* for them to do so.

Wilson's (1987) military preretirement program resulted in reduction of both state and trait anxiety. He recommends that retirement programs focus on dissemination of information about retirement and benefits *and* on the affective part of the retirement experience through small group discussion. The military is uniquely capable of providing such programs as a routine part of the soldier's career. In conducting preretirement seminars during the late 1970s I advised that optimal planning begins on the day of enlistment. The military member engages in a developmental *process* aimed in this direction throughout his/her career. Effective retirement planning considers the desired standard of living, and the means of achieving it. Preparation may include a cushion for the period of time between retirement and reaching a similar total income level in civilian life. It may incorporate investments to supplement retired pay, or a reliance on a spouse's income during the transitional period. Development of recreation skills is also important. Military duty (especially for the more compulsive serviceman or woman) is often a breeding ground for the workaholic with emphasis on devotion to duty. Development of coping resources and skills that will be used in later life, in seeking a new career, in pursuing leisure and recreation, and ultimately in full retirement are the targets of effective military preretirement planning. The development of strategies to deal with problems the family will face is also essential. I have encouraged military members to begin early in their careers by considering *when* they would like to retire and *why*. I suggest they consider the vicissitudes of the service and develop alternate plans should they be forced out earlier than desired.

CRISIS AND CHANGE

The military retiree and family members are faced with a multitude of decisions after at least two decades in which autonomy was only sporadically permitted. Preparation for retirement is potentially the antithesis of previous experiences with the military. Rather than demanding flexibility in response to others' decisions, the retiree is faced with acting in his own behalf. The role shift typically generates considerable stress. The service member's attitude toward retirement may vary from excited anticipation to dejection and denial. The degree of discomfort seems inversely proportional to the perceived degree of control exercised. Retirement tension I've noted among colleagues in the 1990s appears related to a sense of lost control generated by the massive draw-down. If the retiree has prepared for a specific retirement date, readied him or herself for another career or job, and developed a plan for the transition over the course of several years, the change will go more smoothly.

Adding to discomfort over leaving the service are variables related to the particular service member. In terms of Erikson's (1963) developmental stages, the military retiree is in the crisis of generativity versus stagnation. While success and satisfaction in one's vocation results in a sense of generativity, lack of fulfillment or achievement results in stagnation and emotional distress. Breaking with known parameters of the job to begin anew can exacerbate what Jaques (1965) identified as the *midlife crisis*. Contending with the prospect of one's own death, shifting from active to passive mastery, and change from outer to inner world orientation combine with the major life change from one career to another to potentiate a true crisis for many military personnel. In studying retired and retirement-eligible officers, Perreault (1981) found that midlife transition concern was related to age and to lessened satisfaction with self-concept. Identification with co-workers lessened concern for transition. Perreault's work confirms the suggestion that midlife crisis contributes to emotional distress in the process of military retirement.

Personality characteristics associated with a career soldier may hobble him in shifting to retirement. Military personnel may differ from civilians in some basic personality characteristics. Studies of service personnel using the Sixteen Personality Factor Questionnaire (16PF), show a very pragmatic approach to living (Cattell, Eber, & Tatsuoka, 1970). In Holland's (1959, 1966) terms, the military services are *realistic* professions, jobs in which doing things, rather than thinking about things, is important. Holland indicates that each occupational environment is dominated by the type of personality associated with it, suggesting that military professionals are likely to be pragmatists.

Retzlaff and Gibertini (1987, 1988) in studying pilot trainees, found 45% had significant elevations on the Millon Clinical Multiaxial Inventory (MCMI) Narcissistic Scale. Pilots often embody a strong, independent, gregarious disposition that serves effectively in their duty roles, but makes it difficult to accept the lessened significance which many will assume when retiring to civilian life. Such qualities lead some to avoid needed assistance in making the transition. The avoidance of care for symptoms of the *retirement syndrome* was identified by Berkey and Stoebner (1968), who report that "one factor, almost always present in the officer retiree, is that he has never before been a patient at a Mental Health Consultation Service." They continue: "Even then, characteristically, he comes reluctantly, having endured his symptoms for at least six months and often as long as two years" (p. 5).

Good followership and good leadership qualities do not necessarily flow from the same caldron. Yet in a military career, an individual is called upon to make the transition from obedient follower to supervisor and leader if he or she is to progress. Cattell and Stice's (1954) data suggest that bright, conscientious, adventurous, conservative, controlled individuals who are extroverted and nonanxious and who show a somewhat above average degree of tough poise have stronger leadership potential. Vaughan (1964) found conformity lower in those with high independence and extroversion and low anxiety. Both the good leader and the faithful follower are vulnerable to difficulties in the process of retirement, but their concerns differ. For the more *dependent,* the service is a place where following others' instructions is highly rewarded. They entrust preparation for retirement to the service. Denial of the need for personal preparation can lead to shock at retirement; reliance on the service to make decisions can leave one ill prepared to deal with life changes and bereft of others upon whom to rely.

The *aggressive, independent individual* is more likely to lose status in retirement, even though he may have actively prepared. Because he may have stayed on active duty partly for the authority and prestige, he will be older and possibly less competitive for civilian positions than even other military retirees. The status change may tax his ability to draw on himself to adapt.

The *compulsive company man* faces different challenges. Though conformity can bring success in the service, it rarely leads to high prestige. The conflict between dependence and independence suggested by Millon (1981) may keep the service member on duty as resentments grow over failure to rapidly progress. After counseling many such servicemen and women, I've concluded that to minimize the impact of forced or voluntary retirement, the company man must recognize and confront his ambivalence. If resolved in favor of self-efficacy, the compulsive individual may manage retirement much the same as the more aggressive counterpart. If resolved in favor of dependency needs, he is more likely to seek the security of another supportive institution in retirement.

There are other customary changes that all personnel experience in moving from military to civilian status. These include very basic issues like purchasing a daily wardrobe and deciding which haircut actually looks best. Though preparation takes such factors into account early so that the individual may practice adaptation, there are those for whom preparation comes too late or retirement too early. They are more vulnerable to emotional trauma when they make the transition.

After 20 or more years in uniform the career soldier may be blindsided by some of the changes he will undoubtedly experience. Unlike most of our civilian peers, the military men and women *wear* their positions, authority, and prestige. The uniform we put on each day, through ribbons, insignia, and rank displays our military history, where we have served, for how long, what degree of responsibility we hold, and what dangers we've faced. The superficially trivial shift to civilian attire powerfully subjects us to the type of role stripping that medical patients experience when discarding street clothes for hospital gowns. Wearing the uniform in the civilian world was uncomfortable for many of us in the 1970s, following the Vietnam war. However, 1991 saw a major shift in public attitudes toward the man and woman in uniform. Since my own shift to civilian clothes, no one walks up to me in the airport any more and say "thanks," out of the clear blue sky. My clothing no longer distinguishes me from the crowd.

Another of the immediate crises faced by the military retiree is disengagement from what Little (1981) described as intense friendships and intertwining of occupational and friendship roles. Friendships form and dissolve quickly in military life. While one way of coping with this is to remain aloof, another is to dive in fully. The base community and squadron, battalion or ship support quick integration of the new unit member and family. Military moves allow little time for adjustment; you "hit the ground running." A considerable sense of loss and grief can accompany severance of this automatic attachment and acceptance. The active service member and family are provided with a sponsor for each move. The sponsor arranges introductions to the new job, community, schools, social activities, and other families and members of the new organization. There is no sponsor for retirement. Like the newly widowed, the retired member and family are suddenly cast adrift from supports previously taken for granted. Multiple losses and life changes are inherent in retirement from the service. Grief similar to that experienced in divorce or death of a family member may be precipitated by the multiple losses of friends, colleagues, and social activities, as well as the job itself. In retirement, I find myself struggling with the inclination to phone former colleagues or to "drop by to say hello" rather than pursuing my new civilian life. Re-creation of the "old system" (Biderman, 1964) may represent a compromise solution to the potential incapacitation of grief, the impropriety of "dropping in," and the need to grapple with responsibility for one's own future by seeking out new relationships and support systems.

Fortunately, as Beehr (1986) pointed out, emotional adaptation to retirement often mimics the individual's adaptation to the working world. Though the relationship is moderated by the planning, occupational goal attainment, and expectations about retirement, generally, if mental health was good *before* retirement, it tends to be positive *after* retirement. The career military family is tempered by adjusting to the unexpected. They have a wealth of experience with loss and change. They have adapted to alien environments under the worst of conditions, and have not only survived but flourished. My father, a former Marine, once told me that the Eleventh Commandment was "Thou Shalt

Adjust." As the career soldier and family "hit the ground running" during service life, they may be expected to obey the Eleventh Commandment, effectively manage the losses of retirement, and rapidly integrate into a new life style.

TRADITIONAL AND NONTRADITIONAL MILITARY FAMILIES

Though less often seen in the 1990s, there still exist traditional, male-dominant military families in which the wife has functioned throughout the husband's career as homemaker and mother. Retirement concerns in these families differ from those of the less traditional single-parent or two-career family.

The retirement syndrome can be eased or exacerbated by the spouse who eagerly anticipates retirement or fears the future. Larkin (1983) found a significant relationship between health care utilization and life changes perceived by retiring military families. This correlation held for spouses of the retiring military members, not for men alone. The end of involuntary moves, the opportunity to settle in one place and perhaps purchase a first house, or to continue and progress in a career may all be eagerly sought by the spouse. These changes may enhance the degree of perceived (or desired) control held by the mate.

For the more traditional wife, military retirement may precipitate grief at the loss of vicarious social status, automatic acceptance, and a natural social group. There may be anxiety about future security and reduced income as well as the discontinuity of taking on new responsibilities. Though some anticipated changes may be viewed as positive, they place demands on each family member.

One potential problem standing in the way of an active decision to retire is the age of and school plans for the children, who may be either encouraging or discouraging such a major shift in family life. Their concerns for their own futures, including the ability to attend college, place not-so-subtle pressures on the family. The military member may wish to retire at the earliest possible time to initiate a new career. However, the needs and desires of spouse and children may throw the family into strife over the timing, goals, and future roles of family members. For the two-career family, if the nonmilitary spouse has been able to sustain career progression, the financial and role transitions are likely to be less difficult than for the more traditional family.

In some cases both spouses have *military* careers. When one retires, the military career of the still-active service member will tend to dominate family decision making due to forced moves, isolated assignments, and the like. Determining whose career is more important or is more likely to progress is complex when both spouses are officers of the same rank because of the absence of clear cues as to what specific factors lead to promotion. Career planning is sometimes less knotty for married enlisted personnel because progression is largely based on concrete factors such as scores on tests of military and job knowledge or performance reports. When one military member retires and the other remains on active duty, officers and enlisted service members face similar problems in the family situation. Determining whose career should take precedence, with the retired member beginning anew and the spouse still working on a military career, can be frustrating.

In both traditional and nontraditional families a question of the spouse's right to expect compensation in return for his or her personal and family sacrifice during the course of the military member's career can arise at retirement. The feeling that the more traditional spouse has given up life opportunities for a career, further education, family stability, or a sense of unity with the extended family may be stirred up. If it is agreed that there has been sacrifice, the appropriate form of *compensation* for the deprived family member has to be negotiated in the process of planning and retirement.

At the time of retirement, the family has the potential for geographic stability for the first time in decades. This may be both alluring and stressful. Besides precipitating the fantasy of where one might *like* to live, it also arouses the question of what the spouse of the retiree might do in the ensuing years. The specter of wars, enforced separations, involuntary moves to foreign countries, and so on, are all behind the family. For the first time in years, the spouse of the retiree may be able to exercise some choice in his or her own personal development or career progression. This power alignment can create significant role changes for the spouses.

Role changes may be even more substantial for the rare families in which the former service member elects to *fully* retire or *semi*retire. When he or she does not seek or does not find full time work, the retiree has substantial time on his hands. His or her presence in the home, with little or nothing to do, and no role to fulfill may be psychologically damaging to retiree and spouse. In my practice, I have listened to numerous spouses of the semiretired complaining that the retiree is "always under foot, is depressed, or is constantly complaining." In traditional families it is probable that the semiretiree and spouse previously have not spent more than a couple of waking hours together each day. Being thrown into constant close proximity with one another, with a lowered income and little or nothing with which to occupy time, becomes distressing for both. While this phenomenon is common in both military and civilian families, the prime difference lies in the age at which it occurs. If it follows military retirement, it is occurring between ages 37 and 45!

CAREER EFFECTS AND MILITARY RETIREMENT

The whole effect of a military career is greater than the sum of the parts. At the extreme are cases of professional men and women, like one psychologist colleague of mine, who in the course of 25 years has not owned a home or lived in a commercial rental apartment or house. He and his family have lived only in military housing since graduate school. One may naively assume this is not much different from apartment dwelling. However, my friend has not borne the responsibility of painting, repairing broken air conditioners, or even paying the electric or water bill. That same colleague has been compelled to cut the grass to a specific length (in inches) and to open his home periodically for inspection by outsiders. He and his family have also been segregated from those of different rank or social status.

Officer or enlisted, male or female, the service member has long been subject to a set of rules unheard of in civilian life, rules that not only make it unwise to criticize a superior but can actually make it criminal. These rules make quitting the job impossible, make being late to work an offense. They impose lawful limitations on the type of makeup and jewelry that can be worn and create requirements for a woman to wear her skirt at a certain length or hair in a certain fashion. Personal relationships with those of lower or higher status are not only ill-advised, they are illegal. Behavior, in or out of uniform, is subject to the scrutiny of the military justice system. Adultery is not only potentially destructive to the family unit; it can lead to prosecution.

Within this highly structured and necessarily rule-bound environment, the professional soldier has learned to adapt and adjust. He has been compelled to be both diplomat and warrior. He has been reinforced for devotion to duty to the exclusion of all else. To survive and progress, he developed a survival kit that filters his anger or frustration but may stifle expression of feelings. He has subordinated his personal needs for growth, independence, or family stability to the good of the service. Sometimes he has lived with knowledge of the most sensitive secrets of the nation, unable to let even those with whom he is most intimate know the pressures or details of his work. He may have occasionally faced the horrible death or disfigurement of comrades who have willingly placed themselves in harm's way. He may equally have placed his own life on the line countless times. So too, he may have suffered separations from home and family for months or years at a time. For some, those months may have been spent fathoms beneath the surface of the sea, for others in remote and inhospitable countries. That same individual may have gained notoriety for valor in battle or exploits in space, or as a leader of men and women. His or her exploits may have been so sensitive as to be known to only one or two. Some who reach retirement will have spent years in the isolation of a prisoner of war camp, tortured of mind and body.

Regardless of rank, status, fame, achievement, or trauma during their careers, military retirees experience similar changes in separating from the service. The rule book is gone. The individual is free to decide for himself what course he or she will follow. At age 40 or older, he may become, for the first time in his life, responsible for all of the basic details of living which have for so long been managed by the service. For some there will have been an ever-increasing yearning for such independence. For others, a military career will have safeguarded them from taking responsibility for their lives. Still others meet their retirement with considerable ambivalence. For all there is a deluge of new choices. Many feel they have no basis upon which to judge their ability to compete in the civilian world. The competition faced throughout their adult lives was bound by the same traditions and tethered by rules they understood. The new rules may be unclear and may seem entirely alien. A question that looms large for that vast majority who seek a new career is, *Does anyone want what I have to give?*

SUPPORT AND TREATMENT

Strange (1984), in summarizing treatment issues related to the military retiree and his family pointed out that the stress of retirement presents not only the risk of maladjustment but also the opportunity for growth. Military people adapt very well to retirement, on the whole (Houghton, 1987). The vast majority, whether retiring or not, never seek mental health assistance. When they do, they typically overcome a substantial personal aversion to seeking assistance from a care giver. The provider, whether a mental health professional, a preretirement seminar leader, or a physician, should be conscious of the long-standing military tradition of avoiding any form of outside assistance, should a military man or woman seek their services.

Prevention

In the course of the past decade, the stress-coping model (Lazarus & Folkman, 1984; Matheney, Aycock, Pugh, Curlette, & Cannella, 1986; Roskies, 1987) has gained substantial favor in both military work site and hospital-based interventions. A prime factor in acceptance of these approaches by the military population is the absence of a focus on psychopathology, combined with a health promotion and a prevention orientation. The clinician would do well to adopt this model in approaching the impact of military retirement. The stress-coping and prevention model is fulfilled through the implementation of preretirement programs that involve not only the service member but also family members. Important is early discussion of the issues of both practical and emotional preparation, as well as the hazards of retirement.

Treatment

When a service member, retiree, or family member actually seeks mental health care, Strange's (1984) recommendations are as valid today as they were when initially offered. In addition to the therapist's consciousness of the complex issues involved in military retirement, it is important to address problems as soon as possible. Involvement of the family in treatment, since they are also part of the retirement process, can greatly facilitate adjustment of all the members. Strange encouraged clinicians to avoid overtreating their retiring or retired patients. As he notes, mild anxiety and depressive symptoms are an inherent part of the retirement transition and should be considered "reactive."

Future Care

In the managed care environment of the 1990s, cost-effective service delivery to clients facing retirement stress may be best provided in a group setting. Sweet et al. (1989) found the support group format to be an effective means of providing care for early retirees in a Veterans Administration hospital. The more structured format of the preretirement lecture-discussion seminar can be easily tailored to that of a short-term structured group focusing on management of the stress associated with military retirement. Military medical facilities are uniquely situated to offer this form of systematic and recurrent program under the auspices of health promotion. Doing so would offer the potential for delivering care and mutual support to those who could benefit, but who might be very reluctant to seek it out through a psychiatric service or mental health clinic. Larkin's (1983) finding of increased health care utilization by families approaching retirement suggests that such programs might well produce cost savings in health service delivery by reducing the need for medical care for tens of thousands of retirees and family members each year. Research in this area of health promotions has yet to be conducted.

REFERENCES

Abel, B. J., & Hayslip. L. (1987). Locus of control and retirement preparation. *Journal of Gerontology, 42*(2), 165–167.

Beck, S. H. (1982). Adjustment to and satisfaction with retirement. *Journal of Gerontology, 37*, 616–624.

Beehr, T. A. (1986). The process of retirement: A review and recommendations for future investigation. *Personnel Psychology, 39*(1), 31–55.

Bellino, R. (1969). Psychosomatic problems of military retirement. *Psychosomatics, 10*(5), 318–321.

Berkey, B. R., & Stoebner, J. B. (1968). The retirement syndrome: A previously unreported variant. *Military Medicine, 17*(6), 5–8.

Biderman, A. D. (1964). Sequels to a military career: The retired military professional. In M. Janowitz (Ed.), *The new military.* New York: Russell Sage Foundation.

Cattell, R. B., Eber, H. W., & Tatsuoka, M. M. (1970). *Handbook for the Sixteen Personality Factor Questionnaire (16PF).* Champaign, IL: Institute for Personality and Ability Testing.

Cattell, R. B., & Stice, G. F. (1954). Four formulae for selecting leaders on the basis of personality. *Human Relations, 7*, 493–507.

Dorfman, L. T. (1989). Retirement preparation and retirement satisfaction in the rural elderly. *Journal of Applied Gerontology, 8*(4), 432–450.

Druss, R. G. (1965). Problems associated with retirement from military service. *Military Medicine, 130*, 382–385.

Dunning, B. B., & Biderman, A. D. (1973). The case of military "retirement." *Industrial Gerontology, 17*(1), 18–37.

Erikson, E. (1963). *Childhood and society* (2nd ed.). New York: W. W. Norton.

Fuller, R. L., & Redferring, D. L. (1976). Effects of preretirement planning on the retirement adjustment of military personnel. *Sociology of Work and Occupations, 3*(4), 478–487.

Garber, D. L. (1971). *Retired soldiers in second careers: Self-assessed change, reference group salience, and psychological well being.* Unpublished doctoral dissertation, University of Southern California.

Giordano, J. A., & Giordano, N. H. (1983). A classification of preretirement programs: In search of a new model. *Educational Gerontology, 9*(2–3), 123–137.

Greenberg, H. R. (1965). Depressive equivalents in the preretirement years: The old soldier syndrome. *Military Medicine, 130*, 251–255.

Hamrick, K. S. (1989). A model of military retirement behavior with an application to army enlisted infantry retirement costs. *Dissertation Abstracts International, 50,* 04-A.

Holland, J. (1959). A theory of vocational choice. *Journal of Counseling Psychology, 6,* 35–45.

Holland, J. (1966). *The psychology of vocational choice.* Waltham, MA: Blaisdell.

Houghton, G. C. (1987). The relationship of body age and life satisfaction for retired military officers with second careers and those fully retired. *Dissertation Abstracts International, 48,* 10-B.

Jaques, N. E. (1965). Death and the midlife crisis. *International Journal of Psychoanalysis, 46,* 502–514.

Jensen, P. S., Lewis. R. L., & Xenakis, S. N. (1986). The military family in review: Context, risk, and prevention. *Journal of the American Academy of Child Psychiatry, 25*(2), 225–234.

Kaminski-da Rosa, V. (1985). Planning today for tomorrow's lifestyle. *Training and Development Journal, 39*(1), 103–104.

Kamouri, A. L., & Cavanaugh, J. C. (1986). The impact of preretirement education programmes on workers' preretirement socialization. *Journal of Occupational Behaviour, 7*(3), 245–256.

Kimmel, D. C., Price, K. F., & Walker, J. W. (1978). Retirement choice and retirement satisfaction. *Journal of Gerontology, 33,* 575–585.

Knippa, W. B. (1979). *The relationship of antecedent and personality variables to the life satisfaction of retired military officers.* Doctoral Dissertation, University of Texas. *Dissertation Abstracts International, 40,* 3-A.

Kragie, E. R., Gerstein, M., & Lichtman, M. (1989). Do Americans plan for retirement? Some recent trends. *Career Development Quarterly, 37*(3), 232–239.

Larkin, J. (1983). *Health service utilization in the near retirement period by both husband and wife in selected military families. An exploratory study.* Doctoral Dissertation, University of Texas. *Dissertation Abstracts International, 44,* 04-B.

Lazarus, R. S., & Folkman, S. (1984). *Stress, appraisal, and coping.* New York: Springer Publishing Co.

Liptak, J. J. (1990). Preretirement counseling: Integrating the leisure planning component. *Career Development Quarterly, 38*(4), 360–367.

Little, R. W. (1981). Friendships in the military community. *Research in the Interweave of Social Roles, 2,* 221–235.

Matheney, K. B., Aycock, D. W., Pugh, J. L., Curlette, W. L., & Cannella, K. S. (1986). Stress coping: A qualitative and quantitative synthesis with implications for treatment. *Counseling Psychologist, 14*(4), 499–549.

Maze, R. (1992a, March 2). 15 year retirement: Attractive, but a pipe dream? *Air Force Times,* p. 8.

Maze, R. (1992b, March 9). Panel backs cutting 200,000 more active duty jobs by '97. *Air Force Times,* p. 3.

McBride, A. (1976). Retirement as a life crisis: Myth or reality? A review. *Canadian Psychiatric Association Journal, 21*(8), 547–556.

McNeil, J. S., & Giffen, M. D. (1965). Military retirement: Some basic concepts and observations. *Aerospace Medicine, 36*, 25–29.

McNeil, J. S., & Giffen, M. D. (1967). Military retirement: The retirement syndrome. *American Journal of Psychiatry, 123*, 848–854.

Millon, T. (1981). *Disorders of personality DSM-III: Axis II.* New York: John Wiley.

Milowe, I. D. (1964). A study in role diffusion: The chief and the sergeant face retirement. *Mental Hygiene, 48*, 1–107.

Morrow, P. C. (1982). Human resource planning and the older worker: Developing a retirement intentions model. *Journal of Occupational Behaviour, 3*(3), 253–261.

Nowak, C. A., & Brice, G. C. (1984). The process of retirement: Implications for late-life counseling. Family *Therapy Collections, 10,* 106–123.

Odenwald, S. (1986). Pre-retirement planning gathers steam. *Training & Development Journal, 40*(2), 62–63.

Office of the Actuary, Department of Defense. (1991). *DoD Statistical Report on the Military Retirement System* (RCS NO. DDM (A) 1375). Arlington, VA: Department of Defense. Office of the Secretary of Defense, Force Management and Personnel.

Palmore, E. B., Fillenbaum, C. G., & George, L. K. (1984). Consequences of retirement. *Journal of Gerontology, 39,* 109–116.

Perreault, M. M. (1981). Mid-life transition and career change: Retired military in second careers. *Dissertation Abstracts International, 42,* 10-B.

Portnoi, V. (1983). Post-retirement depression: Myth or reality? *Comprehensive Therapy, 9,* 31–37.

Quick, J. F. (1990). Time to move on? *Prevention in Human Services, 8*(1), 239–250.

Retzlaff, P. D., & Gibertini, M. (1987). Air Force pilot personality: Hard data on the "right stuff." *Multivariate Behavioral Research, 22,* 383–399.

Retzlaff, P. D., & Gibertini, M. (1988). Objective psychological testing of U.S. Air Force officers in pilot training. *Aviation Space Environmental Medicine, 59,* 661–663.

Roskies, E. (1987). *Stress management for the healthy Type A: Theory and practice.* New York: Guilford Press.

Rowen, R. B., & Wilks, C. S. (1987). *Pre-retirement planning: A Quality of life issue for retirement.* Paper presented at the Southwestern Social Science Association Annual Meeting, Social Work Section, San Antonio, TX.

Schmitt, N., & McCune, J. T. (1981). The relationship between job attitudes and the decision to retire. *Academy of Management Journal, 24*(4), 795–802.

Shaw, J. A. (1987). Children in the military. *Psychiatric Annals, 17*(8), 539–544.

Shouksmith, G. (1983). Change in attitude to retirement following a short pre-retirement planning seminar. *Journal of Psychology, 114*(1), 3–7.

Siegel, S. R., & Rees, B. Y. (1992). Preparing the public employee for retirement. *Public Personnel Management, 21*(1), 89–100.

Singleton, J. F. (1985). Retirement: Its effect on the individual. *Activities, Adaptation and Aging, 6*(4), 1–7.

Strange, R. E. (1984). Retirement from the service: The Individual and his family. In F. W. Kaslow & R. I. Ridenour (Eds.), *The military family: Dynamics and treatment* (pp. 217–225). New York: Guilford Press.

Sweet, M., Stoler, N., Kelter, R., & Thurrell, R. J (1989). A community of buddies: Support groups for veterans forced into early retirement. *Hospital and Community Psychiatry, 40*(2), 172–176.

Thurnher, M. (1976). Midlife marriage: Sex differences in evaluation and perspectives. *International Journal of Aging and Human Development, 7*(2), 129–135.

Vaughan, G. M. (1964). The trans-situational aspect of conforming behavior. *Journal of Personality, 32,* 335–354.

Wan, T. (1982). *Stressful life events, social support networks, and gerontological health.* Lexington, MA: Lexington Books.

West, J. (1992a, March 2). 11,800 applications for exit bonuses OK'd. *Air Force Times,* p. 3.

West, J. (1992b, March 16). SERB picks 610 cols, 369 Lt Cols. *Air Force Times,* p. 6.

Willis, G. (1992, March 30). Survivor benefits. *Air Force Times,* pp. 12–13.

Wilson, P. (1987). The effect of a small group discussion preretirement education model on the anxiety levels of career marine corps personnel prior to their military retirement. *Dissertation Abstracts International, 48,* 02-A.

CHAPTER TWELVE

Social Policy and Planning and Legislative Considerations

Diana L. Kupchella, MS

The title of this chapter seems to imply that some type of rational and well-thought-out social policy and planning precede and form legislation governing the military. Is this an accurate statement? Or has past legislation in response to immediate and short-term needs formed the social policy and composition of the military? The purpose of this chapter is to raise the political consciousness of the reader as to past, present, and future social issues shaping the U.S. military force. Past and present policies are already history, but the future purpose and form of the Department of Defense (DoD) is yet to be determined.

FACTORS SHAPING THE PAST MILITARY FORCE

Prior to 1973, legislation was in effect that required eligible young men to be drafted into the army. The resulting composition of the armed services reflected this mandated policy. Drafted young men who did not meet certain criteria for deferrment went into the Army. Others avoided the draft by volunteering to join one of the other services. The end result was a military force primarily consisting of men who fulfilled their required commitment of 2 to 4 years and separated back to the civilian world, where often a job and future spouse waited. The usual course was that marriage and family followed one's military service.

In 1973, Congress ended the draft, requiring the DoD to develop other means of attracting and retaining military personnel (P.L. 92-129). The United States continued to perceive a threat from the Soviet Union, and funding was appropriated from the Congress for the DoD to institute new programs and a new image in order to maintain an adequate defense. All of a sudden, the military had to respond to the demands of its potential "customers," and it took on an entirely different facade. Instead of molding the draftee to the demands of the military, the military was being molded by the new draftees and society's demands. The military had to respond to the needs of its members and their families if it had any hope of retaining trained and experienced personnel who had valuable skills. The civilian market was now a competitor rather than a bystander patiently waiting for the promised honorable discharge papers of its work force. As a competitor, the DoD was forced to make some fundamental changes: it opened more job areas for women and, in doing so, relaxed some of its policies concerning women (i.e., allowing them to have dependents); it created more education programs; and it developed more family-oriented programs and policies (day-care centers, youth programs, family advocacy, etc.), thus making itself more attractive to the potential market of American youth. As the years went on, the DoD was held to its chartered responsibility of maintaining an effective war machine with an all-volunteer force that expected the military system to meet all of its and its families needs.

Since 1990, the Cold War has ended, Desert Storm has been fought, and our strongest (recognized) enemy, the Soviet Union, has disintegrated. Congress is struggling with the demands of the American people to cut the military budget and therefore downsize the military forces in favor of spending for domestic purposes. However, there are still external threats to the security of this country, and a strong though smaller military force is still essential. In lieu of reinstating the draft, the military must remain attractive to potential recruits in order to maintain viability. The DoD is forced to continue to walk that fine line of keeping the public happy and maintaining an effective war machine and troops available as manpower for cleanup and rebuilding in the event of a disaster, like Hurricanes Andrew and Iniki in the summer of 1992.

Today, more than ever, Americans are insisting upon recognition of their "rights." Women are demanding equal opportunities with men, including the right to die in battle, and homosexuals are demanding equal rights to jobs in the military. The questions now seem to be, what kind of military force do we currently have, what kind of force do we need for the future, and how do we mold the former into the latter?

COMPOSITION OF THE CURRENT FORCE

Unfortunately, there are no DoD-wide standard sources currently available to accurately describe demographic characteristics of military members and their families. Consequently, information may conflict (Blankinship, Bullman, & Croan, 1990), depending on the source, and definitions vary as well (e.g., is a single parent a service member with a cohabitating minor dependent or a service member with child support responsibilities, or both? The Army has recently developed ("U.S. Army Family Demographics System," 1990) a method of deriving demographic data from the Defense Enrollment Eligibility Reporting System (DEERS), a computerized system that manages persons eligible for military benefits. The Army now has some reliable data available in contrast to the usual "survey and estimate" method to obtain information about family dependents. As the Army is the largest of the services, most demographic studies focus on the Army for predicting military needs and trends as a whole.

In spite of the data collection and availability problems, there are some good estimates on the characteristics/demographics of current military members. In 1985 a database was established in the Army using the DoD Survey of Officer and Enlisted Personnel. The responses to this survey were compared to a similar survey conducted in 1978–1979. Utilizing the findings of these two surveys, the researchers concluded that more married males with children enlisted in the Army in 1985 than in 1979, twice as many females with children enlisted in 1985 (married or not) than in 1979, and the enlistment of single-parent females had tripled. Surprisingly, more officers (male and female) were single at time of entry in 1985 than in 1979.

Rakoff and Doherty (1989) indicated that

... although the vast majority of Army personnel enter unmarried and without children, almost half of the enlisted males and two thirds of officer males are married with children. Only about one quarter of the women in the Army are married with children, but they have fewer years of service and are younger on average. When controlled by length of service, the differences between the males and females are smaller, but males are still more likely to be members of households with spouses

and children than are females. . . . married personnel tend to have a
higher intention of remaining in the Army than do single personnel,
especially males. This is true for both enlisted personnel and officers; at
each years-of-service (YOS) point, the average reenlistment probability
was higher for married men than it was for single men, and more married than single officers expressed an intention to remain in the Army
for a full career. For males, adding children to the family increases
retention intent, except for officers who entered single but had children
during the first 3 years of service. The opposite seems to be true for
females. (pp. vii–viii)

Similar findings are reported by Morrison et al. (Morrison, Vernez,
Grissmer, & McCarthy, 1989). This study found that there were more
female soldiers in 1985, with the rate having risen from 7% to 10% since
1979. They also found that there were more "dual-Army" families.

In 1985, approximately one in ten Army personnel were members of
families in which both spouses were on active duty. Fewer than 1 in 14
were in 1979 (p. 2). An increase in female single parents was found and
the report stated: In 1979, only one of every four custodial single-parent
Army families was headed by a female member; by 1985, the figure was
nearly one in two. (p. 2)

Burrelli (1991) describes today's military as "older (26.4 years for the
average enlistee and 33.4 for officers); more likely to be married (53%);
more heavily black (20.8%) and female (11%); and more reliant on the
reserve 'citizen soldier'" (p. 3).

The all-volunteer force, then, would appear to have converted the
military from a largely single-male, short-term (drafted) fighting force
to increasingly female, married, family- and career-oriented organization. These facts about the current composition of the armed forces has
forced the debate on the purpose of the military to come to the fore-
ground. Is it a war-readiness machine trained and maintained for the
sole purpose of protecting the United States and its vital interests? Or
is it a career opportunity providing a job, health benefits, worldwide
travel, and early retirement for otherwise unemployed families? Or
both?

At present (September 1992) the military is facing a severe downsizing in response to the end of the Cold War and lack of any perceived
global nuclear conflict. What type of military will it be? Some special
interests groups are letting their opinions be known. Current pending
legislation will require equal rights for homosexuals to serve in the
military, women to be allowed the opportunity of serving in combat

roles, single parents being exempt from deployment in the event of conflict, and some similar exemptions in the case of dual military couples with children.

PROPOSED LEGISLATION AND FACTORS SHAPING THE FUTURE MILITARY FORCE

How will legislation shape the U.S. military of the future? In the 102nd Congress, 883 bills or resolutions have been introduced directly affecting military personnel. These measures are a reflection of society's concerns and priorities regarding todays military and its mission. A vast number of these proposed measures amend veterans' benefits. Some are a direct result of Operation Desert Storm, but the large majority of them also attest to the growing number of veterans. With veterans of previous U.S. conflicts as far back as World War I still alive and with current downsizing attempts through actions such as Selective Early Retirement Boards, the number of people affected by such legislation is immense. Indeed, many of these retired military once made career decisions based largely upon promised retirement benefits, including pay, a lifetime of medical/dental care for themselves and their dependents, BX/PX and commissary privileges, and space-available travel (see chapter 11, this volume).

As individuals currently on active duty face career decisions and as career-minded individuals are enticed to enter active duty because of its retirement benefits, they are very likely to examine the government's track record of keeping its' promises to those already retired. The quality of the future career military force may well depend upon those perceptions. On April 9, 1992, after introducing several bills benefiting veterans, Representative Maxine Waters (D-CA) stated:

> Military downsizing is ruining the lives of tens of thousands of people who thought they had a career in the military. The last ten years has seen a continuous erosion in veterans benefits across the board. It does not seem unreasonable to earmark some portion of the projected savings in military spending to those who have sacrificed so much. Veterans have gone from parades to poverty in one short year. (*Congressional Record*, April 9, 1992)

Integrity of the military and governmental policy regarding treatment of those with a military obligation or handling conscientious objectors will also be scrutinized by those considering a military career. H.R. 611 and H.R. 5060 address these issues.

There is an old saying that "if the military wanted you to have a wife (spouse) and children, it would have issued them to you." In order to entice people to join today's military, however, the family has taken center stage. The military has had to become more accommodating to families, including single-parent families. Several bills before the current Congress reflect this policy. Some examples are provisos in bills that seek to prohibit stationing single parents at locations "where facilities for dependents are not reasonably available" (H.R. 738, S 283); prohibit deploying single parents (or more than one member of the family) "to an area in which hostile fire or imminent danger pay is paid" (H.R. 1081); and "provide child care services to all members of the Armed Forces on active duty desiring such services" (H.R. 2848). One bill even expands the traditional definition of "dependent" to grant medical and dental care to minors who are in the legal custody of military members (H.R. 2134). Traditionally, "dependent" to a military member has been rather narrowly defined to include only spouse, biological or adopted minor children, and sometimes a parent.

Women in the military have certainly been at the forefront of public debate. Legislation has been introduced to regulate how soon after childbirth they should be sent to a location geographically apart from their child, to decide whether they should hold combat positions, to protect them from sexual harassment. H.R. 957, H.R. 1024, and H.R. 2376 would all limit the extent to which mothers could be deployed and thus separated from an infant or small children. On December 5, 1991, President Bush signed into law a measure creating the Commission on the Assignment of Women in the Armed Forces (P.L. 102-190). This law removes the legal prohibition against women flying combat missions in the Air Force, Navy, and Marine Corps. Finally, the outrage that followed disclosure of alleged sexual harassment has led to several measures. House Concurrent Resolution 344 calls for a full investigation into the allegations that sexual harassment of women took place at the September 1991 symposium of the Navy's Tailhook Association in Las Vegas. Senate Bill 2973 provides for counseling and treatment of women veterans as a result of sexual trauma or abuse, and Senate Resolution 209 condemns sexual harassment.

Bisexuals and homosexuals are groups who have vocally demanded equal rights in all things, including the military, which has traditionally held that homosexuality is incompatible with military service. Representative Patricia Schroeder (D-CO), upon introducing H.R. 5208, stated, "Department of Defense Directive 1332.14, which says homosexuality is incompatible with military service, is un-American because it arbitrarily excludes and denies Americans equal opportunities, particularly women, who are three times more likely than men to be investigated and discharged under this policy" (*Congressional Record*, May 19, 1992). Likewise, House Resolution 271 and Senate Resolution 236 call for rescinding the DoD directive that bans gay, lesbian, and bisexual Americans from military service.

Current law (P.L. 90-40) requires all U.S. males to register with the Selective Service upon their 18th birthday. Two bills have been introduced that would eliminate this requirement (H.R. 4084 and H.R. 4367). Mandatory Selective Service registration was repealed after the Vietnam War and reinstated during the Carter administration. H.R. 2681, although not exactly eliminating Selective Service, would establish a universal national service under which citizens between 18 and 25 years would perform 1 year of service, either civilian or military.

Other measures have been introduced that would refocus the mission of the U.S. military to more domestic functions. H.R. 1092 and H.R. 1481 would allow military personnel to perform border patrol functions, along with the Immigration and Naturalization Service and the U.S. Customs Service. H.R. 3395 would authorize military personnel to serve as advisors to correctional facilities operated like military boot camps.

The question at this point would seem to be, will the legislative measures listed above mold the size and shape of a military capable of fulfilling its defined mission (whatever that is determined to be), or will tomorrow's military force be simply a reflection of special interest groups demanding their share of the opportunities that a military career offers? A thorough reevaluation of the purpose of the U.S. armed forces would seem to be in order. The American public needs to be educated and actively involved in the decision, and their will (not just that of special interest groups) needs to be conveyed to congressional legislators. Without public involvement, legislation is likely to be made reactively to immediate concerns without any reasonable long-term planning. The future of the military and their families will then be determined by fleeting moods and whims, not a very enticing or stable environment if the government is trying to attract highly competent people to make a career of military service.

LEGISLATIVE PROCESS FOR THE MILITARY

One might now legitimately say that all of this is well and good, but how do new ideas for legislation regarding the military come to be proposed? What means of influence are available to those who will be effected by this legislation? The answer involves rather complex formal and informal systems of communication between lawmakers and the individuals for whom the laws are written.

First of all, the military is a highly organized and defined institution by its very nature. As such, it has very clear-cut internal chains of communication, also referred to as chains of command. These chains specify who may communicate with whom and basically require individuals to communicate problems and concerns to immediate supervisors before going to anyone else (meaning, particularly, anyone outside the institution). If the situation is beyond the control of this supervisor, he/she is expected to relay the problem up to his/her respective supervisor. This process continues until the problem is adequately resolved. On occasion, as this process proceeds, it is discovered that the problem is more widespread than originally thought, as similar input is being received from various parts of the military. In such a situation, the high-ranking officer receiving the multiple input may be able to influence or write military policy within the DoD to an adequate extent, which fixes the problem without legislation. An example of such a situation was recently reported (Willis, 1992) regarding DoD policy on family care plans for military dependents. Media reports during Operation Desert Shield/Storm of single parents and other military members with primary family responsibilities has led the Department to further define and standardize their family care contingency plans. With the Department's successful handling of this problem internally, congressional mandating legislation is unnecessary.

There still, however, may be problems the Department cannot resolve internally because of some existing legislation or that the Department, for whatever reason, chooses not to resolve at present. In such instances, legislation may be required. Such a request moving up the chain of command from supervisor to supervisor will eventually be channeled through the appropriate service secretary in the Pentagon and reach the Office of the Secretary of Defense, who will, if he chooses, make a recommendation to Congress through his annual budget request, which is included in the president's annual budget and is presented to Congress every January. These top military officials, including the president (who is Commander in Chief of all of the armed forces), also have many other formal and informal communication sessions with Congress throughout the legislative cycle, via testimony at committee hearings, letters, proposed committee report language, and the like, providing additional means of communicating military needs during the course of a year. Of course, each military official along the chain of command has the opportunity to review the issue and provide input, as well as decide whether to elevate it or not to the next higher level. This process, as one might easily recognize, can be especially long and tedious, not to mention occasionally unsuccessful.

There are, however, other means by which the military, retirees, dependents, and the general public may make their desires known to legislators. These methods have been outlined in earlier publications (DeLeon, 1983; Portnoy et al., 1983) and are applicable here. Although active-duty military are prohibited from taking any "official" stand outside military channels, there are several professional lobbying organizations that may speak on their behalf and whose primary purpose is to safeguard and improve policies and benefits for current and past military members and their families. Such organizations include, among others, the Non-Commissioned Officers Association, the Reserve Officers Association, the Veterans of Foreign Wars, and organizations for specific services, such as the Air Force Association. In addition, any professional organization, with members in the military or not, can have a very powerful voice in influencing legislation.

Generally, these organizations have some type of ongoing legislative committee whose primary purpose is to screen proposed legislation, meet regularly with legislators and their staffs, and maintain a positive communication channel with those who will support the organization's interests. This ongoing networking with legislators is critical for moving any particular interest item; for elected officials, although interested in passing legislation for the common social good, are also interested in receiving recognition of their efforts and accomplishments for the purpose of their next reelection. Members of organizations' legislative committees who understand this reciprocal process and successfully maintain a positive relationship with legislators, have little difficulty in pushing their organization's agendas, resulting in legislation favorable to their cause. When military members belong to such organizations, their concerns are heard in a timely and very powerful way.

Finally, as private citizens, military members and retirees, like all other citizens, have the right to correspond, phone, or visit their congressional representative or senator directly. This method usually has rather immediate results and is therefore possibly the fastest method by which a military member can obtain results. However, with the potential labeling of the military member as a "troublemaker" when the invariable congressional inquiry follows, and the question being raised as to why the member didn't go through the chain of command first, this method is usually reserved as a last-resort effort.

CONCLUSION

The past policies regarding military service seem to have generally met the military needs of this country. With the exception of Vietnam, all military goals of past conflicts have been met with the existing military force. However, will this situation continue to be true? Is there still a need for a DoD, and should its focus be strictly defense or should it expand its scope to such areas as law enforcement within the United States? Currently, the military does provide employment and career security for a vast number of people; should it be a federal employment and welfare program? What exactly does the American public want the mission of the military to be, and who should serve in the military to accomplish this mission? Current pending legislation, as discussed above, is being debated, and the future of the DoD, as well as the potential security of the American people, is at stake. Decisions will be made. Will they be well thought out and based on the purpose for which the military is designed? The American public will decide.

REFERENCES

Blankinship, D. A., Bullman, S. L., & Croan, G. M. (1990). *The policy program, and fiscal implications of military family research: Proceedings of the 1990 military family research review* (Report No. 6347). Arlington, VA: Military Family Resource Center.

Burrelli, D. F. (1991). *Military deployment and family policy* (Order Code IB91100). Washington, DC: Congressional Research Service.

DeLeon, P. H. (1983). The changing and creating of legislation: The political process. In B. Sales (Ed.), *The professional psychologist's handbook* (pp. 601–620). New York: Plenum.

Morrison, P. A., Vernez, G., Grissmer, D. W., & McCarthy, K. F. (1989). *Families in the Army: Looking ahead* (Report No. 5368). Santa Monica, CA: The Rand Corporation.

Portnoy, S. M., Friedland, S. J., Norman, M. N., Carveric, B. R., Eisman, E. J., Zapf, R. F., & DeLeon, P. H. (1983). Effective state-level advocacy: A model for action. *American Psychologist, 38,* 1220–1226.

Rakoff, S. H., & Doherty, J. H. (1989). *Army family composition and retention* (Report No. 6054). Alexandria, VA: U.S. Army Research Institute for the Behavioral and Social Sciences.

U.S. Army family demographics system (FAMILY). (1990). (Report No. 6350). Alexandria, VA: U.S. Army Community and Family Support Center.

Willis, G. (1992, August 17). New policy targets single parents, dual-service couples. *Air Force Times,* p. 6.

CHAPTER THIRTEEN

Thematic and Universal Considerations

Florence W. Kaslow, PhD

A REALISTIC APPRAISAL OF THE HISTORY OF CIVILIZATION REVEALS THAT WARS are a frequent, recurrent phenomenon. It appears that some country, somewhere in the universe, is always preparing for, engaged in, or recuperating from war. For example, as this is being written (November 1992) there is severe ethnic strife in Bosnia and Croatia (formerly Yugoslavia); Iran is amassing weapons and seems intent on fulfilling an earlier proclamation that it will again become an armed superpower in the Arab world; and the United States and the United Nations are sending troops, as well as food and medical supplies, to famine-stricken Somalia, which is profoundly scarred by internecine struggles. As long as pugnaciousness exists and countries compete for power, dominance, and supremacy by utilizing the weapons of warfare rather than the tools of peaceful negotiation, nations will maintain armed forces and there will be military families that merit attention in the form of rational legislation and effective programs to protect and promote their well-being and minister to the kinds of special dilemmas they encounter, which have been elucidated in the foregoing chapters.

In light of the above, those in the military, whether on active duty or in the reserves, must always be in a state of preparedness and readiness to be deployed. The plight of those in the reserves who assumed they would never be mobilized was one of surprises and even shocks during the Persian Gulf war. It led many to the realization that anyone who volunteers for or is drafted into a military service, in the United States or elsewhere, may be called up and/or dispatched to a war zone or where there has been a natural disaster (like Hurricane Andrew in South Florida) upon short notice. Once one is "in the military," the government can exercise authority over where one goes, what one does, and when and how one does it.

This is a fact of military life—for the trooper and his or her family. Once a person enlists or is conscripted, until the time that individual's retirement occurs, the military system takes charge of making many decisions that vitally effect his/her life. These include, but are not limited to, where and when basic training will take place, the nature of one's work assignment and on-duty hours, the geographic locale in which one will reside and often the type of residence one may occupy, whether the spouse and children (if he/she has them) can accompany the service person if relocation occurs, and whether and when one will be deployed in the event of an emergency. When one joins or is drafted into the armed forces, one forfeits some personal decision-making prerogatives.

This means that, unlike their civilian counterparts, soldiers, sailors, and marines can not decide to fly home from near or far when a spouse has a baby or needs surgery, when a parent has a stroke or coronary, or when the rest of the family is summoned because the specter of death hovers near. Papers need to be filed requesting emergency leave. The final decision rests with the commanding officer, not with the person whose significant family member(s) may be in the midst of a major life cycle event, happy or sad.

Although military family members may rationally understand that a husband, son, father, or brother (wife, daughter, mother, or sister) has agreed to subjugate his or her will to that of the country, it is not uncommon that the absence of a loved one in times of trauma or crisis is resented. Some family members speculate as to why they have to bear the burden alone and whether the trooper really made every conceivable effort to get leave. In turn, the serviceperson often feels torn— aware of his/her overriding commitment to "duty, honor, country" yet guilty over not being available to his/her family of origin or family of creation in times of greatest need. One must learn to live with the ambivalence which results from juggling these divided loyalties.

Often, fears about the serviceperson's being maimed or killed are left unspoken by all; to express such fears is considered a sign that one does not have "the right stuff" (Wolfe, 1979). This shared silence when danger is omnipresent may be a divisive force or serve as another profound bond.

On the home front, many spouses and children experience a sense of pride and honor at the contribution of their close relative to their country. The uniform is a symbol of commitment and belonging; like the flag, it is a tangible sign of being identified with a big and important enterprise. The concept of being dedicated to a "mission" endows many military personnel and their families with an overriding sense of meaning and purpose in life and can provide an additional feeling of congruence between them. Such a sense of purpose mitigates against anomie and isolation and is a characteristic often found to typify healthy families (Beavers, 1977; Kaslow, 1981). When there is a shared devotion to the larger mission, family members strive to rise above narrow personal self-interest and to see themselves in the context of a national perspective and of patriotic larger-than-self goals.

The sometimes split loyalties emanating from the several, occasional conflicting commitments to family of creation, family of origin, service unit such as battalion or squadron, and the larger military establishment often lead to very mixed emotions as to where one is and should be. These multiple allegiances are exemplified in the chapters on the military child, mothers in uniform, parents missing in action, special warriors, and the sustenance of military families.

Usually in the field of marital and family therapy clinicians attempt to facilitate open communication and to eliminate secrecy between partners and between family members on important subjects that are of mutual concern, while concurrently having their patients/clients respect one another's privacy and appropriate personal and intergenerational boundaries. Yet, when a family member is in the armed forces, especially if he serves as a special warrior[1] or in another capacity where secrecy, camouflage, and deception may be essential to national security and the success of a mission, this need for utmost secrecy must be understood, accepted, and safeguarded. This can entail empathizing with a spouse's feeling excluded from much that is significant in her partner's life and from being jealous of the closeness her mate has with his other partner, that is, the one he goes with on special assignments and whose life is therefore integrally entwined with his in a different but also profound "till death do us part" scenario. She, like many other partners of military personnel, realizes that these mutual pledges to each other, particularly in the face of danger, are tight and strong and

---

1. Secret warriors tend to be male only, so this section is written to reflect that fact.

that the excitement they share in high-risk situations is likely to be much more gripping, even at times exhilarating, than that shared by the couple in the course of the ordinary events of married life.

Being conversant with the facts that engulf those in the armed forces and the impact of these circumstances and alliances on the marital and family system dynamics seems essential for practitioners treating military families. While empathizing with the nonmilitary family members, one must also display awareness of and appreciation for the stressful activities undertaken "in the call of duty" by the service person and be able to exhibit multilateral partiality when the need arises (Boszormenyi-Nagy & Spark, 1973).

The serviceperson's spouse, whether in uniform or a civilian, as well as his/her children, is also likely to form some other deep attachments during the periods of separation. The various military bases and family service centers, here and abroad, have numerous kinds of programs to welcome and orient spouses, help them to become acclimated and to feel they also belong, assist them in coping with mobilizations and deployments that involve their partner/parent, and facilitate their getting ready for the return and reentry of the absentee spouse. Frequently, close relationships evolve, particularly within the kind of support groups that were formed during the Persian Gulf war to help families weather the storm at home. Those on the bases were also sharing daily stressful life experiences and anxiety over the safety of their loved ones. The cameraderie was conducive to the development of strong, reciprocal, and valued friendships. These friendships, which proved vital to emotional survival at home, also evoked some antagonism in returning members of the armed forces whose buddies had been killed in action or had departed for other locales. Their spouses' new relationships simultaneously may have been formed because of their absence, yet existed separate from them, and could be of longer duration.

Even couples who had been quite close, affectionate and devoted before lengthy separations occurred because of military tour of duty assignments are likely to feel like strangers when they are reunited. They have lived separate lives, experienced different daily demands, activities and exigencies, and been with totally different groups of people. They grow and change, sometimes markedly if the separation is a long one, and often must get reacquainted. They need to work through any resentment, guilt, and shame either or both have accumulated. For example, if there are psychosexual scars caused or exacerbated by experiences in a war zone, they will need to find ways to cope with the sensitivities, self-recriminations, and/or self-pity emanating from any dysfunction, as well as the dysfunction itself, and to seek appropriate psychological and/or medical treatment. If either has engaged in extramarital behavior, heterosexual or homosexual, they will have to go through accepting responsibility for that behavior, apologizing, making some form of retribution and asking for forgiveness—which may or may not be given—if the marriage is to survive and be reasonably gratifying to both. The partner may require testing for AIDs and other diseases before the "adulterer" is allowed to return to the marital bed. The gala part of the reunion and the feeling of relief that accompanies the homecoming may be followed by much turbulence in reworking and renegotiating the intrafamilial relationships.

In addition to the potential problems already elucidated, the individuals in the part of the family unit that remained together usually have coalesced into a new pattern of interrelating and taken on the tasks and some of the role of the missing member. The spouse, if a wife, frequently has become more independent and self-sufficient and may not want to resume being relegated to second-in-command status. Similarly, the children usually have become more mature and competent and want this to be recognized and respected. In the event that the at-home spouse is the husband, he may have become much more attached to the children while his wife was away and may not want to be replaced in their affections. Thus, the family relationship system is likely to experience some perturbations as it strives to find a new homeostatic balance that is satisfying to all members.

This is not only true when someone comes home from a long tour of duty but also when the soldier, sailor, marine, military nurse, is discharged because their period of enlistment is over or they have been wounded and can no longer serve or because it is time for retirement. In terms of the individual and family life cycle, some of these events may happen well before anticipated and seem very premature and out of sync with those of the same age in the civilian society. Reequilibrating can take a toll on the total family and consume more time and emotional energy than expected, or like many other aspects of life in the armed forces and beyond, early retirement can offer the opportunity for many wonderful challenges and new experiences (Strange, 1984).

When families become military families, flexibility and adaptability are important attributes that enable their relocations and acclimation to new environments, their separations and reunions, and their unexpected reassignments and disruptions to be handled reasonably well. These same qualities facilitate their transition through retirement back into civilian life.

The Vietnam, Korean, and Persian Gulf wars all underscored the imperative need for our country to have rational policies and procedures for dealing with service personnel and their families. Enlightened self-interest necessitates that legislation that effects the well-being of military families be periodically reviewed and revised so that it is relevant to the changing nature of military families; for example, in today's world, when the wife/mother is the active duty member, when the military father has primary custody of his children, when the officer discloses he is homosexual. Numerous relevant support services need to be in place and available at military family service centers, at base psychiatric clinics and hospitals, and quickly deployed to the front lines in times of war or because of humanitarian relief efforts. These services and programs need to be reconsidered periodically and altered when situations warrant, as for example, the addition of family advocacy services to deal with violence in military families (Schwabe & Kaslow, 1984), or of special substance abuse treatment facilities such as the one at Long Beach Naval Hospital in California (Williams, 1984).

Although military families are similar to civilian families in many ways, their life-style and the kinds of exigencies and uncertainties they face differ. Therefore, those engaged in treating military families, in both the civilian and military sectors of our society, need to be conversant with the unique characteristics and dilemmas that they face in order to intervene most efficaciously. All of the issues addressed herein comprise the body of knowledge which bears inclusion in any training program for providers of a vast array of services to military families (above and beyond the usual standard mental health curriculum and internship requirements). And it appears that such services can be delivered effectively only by those who respect the courage, dedication, and patriotism of military families—even if they do not choose this pathway for themselves.

REFERENCES

Beavers, W. R. (1977). *Psychotherapy and growth: A family systems perspective.* New York: Brunner/Mazel.

Boszormenyi-Nagy, I., & Spark, G. (1973). *Invisible loyalties.* New York: Harper & Row. (Reprinted, 1984, New York: Brunner/Mazel).

Kaslow, F. W. (1981). Profile of the healthy family. *Interaction, 4*(1/2), 1–15; *The Relationship, 8*(1), 9–24.

Keith, D. V., & Whitaker, C. A. (1984). C'est la guerre: Military families and family therapy. In F. W. Kaslow & R. I. Ridenour (Eds.) *The military family: Dynamics and treatment* (pp. 147–166). New York: Guilford Press.

Schwabe, M., & Kaslow, F. W. (1984). Violence in the military family. In F. W.

Kaslow & R. I. Ridenour (Eds.), *The military family: Dynamics and treatment* (pp. 125–146). New York: Guilford Press.

Strange, R. E. (1984). Retirement from the service: The individual and his family. In F. W. Kaslow & R. I. Ridenour (Eds.), *The military family: Dynamics and treatment* (pp. 217–225). New York: Guilford Press.

Williams, T. G. (1984). Substance misuse and alcoholism in the military family. In F. W. Kaslow & R. I. Ridenour (Eds.), *The military family: Dynamics and treatment* (pp. 73–97). New York: Guilford Press.

Wolfe, T. (1979). *The right stuff*. New York: Farrar, Straus, and Giroux.

Author Index

Subject Index

Springer Publishing Company

Fourth edition of this classic volume!

FAMILY CONSTELLATION
Its Effect on Personality and Social Behavior

Walter Toman, PhD

Highlighting the newest edition of this book—presented again in Dr. Toman's easy-to-read style—are new interpretations of statistical data, a reader questionnaire, and a fully updated bibliography.

Praise for earlier editions

"From the studies and experiences of a lifetime, Toman has produced a volume full of sagacious insights."
—American Journal of Psychiatry

"This book can be used as a valuable reference tool. When formulating research problems, even those social scientists critical of its psychoanalytic orientation or skeptical of its empirical data will benefit from many of the ideas it contains."
—Journal of Marriage and the Family

"For those who would like to better understand themselves and other persons, Family Constellation *will provide hours of interesting reading, reflection, and discussion."*   **—Youth Leader**

Contents:

Introduction • Persons Comprising a Family • Changes in Family Constellations • Other Influencing Factors • Animal Families and Special Forms of Human Families • Lovers and Spouses • Friendships • Parent–Child Relationships • Relatives • The Data • The Basic Types of Sibling Positions • Parents and Types of Parents • Clinical Cases • Quantitative Aspects, Related Theories, and Other Investigations • Methodological Considerations in Social, Psychological, and Clinical Contexts • Family Data in Clinical Psychological Practice

300pp   0-8261-0496-7   hardcover

536 Broadway, New York, NY 10012-3955 • (212) 431-4370 • Fax (212) 941-7842